D1520842

PERFORMANCE IN THE TEXTS OF MALLARMÉ

le ~~temps~~ D. est en le mystère
de l'équation suivante.

que th

est

le développement des Idées   ou héros

le résumé du th—

comme Idées
            être

d'où   th = mystère

        héros =

pour établir
cette raison

Performance

—— *in the Texts of* ——

Mallarmé

The Passage from Art to Ritual

Mary Lewis Shaw

The Pennsylvania State University Press
University Park, Pennsylvania

FRONTISPIECE: Le "Livre," folio 13. By permission of the Houghton Library, Harvard University.

Library of Congress Cataloging-in-Publication Data

Shaw, Mary Lewis.
   Performance in the texts of Mallarmé : the passage from art to
ritual / Mary Lewis Shaw.
      p.   cm.
   Includes bibliographical references and index.
   ISBN 0-271-00807-5 (acid-free paper)
   1. Mallarmé, Stéphane, 1842–1898—Knowledge—Performing arts.
2. Mallarmé, Stéphane, 1842–1898—Aesthetics.   3. Performing arts in
literature.   4. Avant-garde (Aesthetics)   5. Ritual in literature.
I. Title.
PQ2344.Z5S53   1993
841'.8—dc20   91-18980
                                                         CIP

Published by The Pennsylvania State University Press, Suite C, Barbara Building,
University Park, PA 16802-1003

It is the policy of The Pennsylvania State University Press to use acid-free paper for
the first printing of all clothbound books. Publications on uncoated stock satisfy the
minimum requirements of American National Standard for Information Sciences—
Permanence of Paper for Printed Library Materials, ANSI Z39.48–1984.

For Benjamin and Elizabeth

Contents

Acknowledgments

This book would not have been possible without the loving support of many members of my family, especially Jeffrey Kaplan, Elizabeth Shaw, Frank Franklin, and Doris Willens Kaplan. I also want to thank my friends for their help and encouragement, particularly François Cornilliat, Kathryn Gravdal, Margaret Megaw, and Brigitte Mizrahi. I am grateful to William Waller for his editorial assistance, and to Steven Winspur for his careful reading and insightful comments. I owe much of this study's development to the late Professor Bert M.-P. Leefmans, who introduced me both to Mallarmé and to avant-garde art, to Professor Michael Riffaterre, who taught me how to read critically and who guided the project's earlier stages, and to Tzvetan Todorov, who encouraged me to try to understand not only what Mallarmé was writing, but also why.

Introduction

During the last years of his life Stéphane Mallarmé (1842–98) designed the most ambitious theatrical performance ever conceived. Far greater in scope than either the Wagnerian *Gesamtkunstwerk* or such contemporary mammoths as Robert Wilson's *CIVIL WarS*, this performance was to take place at various intervals over five years and to consist of the ritual consecration of Mallarmé's own ideal Book, *Le Livre*, a text that was to have replaced the Bible during the troubling "interregnum" following the death of God.[1] In our own time, with so many new theories and forms of performance emerging, this project certainly deserves to be well known. But the unequivocally performative aspect of Mallarmé's Book is so difficult to reconcile with his legendary literary purism that the project is hardly ever discussed.

The purpose of this study is twofold. My first aim is to provide those interested in literature and in Mallarmé with a new perspective on the role of performance throughout his texts, an analysis of his aesthetics

---

1. Research I have pursued since the completion of this book has led me to believe that during the 1890s Mallarmé might have been concretely designing this performance as a ritual consecration of the beginning of the twentieth century, the last century before the second millennium. It is true, as Bertrand Marchal has pointed out in *La Religion de Mallarmé* (Marchal 1988), that in an early version of the essay "Solennité" (*La Revue Indépendante*, 1887), Mallarmé had explicitly tied his reflections on the ideal Book with the date 1889 and the opening of centennial celebrations for the French Revolution, referring to "l'Ouverture d'un Jubilé, notamment de celui au sens figuratif qui pour conclure un cycle de l'Histoire, [lui] sembl[ait] exiger le ministère du Poëte" (Mallarmé 1945, 336). However, in the final 1897 *Divagations* version of this essay, Mallarmé deletes the reference to the (now long past) date of 1889, but *conserves* the remarkably pointed reference to such a supremely significant historical "Ouverture." It is this editorial adjustment, along with the original Roman Catholic sense of the term *Jubilé*, and a number of crucial numerical and temporal aspects of Mallarmé's reflections on the Book that have led me to explore the Book as a turn-of-the-century rite. See my development of this argument in "Le Retournement du siècle: Modernisme, débuts et fins" (to be published in the conference proceedings for *Le Tournant du siècle*, held in Antwerp in May 1992) and in the introduction to *Rhétoriques fin de siècle* (Shaw 1992b).

that accounts for the development and significance of this curiously
theatrical Book. Second, this study introduces those interested in music,
dance, and theater to the extraordinarily difficult yet highly rewarding
texts of a poet whose aesthetic theory and literary experimentation antici-
pated much of what has become central to these arts and to their inter-
mixture in performance art.

Despite tremendous critical attention within the field of literature, Mal-
larmé continues to epitomize for most the ivory-tower poet accessible
only to an initiated few. And yet it is widely recognized that the Master of
the Symbolists has engendered more literary offspring than any other
modern poet. In the twentieth century his influence has been equally
important to the development of conservative, avant-garde, abstract, and
concrete poetics and is readily discernible in the work of French poets as
diverse as Paul Valéry, Paul Claudel, Alfred Jarry, Guillaume Apollinaire,
André Breton, Saint-John Perse, Francis Ponge, and Yves Bonnefoy, as
well as in that of such different non-French poets as Gabriele D'Annunzio,
F. T. Marinetti, W. B. Yeats, James Joyce, George Moore, T. S. Eliot, Ezra
Pound, Wallace Stevens, Eugen Gomringer, William Carlos Williams,
E. E. Cummings, Charles Olson, and Louis Zukofsky.

Outside the field of letters and in the broader domain of all the fine
arts, the influence of the hermetic poets' poet has also, paradoxically,
been great. He has, for example, been acknowledged as the favorite poet
and source of inspiration for artists as diverse as the modern classicist
composer Pierre Boulez and the anti-artist Marcel Duchamp. His enig-
matic pronouncements on the essence of literature and other arts and his
texts embodying the poetics of suggestion, dynamism, simultaneity, inde-
terminacy, and chance have been cited in conjunction with myriad dispa-
rate developments in twentieth-century arts.

The multifarious character of Mallarmé's literary legacy may be attrib-
utable in part to the impenetrable quality of his texts, to the fact that he
is among the most difficult of modern poets. It has often been cynically
suggested that his writings lend themselves easily to any and all interpre-
tations because they are quite simply impossible to read. But their force
and diversity of impact undoubtedly lie less in their notoriously obscure
surface than in the cause of this obscurity: the ambiguity that permeates
every aspect of his work and thought.

The depth of this ambiguity can be measured by the broadly contradic-
tory character of twentieth-century Mallarmé criticism. Until the late
1950s critics ranging from Albert Thibaudet to Suzanne Bernard vari-
ously presented Mallarmé as one of the last bastions of French classical
poetry and as a proponent of either Platonic, Hegelian, Schopen-
hauerian, or Swedenborgian idealism; more recent critics have persis-
tently undermined these interpretations of his work. Over the last thirty

years critics have consistently turned to Mallarmé's texts to demonstrate the birth not only of modernist but also of postmodernist practices and thought. Maurice Blanchot, for example, has stressed his foreshadowing of the death of literature and art; Julia Kristeva, his pulverization of traditional concepts of language and the self; and Jacques Derrida, his deconstruction of the metaphysics of presence.[2]

What this superabundance of generally rigorous and often brilliant contradictory criticism suggests is not that Mallarmé's texts are nonsensical but, rather, that their sense is contradictory. At the risk of contradicting myself too much from the standpoint of the traditional criticism and not enough from the point of view of the new, my own analyses will stress that he is, in fact, both an idealist and a postmodernist; that he carefully preserves time-honored conventions regarding language and the self while, at the same time, going beyond these in presenting his work as the "moi projeté absolu"; that he is indeed one of the last champions and practitioners of classical poetry, and yet that his texts are as revolutionary in their forms as any being written today.

The diversity of Mallarmé's impact on the art world at large is also attributable to the beautiful yet tortuous expression of an elaborate aesthetic theory that supports antithetical points of view. As will be shown in considerable detail, his conception of the relationship between literature and the performing arts is particularly paradoxical and complex. Constantly affirming the inseparability of music and poetry and applauding Wagner for his efforts to bring about a total art work, he was nonetheless fundamentally opposed to all his contemporaries' attempts to synthesize music and poetry, and especially to the great composer's conception of the synthetic *Gesamtkunstwerk*. An ardent defender of a dying form of classical ballet, he was also one of the most eloquent eulogists of the innovations of the early modern dancer Loïe Fuller. While he was adamant in his rejection of realistic and naturalistic theater because of their condescension to the vulgar masses' appetite for representation, the forms of theater that attracted him most were the Catholic Mass and such "low-brow" forms of entertainment as circuses, parades, puppet shows, and sideshows.

Mallarmé's aesthetic attitudes toward the visual arts seem considerably less complex. He was a staunch supporter of the Impressionists and a close friend of Edouard Manet and Odilon Redon, who illustrated some of his work. And the few essays that he wrote on visual artists

---

2. These critics' readings of Mallarmé will of course be discussed in the following pages, along with those of such preeminent Mallarmistes as Robert Greer Cohn, Gardner Davies, Jean-Pierre Richard, Jacques Scherer, and innumerable others. Despite (and in some cases because of) my differences with these critics, their analyses have greatly enriched my own.

point to interesting parallels between his own writing and their work.[3]
Un coup de dés, his last complete text published in his lifetime and the
first modern concrete poem, has an extremely important visual aspect.
But the relative lack of both ekphrastic poetry and visual art criticism in
Mallarmé's work and the complete absence of reference to painting and
sculpture in his plans for the Book suggest that the relationship between
literature and these arts does not figure prominently in his aesthetic
theory. Indeed, this relationship is barely touched on at all.

That the relationship between literature and the performing arts is, by
contrast, central to Mallarmé's aesthetics is signaled not only by the
prominent role these arts play in his conception of the ideal Book but
also by the persistent references to music, dance, and theater throughout
his critical writings and most ambitious poetic texts. In the essays col-
lected in *Variations sur un sujet* and *Crayonné au théâtre,* in his 1892
Oxford-Cambridge address "La musique et les lettres," and in "Richard
Wagner: Rêverie d'un poëte français," he continually juxtaposes litera-
ture and the performing arts and defines a reciprocal relationship be-
tween them. He describes these arts as identical contraries that simulta-
neously complete and replace each other: music is "l'Indicible ou le Pur,
la poésie sans les mots" (389); dance, a "poëme dégagé de tout appareil
du scribe" (304); pantomime, a "soliloque muet . . . comme une page
pas encore écrite" (311); and the literary text, a "représentation . . .
[qui] supplée à tous les théâtres" (334).[4] And he links the supplementary
relationship of literature and the performing arts to the unity-in-duality
inherent both in language and the self.

The first chapter of this book gives an overview of this complex
network of relationships and demonstrates that in Mallarmé's writing
the function of artistic performance is broadly equivalent to that of
performative language and ritual. Music is the "dernier et plénier culte
humain" (388); dance, a "rite . . . énoncé de l'Idée" (322); and theater,
"le vrai culte moderne" (875). In Chapters 2 through 5, on music, dance,
theater, and opera, I examine the theory of each of these arts in detail,
showing the relevance of his views to the theories and practices of
twentieth-century artists as different as Claude Debussy and Pierre
Boulez, Martha Graham and George Balanchine, Antonin Artaud and
Bertolt Brecht.

In Mallarmé's most ambitious poetic texts—his unfinished mystery
play *Les noces d'Hérodiade, L'après-midi d'un faune, Igitur,* and *Un coup*

3. These important issues have been quite thoroughly and interestingly discussed (most
recently by Penny Florence in *Mallarmé, Manet, and Redon,* 1986).
4. Unless otherwise indicated, all references to Mallarmé's texts are to the Pléiade edition of
Œuvres complètes (Mallarmé 1945).

de dés—we find a subtle application of the theoretical relationship be-
tween literature and the performing arts that is described in his critical
prose. Although none of these texts is a performance piece in the ordinary
sense, they all refer to supplementary musical and theatrical perfor-
mances. Marring the autonomy of texts that have always been presented
as self-referential literary monuments, these references to performance are
troubling to the degree that critics have attempted to reason them away or
simply left them hanging. Chapters 6 through 10 analyze these references
to performance as integral to the signifying process of these well-known
texts, references that have consistently been treated by Mallarmé scholars
as meaningless but that none of his editors has yet dared erase.

In the last chapters I turn to the Book, the vast literary/theatrical
project mentioned above, analyzing in Chapter 11 *Le Livre,* the posthu-
mously published manuscript in which it is described. The references to
performance are so many, so unliterary, and so direct in *Le Livre* that
they can be neither ignored nor rationally erased. Thus, with the impor-
tant exception of Jacques Scherer's 1957 introduction to the manuscript,
Le Livre in its entirety has been left virtually unanalyzed and treated as
an aberration of literature, as the representation of an impossible, be-
cause inexplicable, Book.[5] The object of my own analysis will be to show
that far from aberrational and inexplicable with respect to Mallarmé's
other literary texts, *Le Livre* is a highly developed attempt to realize the
aesthetic ideal they suggest. In the final chapter I shall discuss the rela-
tionship of this aesthetic ideal to twentieth-century avant-garde perfor-
mance, my examples ranging from Futurist, Surrealist, and Dada theater
to the "happenings" of such contemporaries as Allan Kaprow and John
Cage. I hope to show that, among other things, Mallarmé's Book merits
consideration as one of the first and most fascinating examples of what
has generally come to be known as performance art.

Through performance, Mallarmé attempted to bind his texts to a
theater embracing the whole world. In so doing he naturally transgressed
the traditional boundaries of literature and art. This "purist of poets"
and most celebrated of aesthetes, long considered a great proponent of
"art for art's sake," in fact restored to art something far more ancient:
the function of ritual.

---

5. In recent years, a number of studies have begun to fill this critical gap by underscoring the
importance of *Le Livre* not only in relation to the whole of Mallarmé's work but also in
relation to his influence on others. See, for example, Vincent Kaufmann's *"Le Livre" et ses
adresses* (1986), Bertrand Marchal's *La Religion de Mallarmé* (1988), and Daniel Moutote's
Maîtres livres de notre temps: Postérité du "Livre" de Mallarmé (1988).

Fig. 1. Stéphane Mallarmé, rue de Rome. Courtesy Archives Seuil.

CHAPTER ONE

Performance as Ritual

To perform is to interpret or represent theatrically, as in music, dance, and drama. But to perform is also to bring a reality into being, as in a declaration of war (performative language) or in the carrying out of a ceremonial gesture (ritual) in church. Since the performing arts, performative language, and ritual are inextricably bound in Mallarmé's texts, it is useful to consider the broad theoretical connections among them.

The performing arts, by definition, require the presence in time and space of a performer and a spectator or listener. Thus, it is the intermediary presence of the performer that distinguishes them from literature, the visual and plastic arts (architecture, painting, and sculpture), and from arts conveyed through mechanical reproduction (photography, film, and sound recording). Just as the element of live performance can be subtracted from performing arts through their mechanical reproduction, so can any normally unperformed art be performed, as would have been the case with Mallarmé's ideal Book. Indeed, in the twentieth century, traditionally unperformed arts have increasingly been thus presented in the multimedia works we call performance art. The ultimate aim of this book is to show that Mallarmé's literary experiments anticipate performance art in several important ways.

Mallarmé was, however, a poet and not a performing artist, and his interest in performance undoubtedly arose from his theory of poetry, rather than the reverse. This theory of poetry is more than a manual of style or a set of aesthetic precepts. It is a philosophy of language with an important metaphysical dimension, which is schematically set forth in his *Notes*. Although these *Notes* are among the most problematic and least discussed of Mallarmé's texts, their main points require immediate presentation, for they make Mallarmé's concept of the *performative* aspect of language and poetry relatively clear.

I have said that one of the most remarkable aspects of Mallarmé's work in general is the ambiguous coexistence of (what we now call) "postmodern" and traditional metaphysical worldviews. This ambiguity is quite apparent in the *Notes*, which posit that Being and Language both originate in and re-create a metaphysical principle called "le Verbe." Language, Mallarmé asserts, is the development of *le Verbe* in Being in both its physical (contingent) and ideal (eternal) planes ("le Temps" and "l'Idée"). *Le Verbe*, as the principle of the unity-in-duality and identity-in-difference of spatiotemporal form and atemporal concept, determines the double manifestation of Language as Speech and Writing, whose reciprocal reflections anachronistically engender *le Verbe*.[1]

Because *le Verbe* is brought into Being through the reciprocal reflections of Speech and Writing, Mallarmé asserts, every text must prove its authenticity as Language (i.e., language affiliated to *le Verbe*) by submitting itself to the test of "diction," or *oral performance:*

> Le Vers et tout écrit au fond par cela qu'issu de la parole doit se montrer à même de subir l'épreuve orale ou d'affronter la diction comme un mode de présentation extérieur et pour trouver haut et dans la foule son écho plausible, au lieu qu'effectivement il a lieu au delà du silence que traversent se raréfiant en musiques mentales ses éléments, et affecte notre sens subtil ou de rêve. (855)

Speech, the performance of language, is thus both the origin and the culmination of writing. It is the performance of writing not only in the theatrical sense but also in the second, performative language, sense referred to above, for it is only through its utterance that a writing can realize what it symbolizes, the metaphysical presence of *le Verbe*.

Mallarmé's affirmation that writing must ultimately be transposed into speech before an audience immediately suggests that poetry is itself, for him, necessarily a performing art (a point that has not been sufficiently emphasized in most discussions of his work). Perhaps more inter-

---

1. These points are articulated in a key passage from the *Notes:* "Le Langage est le développement du Verbe, son idée, dans l'Etre, le Temps devenu son mode: cela à travers les phases de l'Idée et du Temps en l'Etre, c'est-à-dire selon la Vie et l'Esprit. D'où les deux manifestations du Langage, la Parole et l'Ecriture (destinées en nous arrêtant à la donnée du Langage) à se réunir toutes deux en l'Idée du Verbe: la Parole, en créant les analogies des choses par les analogies des sons—L'Ecriture en marquant les gestes de l'Idée se manifestant par la parole, et leur offrant leur réflexion, de façon à les parfaire, dans le présent (par la lecture) et à les conserver à l'avenir comme annales de l'effort successif de la parole et de sa filiation: et à en donner la parenté de façon à ce qu'un jour, leurs analogies constatées, le Verbe apparaisse derrière son moyen du langage, rendu à la physique et à la physiologie, comme un principe, dégagé, adéquat au Temps et à l'Idée" (854).

esting than his affirmation of the interdependence of speech and writing, however, is his insistence also on their difference and autonomy. In the passage cited above, he describes writing's transposition into speech not as a moment of unification but as a moment of separation. The oral performance of a text, *la diction,* is not represented as the plenitude of writing, but as its echo, the sign of writing's presence-in-absence. The function of speech as a "mode de présentation extérieur," is thus to reflect the presence of writing elsewhere—that is, on the page and in the silent, intangible realm of "musiques mentales" and dream.

Mallarmé's ambition to bring *le Verbe* into Being by demonstrating the identity-in-difference of writing and speech determines not only his belief in the ultimate necessity of the performance of his poems but also, paradoxically, his special interest in nonverbal performing arts. As we shall see, in both his critical and his poetic texts, the relationship between literature and the performing arts is linked to the double structure of language as writing and speech. And the double structure of language is itself linked to the unity-in-duality (and identity-in-difference) of mind and body within the human Self. However one reads Mallarmé on the question of the Origin of Being, the Being of the Self (both in Time and the Idea) is for him the subject and object of every form of language. And the spectrum of languages on which his writings especially focus moves from the literary text to the nonverbal performing arts.

By virtue of its unperformed and relatively intangible nature, representationally abstract literature is, for Mallarmé, the purest language of the mind. The literary text, or book, as "spiritual instrument" is the superlative medium for expressing immaterial thought. Conversely, by virtue of their sensorial concreteness, the representationally abstract performing arts are the purest languages of the body, superlative media for expressing the inherently corporeal and contingent. Literature and the nonverbal performing arts are the polar extremes of Language, whose reciprocal reflections, more clearly still than those of speech and writing, ritually testify to the presence of *le Verbe* throughout the spectrum of Language and to the unity-in-duality of mind and body that constitutes the Self.

Although Mallarmé's perception of music, dance, and theater as ritual languages of the body stems from his theory of poetry, it is neither unique to him nor theoretically far out in left field. Ritual and the performing arts are, in fact, indistinguishable on the basis of form alone. The distinction between ritual and theater, for example, is generally founded not on form but on a difference between performances that are considered merely entertaining and those implying a more far-reaching impact on the participants' lives. Ritual is perceived to be more efficacious than theater because it plays a critical role in regulating social behavior and in establishing or reaffirming the participants' religious and political beliefs. As theorists of performance such as Richard Schechner (1977, 90) point out, however, there has been an oscillation between the poles of ritual and theater in the history of every type of performance and there is a mixture of entertaining and efficacious elements in all ritual and theatrical events.

However one defines art and ritual, it is difficult to draw a clear boundary between them; some degree of each is always present in the other. But insofar as Western tradition tends to define art as either mimetic or as extrinsically nonfunctional, as "art for art's sake," there is an important difference between art and ritual. Art as the representation of reality implies a distinction between itself and reality. "Art for art's sake" implies a distinction between itself and the sociopolitical and metaphysical dimensions of human life. Ritual implies, on the contrary, the dissolution of such distinctions. Inasmuch as I shall be arguing that Mallarmé looked to theatrical performances as a form of ritual through which to consecrate the truth of his poetic texts, I must clarify what I mean by ritual.

As does the word *art,* the word *ritual* designates a highly diverse range of phenomena, and even though the word will be used here within a limited context, I cannot clarify its meaning by simply offering a more precise synonym. Therefore, I am listing below the primary characteristics of ritual. This list amounts to a custom-made definition of the term, but it also takes into account the prevalent meanings of ritual set forth in dictionaries, encyclopedias, and anthropological texts:[2]

1. Ritual is human behavior that conforms to a particular program of rules. It is neither miscellaneous nor technical action, but action within the context of a symbolic system.
2. Ritual is symbolic yet self-referential. It has the paradoxical character of "representing" itself.
3. Ritual must be performed in the present and in the context of a human (or other corporeal/spiritual) presence whose testimony renders it authentic.
4. Be it verbal or gestural, ritual is considered to constitute more of an action than an ordinary speech act. Although it often contains important verbal aspects, ritual presents itself as more than a language.
5. The performance of ritual is determined by some immutable principle or set of principles that ordains it as essential. These commanding

2. For a concise summary of social scientists' views on ritual, see E. R. Leach, "Ritual," *International Encyclopedia of the Social Sciences* 13 (1968): 520–26.

principles are fundamentally metaphysical, whether rites are seen to be magico-religious or secular, i.e., of a social, political, or psychological order.

These characteristics of ritual apply also to theatrical performance within the context of Mallarmé's aesthetic Ideal. To get a broad view of the type of performance toward which his texts point, let us closely examine the five attributes, looking first at what it means to say that ritual is human behavior within the context of a *symbolic system*. This first point, to be sure, is a very obvious and general truth, for almost any human behavior can be regarded as composed of symbols (or signs) and is therefore arguably symbolic in the broadest sense.[3] Let us linger, nonetheless, in order to establish that ritual does indeed consist of symbols and that its systemic function is properly symbolic.

Since ritual is performed through such a wide variety of media (verbal, gestural, musical, pictorial), it has been argued that the minimal defining element in ritual is the symbol itself. In *The Forest of Symbols* (1967), Victor Turner refers to the symbol as "the smallest unit of ritual which still retains the specific properties of ritual behavior." And the symbol he defines as "a thing regarded by general consent as naturally typifying or representing or recalling something by possession of analogous qualities or by association in fact or thought" (19).

The systemic function of ritual is considered symbolic because rites accomplish their ends representationally rather than technically through a direct process of causation (e.g., turning on the faucet to obtain water as opposed to representing its coming in a rain dance). The functional character of ritual's symbolism has been diversely explored in seminal anthropological studies throughout the twentieth century.[4] It is abstractly but succinctly articulated in Jean Cazaneuve's *Les rites et la condition humaine.* Cazaneuve states that in order for an action to fulfill the requirements of ritual, it must allow "l'accomplissement d'un événement par une efficacité symbolique" (Ryan 1977, 15).

---

3. In the broadest sense, a symbol or sign is simply something that represents something else. I shall use *symbol* and *sign* interchangeably in this broad sense, since even within semiotic theory the distinction between these terms is unclear. Saussure (1972) defines the symbol as a sign that has a natural resemblance or connection to its referent: "Le symbole a pour caractère de n'être jamais tout à fait arbitraire; il n'est pas vide, il y a un rudiment de lien naturel entre le signifiant et le signifié" (101). For Charles Peirce (1966) there is only an arbitrary link between a symbol and its referent. He distinguishes symbols from icons and indices as "signs that represent their Objects essentially because they will be so interpreted" (368).

4. See, for example, Emile Durkheim's *Elementary Forms of Religious Life* (1965), Mircea Eliade's *The Sacred and the Profane* (1959), Arnold Van Gennep's *The Rites of Passage* (1960), and Victor Turner's *The Ritual Process* (1969).

By virtue of its symbolic character, ritual is like a language. Its symbolic function is, however, more limited than that of language itself (which Ferdinand de Saussure designated as the richest and most complex of all semiotic systems). It is with respect to ritual's intrinsic limitations that the second sense of performance, or the notion of the *performative*, comes in. The symbols of language may fulfill various functions: they can be descriptive or can state or constitute what they symbolize. Ritual is not so diverse, for it always uses its symbolic capacity to constitute, or to bring into being, what it symbolizes. Ritual shares this attribute with performative language.

In *How to Do Things with Words* (1975), the speech-act theorist J. L. Austin writes that the performative utterance must *constitute* the action that it describes or states: "to utter the [performative] sentence . . . is not to *describe* my doing of what I should be said in so uttering to be doing or to *state* that I am doing it: *it is to do it*" (6). The utterance "I am killing the enemy" is descriptive. The utterance "I declare war" is performative; it constitutes the act of declaring war.

Thus, contrary to what one might think, the uniqueness of the performative utterance lies not in the degree of its efficacy (in the fact that it constitutes an effective action) but in the fact that this efficacy is dependent on the self-referentiality of the utterance, its explicit reference to itself. In *Problèmes de linguistique générale* (1966), the French linguist Emile Benveniste makes this requirement quite clear: "L'énoncé [performatif] *est* l'acte; celui qui le prononce accomplit l'acte en le dénommant." This gives to the performative utterance "une propriété singulière, celle d'être sui-référentiel, de se référer à une réalité qu'il constitue lui-même. . . . L'acte s'identifie donc avec l'énoncé de l'acte, le signifié est identique au référent" (273–74).

Like performative utterances, ritual actions refer to their own referring as constituting the reality that they designate and bring into effect. A benediction, be it verbal or gestural, such as making the sign of the cross or sprinkling baptismal water, is a blessing that says it is a blessing. The blessing is conferred through its symbolizing process. Many of the social aspects of changes in the life cycle are not only symbolized, but also actually produced through ritual ceremonies at birth, puberty, marriage, and death. Thus, in the context of ritual as in that of performative language, the signified or symbolized is held to be identical to the signifier, and the sign, identical to its referent.

One could undoubtedly argue that rites do not always, in fact, realize what they symbolize. Such rites as prayers for good health and rain dances may, for example, go unanswered. But the fact that a ritual representation does not reconstitute its referent does not necessarily indicate that ritual is otherwise structured. The failure of ritual's reconstruction of reality generally points, rather, to some flaw in the performance of the rite.

In view of their simultaneously symbolic and self-referential character, performative language and ritual must be recognized as sharing a paradoxical relationship to reality. They defer reality by virtue of symbolizing it, yet they are also identical to it in the sense that the reality they symbolize exists only by and through its ritual or performative symbolizing process. Consequently, the ritual symbol should be understood not merely as that which stands for something else but as that which stands for something else which it also is. This is the point I underscored in stating, as the *second* characteristic of ritual, that it has the paradoxical nature of representing itself.

If we are to adhere to the prevailing thinking in contemporary philosophy (such as that of Derrida in *De la grammatologie,* 1967), this paradoxical model of reality, itself inhabited by representation, is peculiar neither to ritual nor to performative language; rather, all being, or presence, is inhabited by representation.[5] While this view may be true, I would still maintain that this paradoxical concept of reality has a somewhat particular relevance to performative language and ritual. In these two modes the identity-in-difference of the sign and its referent is readily recognized and felt to be profoundly meaningful, whereas in most other cases it tends either to be rejected or to lead (as in deconstruction) to the general principle that there can be no such thing as meaningfulness.

In Mallarmé's texts the identity-in-difference of signs and referents is neither rejected nor accepted as a general rule. Yet he often recognizes the existence of this paradoxical relationship within the context of his analyses (or representations) of theatrical performance, and when he does he points to it as Ideal. He repeatedly underscores, for example, the identity-in-difference of the sign and the referent in the essay "Crayonné au théâtre" (1945) as he reflects on the "fundamental traits" of various performing arts. And in so doing, he does not appear to be commenting on the nature of all art but, rather, considering the nature of a pure and unique art form, in short, an aesthetic Ideal:

---

5. For Derrida, being, or presence, is always necessarily its representation; and for him, as for Peirce, the sign, or representer, necessarily carries the structure of alterity or identity-in-difference within it: "La dite 'chose même' est toujours déjà un *representamen* soustrait à la simplicité de l'évidence intuitive. . . . Le propre du *representamen,* c'est d'être soi et un autre, de se produire comme une structure de renvoi, de se distraire de soi. Le propre du *representamen,* c'est de n'être pas *propre,* c'est-à-dire absolument *proche* de soi (propre, proprius). Or le représenté est toujours déjà un *representamen*" (Derrida 1967, 72).

Il est (tisonne-t-on), un art, l'unique ou pur qu'énoncer signifie produire: il hurle ses démonstrations par la pratique. L'instant qu'en éclatera le miracle, ajouter que ce fut cela et pas autre chose, même l'infirmera: tant il n'admet de lumineuse évidence sinon d'exister. (295)

In the chapters to follow we shall see how often Mallarmé's articulation of the symbolic yet self-referential nature of various performing arts leads to an explicit association between them and ritual. (For example, following the passage quoted above from "Crayonné au théâtre," dance is called a "rite," an "expression of the Idea"). For the moment it is important only to note that he variously deems the symbolic, self-constitutive character of the performing arts to be a manifestation of metaphysical presence or nonpresence, that is, of the truth/reality of the Idea or of its existence only as a Fiction. This wavering between the acceptance and rejection of the idea of metaphysical presence reflects, I believe, Mallarmé's profound uncertainty on the question of the Origin, but is also a broad philosophical extension of his recognition of the identity-in-difference of the sign and the referent, of the symbolic and the real.

Returning to our examination of ritual and the performing arts (as perceived by Mallarmé), we must work further to distinguish them from a multitude of other symbolic, self-referential forms such as religious relics, sacred idols, written contracts, and many unperformed works of art. A close look at the *third* characteristic of ritual, that it must be performed in the present and before an authenticating human presence, will help us better isolate Mallarmé's concept of ideal theatrical performance. Performative language shares ritual's requirement of temporal and testimonial human presence, and its theorists can once again help us clarify the attribute.

A performative utterance is a speech act in progress, or the saying of something as opposed to a record of something said. It depends upon the physical *presence* of a speaker who is speaking in the *present*. Benveniste (1966) stresses this point, writing that relative to the speaking subject, the performative utterance must be designated as taking place here and now: "Un énoncé est performatif en ce qu'il *dénomme* l'acte performé, du fait qu'Ego prononce une formule contenant le verbe à la première personne du présent" (274). Thus, "I swear" is a performative utterance, but the utterances "he swears" and "I shall swear" are not.

The performance of ritual depends on similar circumstances. The spatiotemporal presence of the officiant and other participants is a fundamental necessity for the carrying out of any rite. This point may seem self-evident, since rites are performed, but it might be useful to illustrate the principle with an example. Let us consider the marriage ceremony, a rite, whether religious or secular, that persists with force and conse-quences, having effect on our lives. The presence of the officiant and participants in a marriage rite is required, and they are obliged to speak/ act in the present: "Do you take this man?" . . . "*I do.*" "*With this ring I thee wed.*" The officiant concludes the ceremony with a performative utterance that constitutes its referent, the act of marrying the couple: "By the authority invested in me by *x* (e.g., God or the State) *I now pronounce you man and wife.*"

To readers already familiar with Mallarmé, it may seem surprising that I should emphasize the importance of temporal and corporeal hu-man presence within the context of his aesthetic ideal. It can easily be argued that he was a poet more concerned with absence, among the first of modern writers to claim that the "present" does not exist: "il n'est pas de Présent, non—un présent n'existe pas. . . . Faute que se déclare la Foule, faute—de tout" (372). This is not an objection that can be easily disposed of, nor shall I attempt to dispose of it here. As previously mentioned, Mallarmé's thought on the subject of presence is fundamen-tally contradictory. I do not, therefore, hope to resolve this contradiction but only to show that it is in full force throughout his critical and poetic texts. Images of absence generally originate in and replace representa-tions of more or less concrete, objective presence, and "absence" is itself evoked as "presence" by virtue of a syntax that portrays it as the *coming into being* of an essence—for example, the "pure notion," or "idea itself." A famous passage from "Crise de vers" well demonstrates this point:

> A quoi bon la merveille de transposer un fait de nature en sa presque disparition vibratoire selon le jeu de la parole, cependant; si ce n'est pour qu'en émane, sans la gêne d'un proche ou concret rappel, la notion pure.
>
> Je dis: une fleur! et, hors de l'oubli où ma voix relègue aucun contour, en tant que quelque chose d'autre que les calices sus, musicalement se lève, idée même et suave, l'absente de tous bou-quets. (368)

The pure notion is the essence that "emanates" from the near disappear-ance through language of a "fait de nature." The flower rendered absent through speech becomes the (presence of) the ideal flower itself.

In "Sainte," one of Mallarmé's most beautiful poems, the symbol of absence, the "musicienne du silence," is similarly evoked (through "la parole," the poem) as an Ideal presence—the Angel stroking a harp "formée avec son vol du soir"—that originates in and replaces the more concrete image of Saint Cecilia with her missal and viol in a stained-glass window. That the saint is initially manifest as a *tangible presence* is emphasized by the unusual positioning of the verb "Est" at the beginning of the second quatrain. And her image as a tangible presence, like that of her attributes, ultimately fades through the poem's unfolding—variously negated or idealized in the last two quatrains:

> A la fenêtre recelant
> Le santal vieux qui se dédore
> De sa viole étincelant
> Jadis avec flûte ou mandore,
>
> Est la Sainte pâle, étalant
> Le livre vieux qui se déplie
> Du Magnificat ruisselant
> Jadis selon vêpre et complie:
>
> A ce vitrage d'ostensoir
> Que frôle une harpe par l'Ange
> Formée avec son vol du soir
> Pour la délicate phalange
>
> Du doigt que, sans le vieux santal
> Ni le vieux livre, elle balance
> Sur le plumage instrumental,
> Musicienne du silence.
>
> (53)

Even though it may be generally conceded that Mallarmé's poetic images of absence can be interpreted as images of ideal presence, one may wonder what this type of presence has to do with the temporal and corporeal human presence required in ritual and the performing arts. To better understand his conception of the relationship between these two modes of presence, we must focus for a moment on a distinction that he makes between literature and the performing arts. Whereas he considers literature (as we have seen in the above-cited passage from "Crise de vers") as a means of access to the *intangible* presence of the Idea through acts of language that abolish nature, he sees the performing arts as a means of access to the *tangible* presence of the Idea through nonverbal, corporeal acts that conversely nullify *la parole*.

Thus, in Mallarmé's critical texts the woman dancing appears as a physical "incorporation of the Idea" and, therefore, as a kind of negative written sign. She is a woman who, paradoxically "is not a woman, but a metaphor," by virtue of a "corporeal writing" that allows the writing of an ideal, unwritten poem, "poëme dégagé de tout appareil du scribe" (304). The mime also appears as the physical embodiment of an ideal presence and as a kind of inverse, or negative, writer. He is a "fantôme blanc," who writes with his face and gestures a "soliloque muet . . . comme une page pas encore écrite" (310).

Music also appears as a tangible Ideal presence and as a negative form of writing. In the essays "Plaisir sacré" and "Catholicisme" it fills "le brusque abîme fait par le dieu, l'homme—ou Type" (393). And the presence of God, or Man as Ideal type, embodied in music (a presence that is also personified though not personalized, in the physical presence of the conductor or priest), necessarily implies, for Mallarmé, an absence of language. Nonverbal (or unintelligible liturgical) music is "la figuration du divin" (389) insofar as it allows a direct encounter with the ineffable. As such, it is presented as the identical contrary of poetry, "l'Indicible ou le Pur, la poésie sans les mots" (389).

As we shall see in more detail, Mallarmé focuses heavily on the physical presence of the performing artist (in the case of orchestral music, on the conductor, "une *présence* de chef d'orchestre détaille et contient la chimère, en la limite de son geste, qui va redescendre (emphasis mine, 390). And he associates these arts with large audiences ("la foule"). Yet he exempts literature from the requirement of human presence to a maximum degree. At times his insistence on the autonomy of the text goes to the extreme of excluding from its signifying process the necessity of a reader's presence (along with that of the writer). This exclusion is exemplified in the essay "L'Action restreinte," in which he implies that the text reads itself, endowed with a living presence of its own:

> Impersonnifié, le volume, autant qu'on s'en sépare comme auteur, ne réclame approche de lecteur. Tel, sache, entre les accessoires humains, il a lieu tout seul: fait, étant. Le sens enseveli se meut et dispose, en choeur, des feuillets. (372)

Although Mallarmé's texts describe the performing arts as having a profoundly spiritual character (equal to that of literature), they are never exempted from concrete human testimony in this way. On the contrary, he stresses corporeal human presence and intersubjective activity in the performing arts, frequently designating them as superlative forms of ritual, as religious ceremonies or forms of worship. Dance is "la mouvante écume suprême" in the preparatory ceremonies of the Temple

(322); theater, "le vrai culte moderne" (875); and music, "le dernier et plénier culte humain" (388). Thus, the requirement of temporal and human presence that helps us distinguish ritual and performative language from other symbolic and self-referential modes is a crucial element in Mallarmé's distinction between literature and the performing arts.

Given the emergence of "performative" and "ritual" theories of literature in recent criticism, it is important to stress from the outset that I am not setting forth a "performative" or "ritual" theory of the writing or reading of literary texts per se.[6] Nor am I arguing that Mallarmé's texts are, in general, ritualistic or performative in the senses being developed here. On the contrary, I would argue that, for him, the text is not performative merely through its being written or (silently) read; it is not performative unless, or until, it passes through the intermediary of a performer, either in the form of its oral delivery or through its transposition into some other performed mode such as music, mime, or dance.[7] Moreover, it is not the history of an actual passage of literature into the realm of ritual and performance that we shall be exploring in Mallarmé's texts but rather the passage's literary representations. In fact, many of his most important texts cannot be fully understood unless we take into consideration their representations of various supplementary, ritual performances.

Returning to our examination of the third characteristic of ritual, I have said that ritual and theatrical performance, for Mallarmé, must take place in the context of a human (or other corporeal/spiritual) presence whose testimony renders it *authentic*. But what does authenticity consist of? Answering this question, modern theories of ritual and performative language become exceedingly complex. I shall not attempt to resolve all the problems inherent in the requirement of authenticity but

6. Two very different examples of what might be called "ritual" and "performative" literary criticism are Marie-Laure Ryan's *Rituel et poésie* and Barbara Johnson's "Poetry and Performative Language." Ryan (1977) compares the poetry of Saint-John Perse to both ritual and performative language on the ground that his texts reactualize the events they represent. In "Poetry and Performative Language" (1981), Barbara Johnson examines conventional distinctions between these symbolic modes and shows that Mallarmé's prose poem "La déclaration foraine" ironically subverts Austin's theory of performative language by rigorously fulfilling all its requirements (140–58). I shall return to her reading of this poem.

7. There is obviously also an important element of "virtual," or ideal theater, in such poems as *Hérodiade* and *L'après-midi d'un faune,* as Evlyn Gould has recently argued in *Virtual Theater from Diderot to Mallarmé* (1989). However, we shall see that, as Mallarmé's theatrical writing progresses in later works such as *Les noces d'Hérodiade* and *Le Livre,* the plans and requirements for text supplementation by actual theatrical performance become increasingly clear, a fact, which in my view, also casts a different light on the "virtuality" of his earlier theatrical writings.

only to summarize the reasoning behind it, first, with regard to performative language.

Austin and Benveniste agree that in order for an utterance to be effectively performative it must occur under the appropriate circumstances. For Austin (1975) the circumstances are appropriate if those involved (the speaker, the listener, and possibly other witnesses) view them as conforming to the traditions or conventions of their society. The performative utterance necessarily belongs to "an accepted conventional procedure having a certain conventional effect" (14). Benveniste (1966) merely writes that a performative statement, in order to be authentic, must be uttered under contextual conditions that are themselves *perceived as valid:*

> . . . un énoncé performatif n'a de réalité que s'il est authentifié comme *acte.* Hors des circonstances qui le rendent performatif, un tel énoncé n'est plus rien. . . . Cette condition de validité, relative à la personne énonçante et à la circonstance de l'énonciation doit toujours être supposée remplie quand on traite du performatif. (273)

In "What Is a Speech Act?" (1971, 46–53), John Searle meticulously articulates a number of these conditions in describing "how to promise," and he suggests how they might be generalized to apply to other explicitly performative speech acts. The most important among them are related to the authority of the speaker to make the statement under the circumstances in which it is made; the speaker's sincerity and the listener's belief in that sincerity; and the speaker's and listener's belief in the plausibility of the predicated proposition. One can effectively promise only what one intends to do and is capable of doing.

It is only by bringing in the perceived appropriateness and the validity of the surrounding circumstances that theorists of performative language can distinguish authentic performative utterances from those that merely appear so, namely, simulated performative utterances occurring in the "real" world (such as adult fraud or children's games) or in the world of art (such as theater).

The authenticity of ritual is similarly established. The traditions and conventions of society are in part the guarantors of the efficacy of rites. In his introductory essay on ritual in *Day of Shining Red,* Gilbert Lewis (1980) asserts that ritual is "bound by rules which govern the order and sequence of performance. These are clear and explicit to the people who perform it" (7). But whatever the extent to which the forms of ritual are conventionally prescribed, their validity also rests on such difficult-to-pin-down factors as the true status and sincerity of the officiant and the belief of other participants in the plausibility of what is being performed. In ritual, the officiant and others involved do not consider themselves to be faking, playing, or pretending. They are employing a symbolic mode of action, and in this sense they are acting, yet they are acting, paradoxically, "for real." Rites officiated by or for imposters are fraudulent *simulations,* as are those performed by actors in a fictional, make-believe world.[8]

Like the requirement of (temporal and human) presence, the requirement that theatrical performances be deemed by the participants to be authentic, or to participate in reality as truth, may seem difficult to reconcile with many of Mallarmé's texts. That he treats literature and other arts as fictional, is not a point I wish to contest. In "La musique et les lettres," for example, he describes literature as both fraudulent, "une supercherie," and as a game, "A quoi sert cela—A un jeu" (647). It is essential to remember, however, that for Mallarmé (metaphysical) reality itself comes into being through representation. As in ritual and performative language, in his texts it is the play of literature and other self-referential symbolic modes that *under the appropriate circumstances* constitutes metaphysical truth.

Mallarmé does not deny the possibility of inauthentic simulations of reality. His attitude toward all forms of representation is not equally positive. He has, in fact, a very negative attitude toward certain types of aesthetic simulations, particularly theatrical ones, which he often designates by the term *simulacrum.* The simulacrum presents itself as inauthentic, as a mere copy of a reality that it does not itself constitute. It is, in other words, a symbolic form that shows its referent to be wholly exterior, or extrinsic. Mallarmé perceives "realistic" and "naturalistic" art works as presenting themselves in this way and, on this basis, vehemently rejects them.

Mallarmé's negative attitude toward realistic and naturalistic theater is expressed in many of the essays of the collection *Crayonné au théâtre.* He calls contemporary theater a "*simulacre* approprié au besoin immédiat" (298) because it shows *only* a representation of external reality for those unable to perceive it directly:

> La Critique . . . cède-t-elle à l'attirance du théâtre qui montre *seulement* une représentation, pour ceux n'ayant point à voir les choses à même! de la pièce écrite au folio du ciel et mimée avec le geste de ses passions par l'Homme. (Emphasis mine, 294)

---

8. In *The Interpretation of Cultures,* Clifford Geertz (1973, 112) argues that it is precisely ritual's perceived partaking of reality that distinguishes it from art and play.

Mallarmé occasionally also deems ballet guilty of the crime of mere representation. Dance should be a performance of absolute truth, an "incorporation visuelle de l'idée" (306), a "mystérieuse interprétation sacrée" (305). Yet he concedes that to ask more of ballet than the representation of people's everyday life would be to think at cross-purposes with the demands of the public of his day:

> Seulement, songer ainsi, c'est à se faire rappeler par un trait de flûte le ridicule de son état visionnaire quant au contemporain banal qu'il faut, après tout, représenter, par condescendance pour le fauteuil d'Opéra. (305)

Mallarmé's favorable attitude toward pantomime in "Mimique" depends on a unique set of circumstances authenticating its representations that we shall further explore. Silencing, or negating, its accompanying libretto, the mime's gestural performance does not imitate anything that has gone before. Moreover, the particular pantomime play described in "Mimique" does not refer to any extrinsic reality at all. It refers only to its own perpetual "allusions," which illustrate nothing but the Idea. In a "hymen," or marriage of contraries, which is "vicieux mais sacré," the mime represents the circular process of representation that constitutes presence itself. The mime does not then simply represent, rather, he operates "*sous une apparence fausse de présent.*" And as Derrida has pointed out in "La double séance" (1972, 239–40), given the inherent ambiguity of the word *apparence* ("à la fois l'apparaître ou l'apparition de l'étant présent *et* la dissimulation de l'étant-présent derrière son apparence"), what this phrase ultimately articulates is the identity-in-difference of the present and the nonpresent.

Owing to its inherently high degree of (representational) abstraction, music, in Mallarmé's texts, usually escapes the criticism that its representations are only simulative and therefore inauthentic. Indeed, aware that instrumental music does not generally represent things, as does the sign language sometimes employed by the actor, dancer, or mime, he affirms that it requires some form of supplement in order to signify particular objects: its effort to represent the world is vain, he says "si le langage, par la retrempe et l'essor purifiants du chant, n'y confère un sens" (648).

One might consequently expect Mallarmé to favor vocal music and also to appreciate Wagner's attempt to make music signify through leitmotif. In fact, he is clearly more interested in music without words and disapproves of Wagner's effort to give music a representational function. He particularly disapproves of Wagner's musical "magic" because it is used to enchant the audience, which is thus immediately taken in by his dramatic "simulacrum" to the point of believing that what it represents once *was* real.

> Vous avez à subir un sortilège, pour l'accomplissement de quoi ce n'est trop d'aucun moyen d'enchantement impliqué par la magie musicale, afin de violenter votre raison aux prises avec un simulacre, et d'emblée on proclame: "Supposez que cela a eu lieu véritablement et que vous y êtes!" (542)

For Mallarmé, music (like other arts) should not be used to symbolize extrinsic referents, such as things appertaining to the past, whether these be legendary or firmly rooted in history. For music is, in fact, the expression of a higher, eternal form of reality, one whose immediate meaning must be drawn from (or determined by) the body of human beings to whom it is revealed:

> A moins que la Fable, vierge de tout, lieu, temps et personne sus, ne se dévoile empruntée au sens latent en le concours de tous, celle inscrite sur la page des Cieux et dont l'Histoire même n'est que l'interprétation, vaine, c'est-à-dire, un Poëme, l'Ode. (544–45)

As with the other performing arts, it is only when music manifests the continuing life of the Idea that Mallarmé deems its representations to be authentic. And he perceives the Idea as revealing itself in nonverbal music at the moment when it suggests to its listeners, or reflects, the existence of its own contrary face, the signifying yet self-referential "Poëme."

Because Mallarmé is searching for a universal form of myth and ritual, the representations of his ideal theatrical performances are, like those of his ideal poems, necessarily depersonalized and virtually devoid of narrative content. Unlike most practitioners of ritual, he relies little on historical and social conventions to guarantee the authenticity of his rites and texts. Rather, he leaves their symbolism as open-ended as possible so that (through the process of their reciprocal reflection) all can participate in the realization of their own concepts of truth.

As is often the case with ritual, theatrical performance has thus, for Mallarmé, the particular function of symbolically *rendering true* both that which the human mind perceives as "inscribed" in nature (i.e., "la Fable . . . inscrite sur la page des cieux," "la Pièce écrite au folio du ciel") and that which is (literally) written within a verbal text. Indeed, the demonstration of the identity-in-difference of these two kinds of writing seems to rest, for him, on some form of theatrical performance.

The intermediary role of performance in demonstrating the identity-in-difference of "natural" and textual writing brings us to the *fourth* characteristic of ritual: the fact that it presents itself as more than a language. Ritual usually incorporates many nonlinguistic elements, and however numerous and important its verbal elements may be, it is generally thought to communicate differently than language ordinarily does.

Many anthropologists have stressed that it would be erroneous to compare the symbolic efficacy of ritual to that of language understood as a decipherable system of signs. Lewis (1980) warns against overemphasizing the code-like and communicative functions of ritual that lead us to interpret it as though it were a linguistic message:

> The "meaning" of a ritual performance or a play is much further off from the meaning of a purely linguistic message than it is from the "meaning" of an event. We interpret a ritual or the performance of a play rather in the way we interpret an event at which we are present or in which we take part: we do not "read" the event as we experience it or as we reflect on it; we do not "decode" it to make sense of it or understand it. We are affected by it. . . . By notions about code and the communication of messages or information, we are led to a preoccupation with the intellectual aspect of the response to ritual so that other aspects of the response which ritual brings about are neglected. (34)

Paradoxically, this kind of distinction between ritual and language, between verbal signs and ritual symbols, is both readily accepted and extremely difficult to justify. To rationalize it we must ask ourselves, among other things, in what precisely ritual's affectivity consists, what the nonintellectual aspects of our response to ritual are, and whether linguistic messages are not just as capable as ritual of eliciting them. It seems to me that as soon as one subjects Lewis's (and others') distinctions between ritual and linguistic messages to critical examination, they fail. Poetry, to give only one example, can certainly be understood as a form of linguistic message, and even though we may decode, read, and reflect on it, it can affect us as much as ritual and elicit an equally powerful nonintellectual response. Moreover, it is arguable that symbols, regardless of their linguistic or nonlinguistic character, do not fit the pattern of being decipherable, that is, of signifying particular or specific things.[9] This being said, I do not perceive Lewis's distinction between our experience of ritual and language to be completely false or worthless, nor, it seems, do many others who have reflected on the nature of ritual at great length.

In the conclusion to his analysis of mythology in *L'homme nu* (1971), Claude Lévi-Strauss, for example, sharply distinguishes myth from ritual on the basis of the relationship of each to language. He presents mythology as a type of language because it verbally expresses basic structures inherent in the human mind. For him the ultimate signified of all myths (like that of language in general) is, in fact, the human mind. This is clearly stated in *Le cru et le cuit* (1964):

> Et si l'on demande à quel ultime signifié renvoient ces significa-
> tions qui se signifient l'une l'autre, mais dont il faut bien qu'en fin
> de compte et toutes ensemble, elles se rapportent à quelque chose,
> l'unique réponse que suggère ce livre est que les mythes signifient
> l'esprit, qui les élabore au moyen du monde dont il fait lui-même
> partie. (346)

But Lévi-Strauss characterizes ritual (as opposed to myth) as fundamentally nonlinguistic. He presents it as a predominantly nonverbal, nonanalytical mode of expression and communication, whether or not words are pronounced within a given rite. Although ritual is clearly representational, he considers it more comparable to music than to myth, because of its great dependency on corporeal gestures and object manipulation: "le rituel, comme la musique à l'autre bout du système, passe définitivement hors du langage" (1971, 600).

If the function of ritual is not, like that of myth and language, to signify concepts and, ultimately, the nature of the human mind, what is it? According to Lévi-Strauss, ritual has the ambiguous function of *adding to, yet replacing* language. It thus plays in relation to language the paradoxical role of the *supplement,* which Derrida (1967) defines and attributes to all signs (in relation to all things) in *De la grammatologie:*

> ... le concept de supplément—qui détermine ici celui d'image
> représentative—abrite en lui deux significations dont la cohabita-
> tion est aussi étrange que nécessaire. Le supplément s'ajoute, il est
> un surplus, une plénitude enrichissant une autre plénitude, le
> *comble* de la présence. Il cumule et accumule la présence. . . .
> Mais le supplément supplée. Il ne s'ajoute que pour remplacer. Il

9. See, for example, Dan Sperber's *Le symbolisme en général* (1974, 28).

intervient ou s'insinue *à-la-place-de;* s'il comble, c'est comme on comble un vide. S'il représente et fait image, c'est par le défaut antérieur d'une présence. . . . Le signe est toujours le supplément de la chose même. (208)

For Lévi-Strauss (1971) ritual adds concreteness to language by substituting gestures and things for their verbal/analytical expression.

En ce qui concerne les gestes et les objets, tous les observateurs ont noté avec raison que le rituel leur assigne une fonction s'ajoutant à leur usage pratique et qui parfois le supplante; gestes et objets interviennent *in loco verbi,* ils remplacent des paroles. Chacun connote de façon globale un système d'idées et de représentation; en les utilisant, le rituel condense sous forme concrète et unitaire des procédures qui, sans cela, eussent été discursives. . . . Le rituel substitue plutôt les gestes et les choses à leur expression analytique. Les gestes exécutés, les objets manipulés, sont autant de moyens que le rituel s'accorde pour éviter de parler. (600)

Marcel Mauss seems also to subscribe to this point of view, maintaining that every rite either explicitly or implicitly constitutes some sort of statement: "Tout geste rituel comporte une phrase, car il y a toujours un minimum de représentation, dans laquelle la nature et la fin du rite sont exprimées au moins dans un langage intérieur. C'est pourquoi nous disons qu'il n'y a pas de véritable rite muet" (Todorov 1978, 276).

Here a problem arises, for if nonverbal rites both complete and replace language, one might assume that any verbal element contained within a rite was redundant. Though the rituals of others appear characteristically redundant, this conclusion is difficult to accept, since many rites are predominantly verbal and still more explicitly contain words on which the efficacy of their representations clearly depends. Thus, Lévi-Strauss's emphasis on the nonlinguistic, nonanalytical aspect of ritual, like Lewis's, appears at best highly problematic and at worst untenable.

Fortunately, my purpose is not to support the truth of the above-cited distinctions between ritual expression and verbal language but only to show that Mallarmé makes such distinctions. In his critical texts the performing arts, considered as languages of the body, are represented as fulfilling a ritual function insofar as they supplement—that is, both add (concreteness) to and replace—(the analytical character of) literary language.

This point may already have become apparent from several previously cited quotations in which Mallarmé describes dance and mime as corporeal forms of (paradoxically unwritten) writing that render any verbal complement unnecessary or vain. For him, the marvel of music is also that it ultimately signifies by evoking through the senses its own ideal conceptual translation. Since he recognizes that nonverbal performing arts are capable of supplementing the intelligibility of poetry, it is not surprising that he should believe poetry capable, in turn, of supplementing the sensory effects of music and other performing arts.

Thus, just as anthropologists have insisted on the autonomy of verbal language and ritual's concrete symbolism, Mallarmé insists that literature and the performing arts are self-sufficient symbolic modes. One must then finally wonder what compels ritual performances to frequently incorporate language and what motivates Mallarmé's special interest in the performing arts and his representations of supplementary performances in several of his poetic texts. I would say that what compels the copresentation of verbal and corporeal modes of expression, both in Mallarmé's texts and in ritual in general, is the ritual practitioner's recognition of a need for both these "languages," however redundant, or repetitive, they might seem.

The need for both verbal and nonverbal languages in ritual can perhaps be better explained if we focus, finally, on the *fifth* characteristic of ritual, on the fact that its performance is ordained by metaphysical principles. Like ritual performances, metaphysical principles are themselves generally perceived not as tautologies but as productive and meaningful superabundances, composed of at least two aspects that are at once different and the same. The unity-in-duality (or identity-in-difference) of matter and spirit in *le Verbe* is a contextually relevant example.

Now, whether or not such a thing as metaphysical unity-in-duality exists, the fact that humanity conceives of it and celebrates it in ritual performances is probably closely related to the belief that duality is inherent to humanity's own being. It is a time-honored convention that there is opposition and conflict between the human body and mind (or spirit), between the sensorial and the intelligible, and, more generally, as Lévi-Strauss (1971) puts it in discussing the purpose of ritual, between life and its analysis in thought:

> Le rituel n'est pas une réaction à la vie, il est une réaction à ce que la pensée a fait d'elle. Il ne répond directement ni au monde, ni même à l'expérience du monde; il répond à la façon dont l'homme pense le monde. Ce qu'en définitive le rituel cherche à surmonter, n'est pas la résistance du monde à l'homme mais la résistance, à l'homme, de sa pensée. (609)

The "redundancy" of verbal and corporeal languages in ritual can thus be understood as a necessary opulence that allows participants to continually mediate oppositions (perceived or experienced) within their own being and thus to render their being consistent with that of a transcendent principle in which contraries comfortably coexist. Along with other fundamental oppositions verbal-corporeal ritual continually mediates those between (the self's) mind and body and those between the self and the external material and transcendent worlds. And it achieves this symbolically, i.e., by representing humanity in the process of mediation.

For Mallarmé, this process is ideally carried out through the transposition of literature into the performing arts (and vice versa). Considered as symbolic modes of expression and communication in which the sensorial and intellectual aspects of the Idea, the self, and the world are equally present and yet conversely manifest, literature and the performing arts reflect each other as identical contraries. As was previously mentioned and will be further shown in detail, Mallarmé perceives the former art as the superior medium through which to create an image-in-the-world of the self/Idea in its mental or spiritual aspect; he perceives the latter arts as the superior media through which to create an image-in-the-world of the self/Idea in its corporeal or sensorial aspect. Together, by bridging their opposition, literature and the performing arts thus provide, for him, a bridge between the corporeal/spiritual self and the physical and Ideal worlds. Together, they reflect and project into the world the identity-in-difference of all Being and the Self.

In the next four chapters, on the nature of music, dance, theater, and opera in Mallarmé's criticism, we shall see that although he prefers and practices Spartan intellectuality and verbal purism in poetry, he is primarily attracted by the opposing features in the performing arts. In later chapters we shall also see that it is a deep-rooted awareness of the mind/body duality that motivates him (like many other practitioners of ritual) to insist on a mysterious, indefinable difference between the written word and the corporeal languages of theater and to add to his poetic texts representations of supplementary performances.

CHAPTER TWO

Music:
"Le dernier et plénier culte humain"

Music played an important yet ambiguous role in relation to the French poetry of the late nineteenth century. This point is evident in Valéry's well-known definition of Symbolism: "Ce qui fut baptisé le symbolisme, se résume très simplement dans l'intention commune à plusieurs familles de poètes (d'ailleurs ennemies entre elles) de reprendre à la musique leur bien" (1924, 105).[1] In René Ghil's *Traité du verbe* (1886), we find the harmonics of poetry explicitly modeled on those of music (vowel sounds assimilated to the timbres of various musical instruments), but as a general matter, the making of music in Symbolist poetry did not result from an actual recapturing of musical riches. Rather, as was recommended in Verlaine's famous "Art poétique," "de la musique avant toute chose" simply implied the rejection of classical poetic conventions in order to release through fluid and semantically imprecise verse the images, rhythms, and sonorities buried in the psyche or soul. Mallarmé was, of course, at the forefront of this literary movement. He was interested in music from several points of view and became caught up in the enthusiastic theorizing about the relations between music and poetry inspired by Wagner.

Mallarmé's concepts of "musicality" and of the relationship between music and poetry are exceedingly complex unlike those of such contemporaries as Verlaine and Ghil. Contrary to what has often been argued, his writings do not show him to have a purely abstract, intellectual interest in music derived solely from a jealous preoccupation with its

1. In "Crise de vers" Mallarmé similarly described the poetic research of his time. He and his contemporaries sought "un art d'achever la transposition, au Livre, de la symphonie ou uniment de reprendre notre bien" (367).

exemplification of his own poetic techniques.[2] Music is for him neither greater nor lesser than poetry, neither absolutely analogous to nor different from it. Rather, by virtue of these arts' varying degrees of sensorial concreteness and representational abstraction, he considers them to be at once identical and contrary and to fulfill in relation to each other the paradoxical function of the supplement (in the sense, earlier defined, of that which both replaces and completes). The supplementary relation of music and poetry is for him an aesthetic manifestation of the unity-in-duality of mind and body, a relationship on which he patterns his concept of the Idea. For Mallarmé, music and literature equally manifest the Idea (he is like neither Schopenhauer nor Hegel in this respect), albeit in contrary ways. The literary text is the Idea's sacred sarcophagus; music, its ritual celebration.

The complexity of Mallarmé's theory of the relationship of music and poetry to the Idea is often reflected in the paradoxical rhetoric through which it is expressed. As we shall see, in several key passages where this relationship is defined, unexpected and ambiguous shifts between literal and figurative references to music impede the reader's capacity to distinguish between music and poetry and the Idea even as distinctions between them are being made. These difficult passages require close reading, because they are the most radical and forceful expressions of Mallarmé's theory. First, however, it will be useful to explore some of his less ambiguous articulations of the similarities and differences between music and poetry.

In one of Mallarmé's first critical essays, "Hérésies artistiques: L'art pour tous" (1862), music is treated as comparable to poetry in its capacity to evoke an almost religious aesthetic feeling. But it is seen as different from poetry in that it achieves this feeling through a nonlinguistic code, the arcane symbols of the musical score. Mallarmé suggests that the poetic text, in order to preserve its own sanctity, should follow

2. In the interest perhaps of safeguarding the idea that Mallarmé had an all-exclusive passion for poetry, several critics have implied that he neither liked nor understood music. Suzanne Bernard is perhaps the most emphatic proponent of this point of view. In *Mallarmé et la musique* (1959), she makes light of the range of references to various kinds of music thoughout his critical prose, insisting that he showed little or no interest in music before his theoretical initiation to it via *La Revue Wagnérienne* and his exposure to symphonic music at the "Concerts Lamoureux," both occurring in the mid-1880s. She also conjectures that he was insensitive to the aesthetic feeling that music evokes: "je ne serais pas éloignée de croire que Mallarmé écoutait la musique d'une manière purement intellectuelle" (42). Though his arguments are more nuanced, Jacques Scherer (1947) seems to share this attitude: "Si Mallarmé aime la musique—d'un amour intellectuel, d'un amour de tête—il pense que la poésie lui est supérieure" (254).

music's example by enveloping itself in mystery and becoming impenetrable to the uninitiated.

In a much later essay, "Le mystère dans les lettres" (1896), we again find Mallarmé holding up music as an example for poetry, here not only on the ground that it effectively creates and preserves mystery but also on the basis of certain techniques through which it does so. To inject more mystery into literature, he suggests, poets should look to modern music, whose themes do not give themselves away easily. In poetry as in music the theme can be revealed at the outset for a brief moment and then be hidden away or be diffused into a number of obscuring echoes: "On peut . . . commencer d'un éclat triomphal trop brusque pour durer; invitant que se groupe, en retards, libérés par l'écho, la surprise" (384). Or, conversely, the poem or piece can begin in an obscure fashion, suspending the revelation of its theme till the end: "l'inverse: sont, en un reploiement noir soucieux d'attester l'état d'esprit sur un point, foulés et épaissis des doutes pour que sorte une splendeur définitive simple" (385). These techniques can be generally described as condensation and dispersal. They occur in symphonies, in which a chord or harmonic structure can either generate or resolve a melody, and in poetry, in which elements of an either initially or finally expressed matrix are disseminated throughout the text.

In describing contemporary experimentation in poetry, in fact, Mallarmé often refers to analogous innovations in music, showing his awareness that the two arts have a similar history. In "Réponses à des enquêtes" he compares the Symbolists' break with the Alexandrine to modern music's deviations from classically structured melodies and rhythms: "en musique, la même transformation s'est produite: aux mélodies d'autrefois très dessinées succède une infinité de mélodies brisées qui enrichissent le tissu sans qu'on sente la cadence aussi fortement marquée" (867). Here, he is undoubtedly referring to the fragmentary, unfinished quality of "Impressionist" musical compositions such as those of Debussy.[3]

Mallarmé uses metaphor as well as comparison to articulate similarities between music and poetry. His 1865 article "Symphonie littéraire," for example, is structured something like a symphony. There are three parts related by a common theme—the salvation of the narrator's soul through great poetry—and each part, or "movement," is devoted to one of his three principal mentors, Théophile Gautier,[4] Charles Baudelaire, and

---

3. See *Mallarmé et la musique* (Bernard 1959) and *The Tuning of the Word* (Hertz 1987) for thorough analyses of the structural similarities between Impressionist music and Symbolist poetry and for comparisons of Debussy's *Prélude* and Mallarmé's *L'après-midi d'un faune*.

4. The title of the essay is itself an homage to Gautier recalling his own literary symphony, "Symphonie en blanc majeur" (Gautier 1948, 22).

Théodore de Banville. Throughout the essay poetry is designated as music whenever its aesthetic affectivity surpasses the expression of ordinary language and shifts into the register of the divine. The narrator's reading of Gautier causes him to experience "une harmonie surnaturelle" and to offer to the poet, in turn, "un grand hymne," one that results paradoxically from his own (feigned) inability to find the proper language with which to eulogize the poet:

> Maintenant qu'écrire? . . . Je ne saurais même louer ma lecture salvatrice, bien qu'à la vérité un grand hymne sorte de cet aveu, que sans elle j'eusse été incapable de garder un instant l'harmonie surnaturelle où je m'attarde: et quel autre adjuvant terrestre, violemment, par le choc du contraste ou par une excitation étrangère, ne détruirait pas un ineffable équilibre par lequel je me perds en la divinité? Donc je n'ai plus qu'à me taire. (262)

Baudelaire's poetic play of "correspondances" affects him similarly. It is an "hymne élancé mystiquement comme un lis," eliciting an equally mystic response—a synesthetic experience of "ineffable holiness," in which he hears the angels sing:

> . . . des anges blancs comme des hosties chantent leur extase en s'accompagnant de harpes imitant leurs ailes, de cymbales d'or natif, de rayons purs contournés en trompettes, et de tambourins où résonne la virginité des jeunes tonnerres: les saintes ont des palmes. (264)

The "movement" on the theme of Baudelaire ends on a musico-religious note: "j'entends éclater cette parole d'une façon éternelle: *Alleluia!*" (264).

The "divine" Théodore de Banville is compared to Apollo, the god of music and poetry, and is metonymically represented as "la voix même de la lyre" (264). Here, as in the preceding movements, a subtle equivalence is finally established between the narrator and his mentors as well as between poetry, music, and the divine: "Tout ce qu'il y a d'enthousiasme ambrosien en moi et de bonté musicale, de noble et de pareil aux dieux, chante, et j'ai l'extase radieuse de la Muse!" (264).

The exploitation of musical metaphor in "Symphonie littéraire" is striking only by virtue of its quantity. The trope itself is highly conventional and overdetermined by the fact that music and poetry share several elements of a common vocabulary that is often also the lexicon of the divine: the "hymne" is a sacred song as well as a sacred text; the "lyre" is a metonym for the god of music and poetry as well as being the particular symbol of lyric poetry (in the sense of poetry of the self); the source of divine inspiration for the poet is the "muse" from which the term *music* is itself derived.

In his later criticism Mallarmé continues to employ musical metaphors but in a manner somewhat less conventional and with a greater degree of catachresis. For example, he describes the actors in Edouard Dujardin's *Fin d'Antonia* as playing "très mélodiquement, en toute suavité; mus par l'orchestre intime de leur diction" (326).[5] Here, musical vocabulary places an accent on the fluidity resulting from finely nuanced articulation.

In "Crise de vers" Mallarmé depends almost exclusively on musical imagery to describe new developments in poetry:

> Le remarquable est que, pour la première fois, au cours de l'histoire littéraire d'aucun peuple, concurremment aux grandes orgues générales et séculaires, où s'exalte, d'après un latent clavier, l'orthodoxie, quiconque avec son jeu et son ouïe individuels se peut composer un instrument, dès qu'il souffle, le frôle ou frappe avec science; en user à part et le dédier aussi à la Langue. . . .
> Toute âme est une mélodie, qu'il s'agit de renouer; et pour cela, sont la flûte ou la viole de chacun.
>
> Selon moi jaillit tard une condition vraie ou la possibilité, de s'exprimer non seulement, mais de se moduler, à son gré. (363)

Here he presents classical verse forms such as the Alexandrine as the orthodox instruments of the poet. (The choice of organ as metaphor is no doubt motivated by its role in supporting, or accompanying, the accepted doctrine of the community in the church.) By contrast, free verse is presented as a more readily individualized instrument, which, unlike the Alexandrine (or organ), can be played however one chooses. The poet's newfound freedom is emphasized by the presentation of a choice of metaphorical musical instruments ("la flûte ou la viole"), by the statement of his capacity to shift between them (he may now "blow," "strum," or "strike") and to modulate his self-expression as he pleases. This (formal) freedom of expression stems from the recognition that

5. We find a similar metaphor in *La dernière mode:* dramatic verse makes a music of its own: "Quelle musique dans ces quatres actes, exquise, rêveuse ou brillante, pour peu que l'une de vous, Mesdames, veuille, le piano fermé, ouïr, au rythme seul des vers, la passion, animant leur dialogue, s'en dégager!" (820).

what is worthy of poetry is not imposed from without but contained within each poet's soul. When poetic expressivity becomes completely modeled on the diversity of form and feeling within each individual, lyric poetry finally comes into its own.

Mallarmé's choice of a musical code to communicate this achievement is, once again, partially determined by the encounter of the semes of subjectivity, musicality, and poeticalness in the term *lyric* (implicit in this passage). The musical metaphors may also stem, however, from the fact that the "crisis in poetry" being described corresponded to a similar upheaval of conventionally consecrated forms in music. As David Michael Hertz has shown in *The Tuning of the Word* (1987), the tonal ambiguity and abandonment of the symmetrical musical period in the works of Wagner and Debussy can be closely correlated to the open-ended suggestiveness and undermining of artificial symmetry characterizing the Symbolists' style.

We must now turn to Mallarmé's articulation of the differences between music and literature. In several of the essays already discussed he goes so far as to describe them in terms of binary oppositions. In "Le mystère dans les lettres" he underscores an opposition that is clearly central from the perspective of a poet, in designating music and literature as the "contradictory," or antithetical, constituents of language "la parole":

> L'écrit, envol tacite d'abstraction, reprend ses droits en face de la chute des sons nus: tous deux, Musique et lui, intimant une préalable disjonction, celle de la parole, certainement par effroi de fournir au bavardage.
>
> Même aventure contradictoire, où ceci descend; dont s'évade cela: mais non sans traîner les gazes d'origine. (385)

The dichotomy articulated here is one of sound and sense: the literary text is presented as aphonal but verbal, and music, as nonverbal sound. For Mallarmé music does not require the accompaniment of words; it communicates its own essence directly as "l'indicible ou le Pur, la poésie sans les mots!" (389). This is because music allows the simultaneous completion (i.e., the concretization) and the ideal translation of language.

> Les déchirures suprêmes instrumentales, conséquence d'enroulements transitoires, éclatent plus véridiques, à même, en argumentation de lumière, qu'aucun raisonnement tenu jamais; on s'interroge, par quels termes du vocabulaire sinon dans l'idée, écoutant,

les traduire, à cause de cette vertu incomparable. Une directe adap-
tation avec je ne sais, dans le contact, le sentiment glissé qu'un mot
détonnerait, par intrusion. (385)

For Mallarmé the separation of language into music and literature is a
positive and necessary achievement because it results in the creation of
two aesthetic modes of expression more integral, or pure, than ordinary
writing and speech and capable therefore of a second and more significant
complementarity.[6] In this respect he shares the attitude of modern compos-
ers such as Anton von Webern who describe music not as the mere accom-
paniment but as the necessary supplement to verbal expression:

> Il y a eu absolument une nécessité pour le surgissement de ce que
> nous appelons musique. Quelle nécessité? Dire quelque chose,
> émettre, exprimer une pensée qu'on ne peut exprimer que par les
> sons. Cela n'a pas pu être autrement. Pourquoi ce travail si on
> peut dire la même chose avec des mots? . . . On veut communi-
> quer en sons quelque chose qu'on ne peut pas dire d'une autre
> manière. En ce sens, la musique est un langage. (Stoïanova 1978,
> 33)

Mallarmé's perception of music and literature as aesthetic refine-
ments of the identical contraries of language is fundamentally related to
his perception of the identity-in-difference and unity-in-duality of mind
and body within the Self. As we shall see, he presents the literary text
as "l'instrument spirituel," the superlative means of the mind's self-
expression and cognition, and music as an ideal means of self-
expression and cognition for the body.

Mallarmé often focuses on the materiality of music, the fact that it
springs forth from objects that are struck, brushed, or blown. Referring,
for example, to music in its "ordinary sense" he specifies its *performed*
character and the *materials* of which musical instruments are made, "la
limitant aux *exécutions concertantes* avec le secours des *cordes*, des
cuivres et des *bois*" (emphasis mine, 648). This is because he associates
music more closely than literature with the natural, physical world. In
fact, it is in the sound of the lowliest creatures that he finds the purest
form of song. The human voice is for him inevitably inhabited by dual-

---

6. Purity, or integrity, of genre is one of the most important qualities Mallarmé seeks in art.
In his preface to Léopold Dauphin's *Raisins bleus et gris*, he clearly states his approval of the
segregation of music and literature, applauding the fact that Dauphin (primarily a musician)
chose not to set his verse to music (859).

ity, for whether or not human music is verbal, he perceives it (as we have just seen) as evoking words and thought. In a letter to Eugène Lefébure, he contrasts the unity of the cricket's song to the decomposition of "matter and spirit" reflected in the human voice:

> . . . combien plus une [la chanson du grillon] surtout que celle d'une femme qui marchait et chantait devant moi, et dont la voix semblait transparente de mille mots dans lesquels elle vibrait et pénétrée de néant. Tant de bonheur qu'a la terre de ne pas être décomposée en matière et en esprit était dans ce son unique du Grillon. (1953, 92–93)

Although the art of music is inherently impure, originating from an impure source, it is, nevertheless, for Mallarmé primarily expressive of nature. In an article on Banville he points out that the orchestra conjures up natural landscapes in a direct, or immediately apprehensible, way:

> . . . observez que les instruments détachent, selon un sortilège aisé à surprendre, la cime, pour ainsi voir, de naturels paysages; les évapore et les renoue, flottants, dans une état supérieur. Voici qu'à exprimer la forêt, fondue en le vert horizon crépusculaire, suffit tel accord dénué presque d'une réminiscence de chasse; ou le pré, avec sa pastorale fluidité d'une après-midi écoulée, se mire et fuit dans des rappels de ruisseau. Une ligne, quelque vibration, sommaires et tout s'indique. (522)

Nature is at once present and absent in music, transposed through the work of musical instruments into a superior state. In this passage the union of contraries that music achieves—the marriage of nature and nonnature—is conveyed in the image of the "ruisseau" (a metaphor for the melodic line) in which the prairie (a metonym for "les paysages") is reflected ("se mire et fuit") and divided by the line ("ruisseau") from itself. Thus, what we experience in music is fundamentally the "cime," the line or horizon *between* the natural and imaginative worlds. We experience it also in literature, but the horizon is seen not from the perspective of the natural world but from that of the mind, "l'esprit."

Mallarmé also closely associates music and nature in "Bucolique," describing them as the double "adjuvant" (which is to say the double "supplement") of literature:

> Le double adjuvant aux Lettres, extériorité et moyen ont, envers
> un, dans l'ordre absolu, gradué leur influence.
>
>   La Nature—
>
>   La Musique—
>
> Termes en leur acception courante de feuillage et de sons. (402)

During different periods of his life the poet has found in nature and
music a retreat from mundane existence and the opportunity to come
into sensorial contact with the Idea:

> La première en date, la nature, *Idée tangible* pour intimer
> quelque réalité aux sens frustes et, par compensation, directe, com-
> muniquait à ma jeunesse une ferveur que je dis passion comme, son
> bûcher, les jours évaporés en majestueux suspens, elle l'allume
> avec le virginal espoir d'en défendre l'interprétation au lecteur
> d'horizons. (Emphasis mine, 402)

The poet's experience of contemplating the book of nature inspires in
him the unremitting desire to read it, to penetrate the mystery of the
sunset (the cycles of darkness and light). In later life the desire to inter-
pret nature is experienced while hearing music. In music he beholds
again the sunset, as a symbol of the central enigma of life (the fact that its
contradictions—its cycles of presence and absence—cannot be fully rec-
onciled or grasped):

> Aussi, quand mené par je comprends quel instinct, un soir d'âge,
> à la musique, irrésistiblement au foyer subtil, je reconnus, sans
> douter, l'arrière mais renaissante flamme [le bûcher de la nature]
> où se sacrifièrent les bosquets et les cieux. (402)

Music provides the poet with a semirefined version of the spectacle of
nature ("semi," because nature is still easily perceivable therein). Further-
more, it has the particular value for the poet (who seeks to create an
absence of nature, to abolish it through his text), of exemplifying a
technique, (a "moyen") for nature's refinement:

> Esthétiquement la succession de deux états sacrés, ainsi
> m'invitèrent-ils—primitif, l'un ou foncier, dense des matériaux
> encore (nul scandale que l'industrie l'en émonde ou le purifie):

> l'autre, ardent, volatil dépouillement en traits qui se correspon-
> dent, maintenant proches la pensée, en plus que l'abolition de
> texte, lui soustrayant l'image. (403)

As Jean-Pierre Richard (1961a) has pointed out, for Mallarmé music
has the special capacity to "vaporiser un être" (392) thereby expressing
"l'univers des essences concrètes" (416). Acting on the materials of the
world, music transforms matter into energy: "Installée à l'origine de
l'objet, la musique le rend irradiant, persuasif, *suave*. Elle expire hors de
lui comme un climat concret de vraisemblance" (399). Since the poetic
imagination transposes the sense perception of the material world into
thought, it is not surprising that Mallarmé should have considered music
to be a kind of industrial,[7] aesthetic intermediary between nature (which
for him is tangible presence) and literature (which for him is the absence
of the tangible); between sensory experience and thinking; between "le
corps" and "l'esprit."

Mallarmé also closely associates music with the human body. This
association shows clearly in his comments on the concert soloist Geor-
gette Leblanc. He again emphasizes the *performative* aspect of music,
stressing that it is a *corporeal* form of expression that should not be
abstracted from its origin. Like Stravinsky, Mallarmé insists that "it is
not enough to hear music but that it must also be seen" (Stravinsky
1947, 128). The singer is not merely the miming vehicle of the music; she
is its actual source.

> A l'encontre de la loi que le chant, pur, existe par lui, rend
> l'exécutant négligeable, une interprète, de très loin, revient, avec
> mystère, s'y adapter, plus comme instrument, ni actrice, en tant
> que le spectacle humain visible, ou personnage, de la Voix qui
> baigne une face expressive, ruisselle, avant dispersion, au vol nu
> aussi de bras, les exalte et mesure ou s'écoule en la sombre
> tunique selon des attitudes que je nommerais d'une mime musi-
> cale, sauf qu'elle-même est la source lyrique et tragique. (861)

---

7. In notes following "La musique et les lettres," Mallarmé states that music is the aesthetic
correlative of industry as literature (more abstract) is the aesthetic correlative of finance. "La
vérité si on s'ingénie aux tracés, ordonne industrie aboutissant à Finance, comme Musique à
Lettres, pour circonscrire un domaine de Fiction, parfait terme compréhensif. La Musique sans
les Lettres se présente comme très subtil nuage: seule, elles, une monnaie si courante" (656).

Like literature, through which, Mallarmé asserts, the mind seeks to find its own reflection in the world,[8] music has an important self-cognitive function. Leblanc demonstrates this function concretely in her gestures, which point back to herself. She embraces the Idea (represented here as an imagined other person) and then makes contact with her own body, which generates this illusory presence:

> L'étrange et passionnante femme accentue la notion que l'art, dans ses expressions suprêmes, implique une solitude, conforme, par exemple, au mouvement, pour étreindre quelqu'un n'existant qu'en l'idée et vers qui le cri, de rabattre un geste ployé et le contact de mains sur sa poitrine à soi. Toute une volonté se compose harmonieusement aux dons plastique et d'organe, ici souverains. (861)

As is explicitly stated in this passage, the will to contact the Idea expressed in music is primarily plastic and organic. Thus, whether music be symphonic or vocal, verbal or nonverbal, the product of an individual or a group, its aesthetic sovereignty resides, for Mallarmé, as much in its sensorial concreteness as in its representational abstraction.

As we shall now see in several key passages in which references to music, literature, and the Idea are ambiguously combined, Mallarmé consistently presents the first two as identical yet contrary modes of human experience. The identity-in-difference of these arts and their mutual interpenetration reveals for him the irresolvable mystery of being,[9] an enigma that is itself projected into a metaphysical principle, the Idea.

In "Crise de vers" the term *Musique* points to the Idea as the principle of universal harmony. Ideal *Musique* is neither literal music nor poetry but an end to which they serve as means:

> . . . ce n'est pas de sonorités élémentaires par les cuivres, les cordes, les bois, indéniablement mais de l'intellectuelle parole à

---

8. The self-cognitive function of literature is defined in "La musique et les lettres": "Avec véracité, qu'est-ce, les Lettres, que cette mentale poursuite, menée, en tant que le discours, afin de définir ou de faire, à l'égard de soi-même, preuve que le spectacle répond à une imaginative compréhension, il est vrai, dans l'espoir de s'y mirer" (648).

9. In *La révolution du langage poétique* (1974), Kristeva sometimes describes the dialectic that constitutes the signifying process in terms of this interpenetration of music and literature. In her view Mallarmé's texts point to and reveal not only the conscious, verbal, symbolic expressivity of traditional poetic language but also the unconscious, nonverbal expressivity of the "chora sémiotique," which she associates with the feminine and with music (29, 473).

son apogée que doit avec plénitude et évidence, résulter, en tant que l'ensemble des rapports existant dans tout, la Musique. (367–68)

On one level the passage implies that poetry, as "l'intellectuelle parole à son apogée," more fully and clearly than music manifests universal harmony—the interconnectedness *of* all things *in* all things—through its unification of sounds and concepts. However, on another level (one that takes the specific language of the text into account), this message is contradicted, for the very choice of *Musique* as metaphor for "l'ensemble des rapports existant dans tout" significantly deconstructs the distinction between music and poetry initially made. This dissolution of difference through contradiction is hardly fortuitous, since it well conveys the central message that the ensemble of relationships exists in *everything* and, thus, in poetry and music alike.

In "Planches et feuillets" we find musical metaphors pointing to the Idea as essence, or ideality of form. A successful performance of Maeterlinck's play *Pelléas et Mélisande* creates for the spectator a form of music that is silent because it transcends representation and, with it, all particular manifestations of form:

Ces tableaux, brefs, suprêmes: quoi que ce soit a été rejeté de préparatoire et machinal, en vue que paraisse, extrait, ce qui chez un spectateur se dégage de la représentation, l'essentiel. Il semble que soit jouée une variation supérieure sur l'admirable vieux mélodrame. Silencieusement presque et abstraitement au point que dans cet art, où tout devient musique dans le sens propre, la partie d'un instrument même pensif, violon, nuirait, par inutilité. (330)

Though the performance is concrete, its representation is so abstract that it seems almost not to be one but rather to be, paradoxically, the *embodiment* of its own Idea (or essence), which cannot be reduced to its tangible substance. Mallarmé chooses a musical code to express this notion because, as we have seen, music connotes for him at once a high degree of (representational) abstraction and (material) concreteness. It thus well symbolizes the nature of a thing whose material representation is so close to its abstract essence that its representational value appears unnecessary. The uselessness (or surplus) of the musical accompaniment in the "admirable vieux mélodrame" (commented on by Mallarmé in the essay "Crayonné au théâtre")[10] is extended here into an "inutilité" not only of music in the restricted sense but also of music as materiality in general, since "musique dans le sens propre" (an allusion to the term's Greek etymology of *mousike,* "art of the muses") is divine and therefore silent, requiring no tangible representation.

In "Solennité" the book of poetry is also presented as conjuring up, in its blank spaces ("le ciel métaphorique qui se propage à l'entour de la foudre du vers"), a type of Ideal *Musique* that once again designates essence, an essence now clearly identified as contained within the self:

> ... ce spirituellement et magnifiquement illuminé fond d'extase, c'est bien le pur de nous-mêmes par nous porté, toujours, prêt à jaillir à l'occasion qui dans l'existence ou hors l'art fait toujours défaut. Musique, certes, que l'instrumentation d'un orchestre tend à reproduire seulement et à feindre. (334)

Articulated again here is the irony that music (in the literal sense) appears to reproduce tangibly what cannot be apprehended, the ineffable, unrepresentable core of the self. By virtue of its high degree of (representational) abstraction, music assumes the position of the poetic blank signifying the unsayable, "l'Indicible ou le Pur, la poésie sans les mots!" (389). This incorporation of the essence of self is necessarily "feinte," for music being concrete form cannot possibly incorporate pure essence (which precedes and transcends being-as-substance). Although the characterization of literal music as *feinte* may appear derogatory, Mallarmé's language is once more fundamentally ambiguous, for the choice of *Musique* as metaphor strongly suggests that there is, in fact, no better representation of the unrepresentable than its simulated presence in music.

In a passage from "Le Livre, instrument spirituel" there is a highly significant ambiguous shifting between the metaphorical and non-metaphorical references to music (a shifting whose importance is signaled from the outset by the essay's title).

---

10. Mallarmé attributes an ironical function to music in melodrama because it exaggerates the dramatic impact of certain moments to the point of distracting us from the seriousness of the play. The music is a *surplus* of drama; it does not support or comply with the drama so much as mock it: "un ambigu sourire dénoue la lèvre par la perception de moqueries aux chanterelles ou dans la flûte refusant la complicité à quelque douleur emphatique de la partition et y perçant des fissures d'espoir et de jour" (296).

> Un solitaire tacite concert se donne, par la lecture, à l'esprit qui
> regagne, sur une sonorité moindre, la signification: aucun moyen
> mental exaltant la symphonie, ne manquera, raréfié et c'est
> tout—du fait de la pensée. La Poésie, proche l'idée, est Musique,
> par excellence—ne consent pas d'infériorité. (380–81)

The "concert" in question is clearly metaphorical; musical vocabulary is
used at first to represent the experience of (silently) reading a poetic text
and then to designate an aesthetic Ideal. But in striking alternations from
metaphor to comparison the literal sense of music is also retained. In the
final sentence, for example, *Musique* shifts from being (metaphorically)
Poésie to being its Other, a rival art form approaching the Idea.

In a letter to Edmund Gosse we find an explicit definition of Music as
Idea, accompanied by both a mystical and an etymological justification:

> Je fais de la Musique, et appelle ainsi non celle qu'on peut tirer du
> rapprochement euphonique des mots, cette première condition va
> de soi; mais l'au-delà magiquement produit par certaines disposi-
> tions de la parole; où celle-ci ne reste qu'à l'état de communication
> matérielle avec le lecteur commes les touches du piano. Vraiment
> entre les lignes et au-dessus du regard cela se passe en toute pureté,
> sans l'entremise des cordes à boyaux et des pistons comme à
> l'orchestre, qui est déjà industriel; mais c'est la même chose que
> l'orchestre sauf que littérairement ou silencieusement. . . . Em-
> ployez Musique dans le sens grec, au fond signifiant Idée ou
> rythme entre les rapports. (R.-A. Lhombreaud 1951, 358)

Ideal Music lies "au-delà" de "la parole"; *la parole* is not *la Musique*
but instead is what produces it under certain circumstances (through
"certain [poetic] dispositions"). The art of poetry, then, stands in the
same relationship to the Idea as the art of music. Both allow the manifes-
tation of the Idea, here defined as the "rythme entre les rapports." In this
definition of the Idea (very similar to the earlier cited "ensemble des
rapports existant dans tout"), the term *rythme* underscores the dynamic,
unstable quality of the Idea, the fact that it results from an unlimited
number of relationships that are themselves ever in flux.

As Kristeva has pointed out in *La révolution du langage poétique,*
Mallarmé's Idea seems most often to designate "une infinité differenciée
et polymorphe," presupposing, rather than any fixed intelligible fullness,
a recurring mysterious void (1974, 537). Thus, while his Idea may be
related in various respects and contexts to such important antecedents as

Plato's "Idea," Hegel's "Spirit," and Schopenhauer's "Will," it should not be equated with any of these.

As the preceding examples show, the Mallarméan Idea does not exist as such. It is an unrepresentable enigma of human origin, which the analyzed passages simply point to in articulating the identity-in-difference of music and poetry through a combination of literal and metaphorical language. It is important to note, moreover, that the persistent shifting and differentiation in these passages between literal music and *Musique* (a figurative term, which the text ironically designates as proper) function to articulate not only the identity-in-difference of music and poetry but also that of figurative and nonfigurative language on which the play of metaphor itself depends.

We find the most developed analysis of the relationship between music and literature in "La musique et les lettres." This piece, originally a lecture delivered at Oxford and Cambridge in 1894, brings together most of the important points we have seen articulated elsewhere in Mallarmé's prose. In several dense and difficult-to-unravel passages, rich both in musical metaphors and musico-poetic techniques,[11] he describes music and literature as manifestations of the human pursuit of the Idea in the universe, an ironic pursuit in view of the fact that it exists there only as a projection of something inherent in the self.

The comparison between music and literature is elicited by a question: "Quelque chose comme les Lettres existe-t-il; autre (une convention fut, aux époques classiques, cela) que l'affinement, vers leur expression burinée, des notions en tout domaine" (645). The answer is affirmative because, the narrator explains, literature has a distinctive or particular function—to add "something other" to the material world: "*Autre chose* . . . ce semble que l'épars frémissement d'une page ne veuille sinon surseoir ou palpite d'impatience, à la possibilité d'autre chose" (647).

11. Throughout the essay we find frequent unexpected inversions, vague or ungrammatical prepositions and pronouns, and all-pervasive deviant punctuation that does not serve the logic and clarity of the phrase but, rather, renders it more "musical" and obscure by diverting the reader's attention to either natural or artificially created rythmic groups. This is true of nearly all of Mallarmé's late prose. Even the relatively clear passage from "La musique et les lettres" cited in the next paragraph, "Quelque chose comme les Lettres existe-t-il . . . ," shows some of these elements. There is an inversion within the parenthetical expression "(une convention fut, aux époques classiques, cela)," and owing to the vagueness of "cela"—which normally points back to a preceding statement but which here seems to point to what follows—we are uncertain what the expression modifies. Was the classical convention merely that something such as literature exists, or that something such as literature exists other than the expression in writing of all notions? The inversions call for several commas that break the flow of the sentence. For a thorough analysis of Mallarmé's grammar and prosody, see Scherer's *L'expression de Mallarmé* (1947).

That "something other," at once the instigator and end product of literature, is, Mallarmé reveals, actually founded on nothingness:

> Nous savons, captifs d'une formule absolue que, certes, n'est que ce qui est. Incontinent écarter cependant, sous un prétexte, le leurre, accuserait notre inconséquence . . . car cet *au-delà* en est l'agent, et le moteur dirais-je si je ne répugnais à opérer, en public, le démontage impie de la fiction et conséquemment du mécanisme littéraire, pour étaler la pièce principale ou rien.

He calls the poet's transformation of nothingness into an unattainable metaphysical Idea a form of literary trickery, a game: "je vénère comment, par une supercherie, on projette, à quelque élévation défendue et de foudre! le conscient manque chez nous de ce qui là-haut éclate." It is, however, a form of self-delusion that he accepts and one that he feels humanity has the right to, insofar as the universal void that it fills with the attractive, illusive Idea corresponds to—is indeed in a sense extracted from—a desiring void within the self.

> En vue qu'une attirance supérieure comme d'un vide, nous avons droit, le tirant de nous par de l'ennui à l'égard des choses si elles s'établissaient solides et préponderantes—éperdument les détache jusqu'à s'en remplir et aussi les douer de resplendissement, à travers l'espace vacant, en des fêtes à volonté et solitaires. (647)

Thus, it is not the desire to express what exists, "ce qui est," but the desire to express what is *not* that sets off the mechanism of literature or fiction.[12] For Mallarmé (unlike for Hugo, Baudelaire, and Rimbaud) the art of the poet is neither Promethean nor demiurgic; the world of real existence is already clearly manifested and complete. Rather, the poet's art is to draw connections between those elements that do exist in order to create a transcendent presence and order of relationships, "l'ensemble des rapports existant dans tout." In order to escape the boredom ("l'ennui") inherent in the human perception of concrete existence, the poet masks the differences that allow the perception of be-

---

12. This self-deceiving mechanism is more clearly described in an 1866 letter to Henri Cazalis: "Oui, je le sais, nous ne sommes que de vaines formes de la matière—mais bien sublimes pour avoir inventé Dieu et notre âme. Si sublimes, mon ami! que je veux donner ce spectacle de la matière, ayant conscience d'être et cependant, s'élançant forcément dans le rêve qu'elle sait n'être pas, chantant l'âme et toutes les divines impressions pareilles qui se sont amassées en nous depuis les premièrs âges, et proclamant devant le Rien qui est la vérité, ces glorieux Mensonges" (1953, 65).

ings with a fictional presence that implies their interconnectedness and unity. His text accomplishes this masking by weaving relationships between things, by adjoining opposites such as black and white, darkness and light.

Mallarmé describes this infinite tracing of connections that achieves the impossible, the establishment or "instituting of the Idea," in terms of a silent, chimerical, melodic line:

> Chiffration mélodique tue, de ces motifs qui composent une logique, avec nos fibres. Quelle agonie, aussi, qu'agite la Chimère versant par ses blessures d'or l'évidence de tout l'être pareil, nulle torsion vaincue ne fausse ni ne transgresse l'omniprésente Ligne espacée de tout point à tout autre pour instituer l'idée; sinon sous le visage humain, mystérieuse, en tant qu'une Harmonie est pure. (648)

The Idea "instituted" in the poetic text resides in the singular human capacity to perceive the unperceivable, to hear in poetry, for example, a "chiffration mélodique tue." It is the human experience of the void, "les blessures," that allows both difference (duality) in the universe and its resolution in unity. From the angle of human perception only, "sous le visage humain," the continuity of Being ("l'omniprésente Ligne") becomes a discontinuity (the complication of the Line) in a Harmony, which is then, paradoxically, perceived as pure. The Idea and the mystery can thus be described as the human perception of identity-in-difference.

If Mallarmé has recourse to musical metaphor in describing the phenomenology of the text, it is because music provides the perfect structural model for this interweaving. The melodic line in its trajectory from point to point responds to our sense both of unity and duality, now revealing itself as a continuous line, now obscuring itself in complex harmonies.[13] We find the connection of opposites in orchestral arrangements "où succède à des rentrées en l'ombre, après un remous soucieux, tout à coup l'éruptif multiple sursautement de la clarté, comme les proches irradiations d'un lever de jour" (648).

Music and poetry are then equally capable of communicating the Idea. Just as in "Le mystère dans les lettres" music's autonomy from words is declared—insofar as it inevitably evokes from the listener its own ideal linguistic translation—in "La musique et les lettres," we see

---

13. Baudelaire, in "Le Thyrse," a prose poem dedicated to Franz Liszt, similarly describes music as the simultaneous expression of unity and duality (1955, 1039).

that literature—insofar as it reappropriates music's structural system, or "apparatus"—can achieve ideal music without the help of sound:

> Je réclame la restitution, au silence impartial, pour que l'esprit essaie à se rapatrier, de tout—chocs, glissements, les trajectoires illimitées et sûres, tel état opulent aussitôt évasif, une inaptitude délicieuse à finir, ce raccourci, ce trait—l'appareil; moins le tumulte des sonorités, transfusibles, encore, en du songe. (649)

Music and literature should not then, for Mallarmé, explicitly collaborate, though they are implicitly interacting forces. They are reciprocal means of Mystery, the powers of one calling on the powers of the other. Music, associated with the work of the senses, provokes an action or reaction from the intellect, "l'entendement," and literature, associated with the intellect, stimulates the senses in turn:

> Alors, on possède, avec justesse, les moyens réciproques du Mystère—oublions la vieille distinction, entre la Musique et les Lettres, n'étant que le partage, voulu, pour sa rencontre ultérieure, du cas premier: l'une évocatoire de prestiges situés à ce point de l'ouïe et presque de la vision abstrait, devenu l'entendement; qui, spacieux, accorde au feuillet d'imprimerie une portée égale. (649)

This interaction is further developed in a decisive passage in which the respective domains of music and letters are clearly specified. Music is explicitly associated not only with the senses but also with darkness, obscurity, and the unconscious, while literature is associated with lightness, clarity, and conscious thought. Here the appropriate modes of delivery for what Mallarmé describes as this single double-faceted genre are also pointed out. Music must be communicated theatrically to a crowd by means of a *performance,* while literature communicates to the individual by the sole means of the *book,* or text.

> Je pose, à mes risques esthétiquement, cette conclusion . . . que la Musique et les Lettres sont la face alternative ici élargie vers l'obscur; scintillante là, avec certitude, d'un phénomène, le seul, je l'appelai, l'Idée.
>
> L'un des modes incline à l'autre et y disparaissant, ressort avec emprunts: deux fois, se parachève, oscillant, un genre entier. Théâtralement pour la foule qui assiste, sans conscience, à l'audition de sa grandeur: ou, l'individu requiert la lucidité, du livre explicatif et familier. (649)

Like the work of the mind and the senses—lightness and darkness, conscious and unconscious thought—music and literature, the performance and the text, though inextricably bound together, are not, Mallarmé intimates, simultaneously apprehensible. Rather, like two sides of a coin, each manifestation of the Idea implies the presence-in-absence of its other, contrary face.

This relationship of presence-in-absence is very familiar to readers of Mallarmé, because he frequently evokes it throughout his critical and poetic texts. An example especially relevant to the present discussion is the earlier cited famous passage from "Crise de vers" in which the poetic (or verbal expression) of "une fleur" gives way to the ideal flower's musical evocation. Pierre Boulez (1966), who like Debussy was greatly influenced by Mallarmé and who musically rendered several of his poetic texts, describes his own setting of poetry to music along contrary but parallel lines:

> Progressivement, les rapports de la voix et de l'instrument sont inversés par la disparition du verbe. Idée à laquelle j'attache un certain prix et que je décrirai ainsi: le poème est centre de la musique, mais il est devenu absent de la musique, telle la forme d'un objet restitué par la lave, alors que l'objet lui-même a disparu— telle encore la pétrification d'un objet à la fois REconnaissable et MEconnaissable. (57–62)

Motivating all of Mallarmé's metaphorical and comparative references to music are fundamental similarities between music and literature, which (as we have seen) are also shared by ritual. These are all modes of expression and communication extracted from the materials of everyday life (e.g., sounds and language) but then forged into autonomous symbolic systems.[14] These symbolic systems are also similar with respect to their referents, which are immanent creations, woven out of internal relations. Like ritual, music and literature are, for Mallarmé, self-referential. They do not merely represent what is thought to already exist in the world; rather, they create a form of Being where there is nothingness—a truth/fiction that constitutes the Idea.

In Chapter 1 we saw that Lévi-Strauss described ritual as mediating between "le vivre et le penser" (1971, 603). In "Bucolique" Mallarmé

---

14. Valéry often emphasized this structural or formal identity, stating that poetry ought to be to language what music is to sound: "Comme le monde des sons purs, si reconnaissables par l'ouïe, fut extrait du monde des bruits pour s'opposer à lui et constituer le système parfait de la Musique, ainsi voudrait opérer l'esprit poétique sur le langage" (Valéry 1950, 48).

assigns this mediating function to music. Furthermore, as we have noted, he looks on music (as others have looked on ritual) as a concrete and sense-oriented language of gesture and object manipulation striving toward the communication of a metaphysical principle. Thus, we should not be surprised to find in his critical writing an explicit association between music and ritual—an association which, of course, has long existed in religions throughout the world.[15]

Mallarmé describes music as ritual in an 1893 essay entitled "Plaisir sacré."[16] He begins with an association between music and nature similar to the one he previously analyzed in "Bucolique." When summer turns to autumn, the crowds abandon the spectacle of nature, only to find its reflection in music at the theater:

> Un vent ou peur de manquer à quelque chose exigeant le retour, chasse, de l'horizon à la ville, les gens, quand le rideau va se lever sur la magnificence déserte de l'automne. Le proche éparpillement du doigté lumineux, que suspend le feuillage, se mire, alors, au bassin de l'orchestre prêt.
>
> Le bâton directeur attend pour un signal. (388)

The narrator contemplates the audience and sets out to discover why music, in his time, is gaining such great influence over the masses. Crowds converge at the symphony, and it seems that this gathering is not motivated primarily by the appreciation of beautiful music: "le mélomane quoique chez lui, s'efface, il ne s'agit d'esthétique mais de religiosité" (388).

People seem to be gathering at the symphony under the pressure of two different principles: one ritual, the other mundanely social. And the narrator asks himself whether the musical event taking place is really an "office" or whether it is merely "un déversement par exemple d'inanité dans de l'absence" (389). He concludes that it may be rightly regarded as both, in short, that elite French society has chosen the symphony to be its "sacred pleasure." "Ah! le bien dire: du moins, le Français, utilisateur et social, plutôt que dilettante, fit cela de la symphonie" (390). With faces showing ecstasy, "des yeux, perdus, extatiquement, hors de leur curiosité," the members of the audience reveal that they are unconsciously

15. For a general discussion of music's ritual functions, see Bruno Nettl's *Music and Primitive Culture* (1956, 6–7).

16. This essay is grouped with others concerning ritual and performing arts, collected under the title "Offices" in *Variations sur un sujet*.

taking part in a ritual. To sit as though enraptured at the symphony is to "prendre part, selon le prétexte convenu, à la figuration du divin" (389). But what is the nature of this divinity? It is the mystery lying latent within the crowd itself, the enigma of human nature, which, divided from within (into mind and body), cannot fully know itself. The crowd projects this inherent unknown outward and elevates it to the status of the divine; whereas, in fact, what it confronts in music is the tangible expression of an element of mystery that it holds within—the corporeal, unconscious, and thereby unsignifiable aspect of the self:

> La foule qui commence à tant nous surprendre comme élément vierge, ou nous-mêmes, remplit envers les sons, sa fonction par excellence de gardienne du mystère! Le sien! elle confronte son riche mutisme à l'orchestre, où gît la collective grandeur. Prix, à notre insu, ici de quelque extérieur médiocre subi présentement et accepté par l'individu. (390)

In the closing passage of the essay Mallarmé again clearly identifies music with the material, unconscious aspect of the self, employing Baudelairean "correspondances" to fuse the crowd's sense of a supernal presence, the sounds of musical instruments, the undulations of the melodic line, and various aspects of the women's dress:

> Parure—si la foule est femme, tenez, les mille têtes. Une conscience partielle de l'éblouissement se propage, au hasard de la tenue de ville usitée dans les auditions d'après-midi: pose, comme le bruit déjà de cymbales tombé, au filigrane d'or de minuscules capotes, miroite en le jais; mainte aigrette luit divinatoire. L'impérieux velours d'une attitude coupera l'ombre avec un pli s'attribuant la coloration fournie par tel instrument. Aux épaules, la guipure, entrelacs de la mélodie. (390)

It is not fortuitous that Mallarmé resorts finally to a code of divine fashion to answer the questions posited in the essay. As anyone familiar with his fashion journal, *La dernière mode,* is well aware, he often uses this strategy to equate what appears to have the least significance—the frivolous and the superficial—with what is most sacred and profound. If despite its mundane social aspects "la Musique s'annonce le dernier et plénier culte humain," it is because in its ephemeral manifestations and through its presence at each performance the crowd finds an aesthetic extension of the body, which is the tangible aspect of the Idea.

CHAPTER THREE

Dance:
"Rite . . . énoncé de l'Idée"

Although dance appears less frequently in Mallarmé's writings than music, the essays of *Crayonné au théâtre* reveal him to have been at least equally interested in it.[1] Many of his positive statements about music are echoed with respect to dance, sometimes with even greater hyperbolic force. Ballet, for example, he labels the "adjuvant et le paradis de toute spiritualité" (305).

In fact, much of what Mallarmé says about the performing arts in general seems best exemplified by dance. It is not surprising, then, that his dance criticism has been more widely appreciated outside the field of French literature than has his criticism of other performing arts. Though his dance essays constitute no more than a few pages, he has come to be considered an important theorist of dance.[2]

These essays set forth a complex and original view of dance as ritual and as a poetry of the body. Dance is explicitly designated as a "rite . . . énoncé de l'Idée" (295) and as "la forme théâtrale de poésie par excellence" (308). In his essay on Wagner, in fact, Mallarmé deems dance

---

1. In his autobiographical letter to Verlaine, Mallarmé states that ballet and organ music (along with outings in nature), constitute his favorite pastimes. He calls these "mes deux passions d'art presque contradictoires" (664)—contradictory, no doubt, because organ music is heavy and auditory while ballet is visual and light. We shall see, however, that in general Mallarmé tends to equate music and dance.

2. The critic André Levinson was perhaps the first to bring these essays to the attention of the dance public, labeling Mallarmé a "metaphysician of Ballet" in a 1923 article for *La Revue Musicale*. Many of Mallarmé's statements on dance are rearticulated in the essays of his disciple Paul Valéry and also paraphrased in Valéry's well-known Socratic dialogue *L'âme et la danse* (1957). Frank Kermode discusses Mallarmé's writings on Loïe Fuller at length in "Poet and the Dancer before Diaghilev" (1962). The inclusion of Mallarmé's essay "Ballets" in the anthology *What Is Dance? Readings in Theory and Criticism* (Copeland and Cohen, 1983) indicates a widespread recognition of his contribution to dance theory.

among all theatrical arts to be "seule capable, par son *écriture sommaire, de traduire le fugace et le soudain jusqu'à l'Idée*" (emphasis mine, 541).

In identifying dance with ritual, Mallarmé was participating in a modern primitivist tradition buttressed by such theoretical works as Nietzsche's *The Birth of Tragedy* (1872), Jane Harrison's *Ancient Art and Ritual* (1913), and Suzanne Langer's *Feeling and Form* (1953). This tradition, which stresses the ritual origins of dance and its special capacity to achieve the integration of mind and body and of self and world, was central to the development of modern dance.[3] Indeed, several of its pioneers (or as they are often called, "priestesses")—Isadora Duncan, Ruth St. Denis, and Martha Graham—held forth as their models ancient Greek, Oriental, and American Indian ritual dances. Mallarmé was not, however, wholly in line with this tradition. Indeed, insofar as he stressed dance's impersonal nature as an abstract bodily writing, he was pointing away from the primitivist tradition and in the direction of such modern formalists as George Balanchine and Merce Cunningham.

Of great interest in Mallarmé's dance criticism is the manner in which it equally emphasizes and *allies* the seemingly contradictory views of dance that we associate with these traditions. In his dance theory as well as in his own projects combining dance and poetry, he is perhaps closest to the world of contemporary avant-garde dance, in which dance and poetry, primitivism and formalism, often coincide.

Mallarmé's essays are reactions to disparate late nineteenth-century dance forms. In "Ballets" he discusses *Viviane* (choreographed by Luigi Manzotti in 1884) and *Les deux pigeons* (choreographed by Louis Mérante in 1886). In "Autre étude de danse, Les fonds dans le ballet" and a short untitled essay, he analyzes one of the earliest examples of modern dance, the stunning veil dances of Loïe Fuller, who, highly acclaimed in 1890s Paris, came to personify Art Nouveau.[4] As is evident even in the title of his initial essay on Fuller, however, Mallarmé does not

---

3. The identification of dance with ritual is less relevant to the development of modern ballet. It is interesting, however, to note the critical role played in the modern ballet repertoire by *Le sacre du printemps*. We need only to think of the revolutionary impact of Nijinsky's original 1913 production and of the subsequent reworkings of the ballet by such major choreographers as Léonide Massine and Maurice Béjart. (Paul Taylor, Richard Alston, and Martha Graham also rechoreographed this ballet.)

4. "Ballets" was first published in 1886 and "Autre étude de danse," in 1893. Other essays including significant discussions of dance are "Crayonné au théâtre" (1887) and a short article on Wagner entitled "Parenthèse" (1886–87). Fuller's influence on the Art Nouveau movement is documented and illustrated in Margaret Haile Harris's catalogue for the Virginia Museum's 1979 exposition, *Loïe Fuller: Magician of Light* (1979).

draw a sharp distinction between these two kinds of dance. Rather, he considers dance very broadly and primarily in terms of its relationship to poetry.

In describing the similarities and differences between dance and poetry, Mallarmé uses both metaphor and comparison, often shifting rapidly between them. This shifting occurs most strikingly in "Ballets," in which he stresses, first, the similarity of dance to poetic writing—stating explicitly that the dancer is a metaphorical figure and that in dancing she writes—and, second, the fundamental distinction between such "dance writing" and writing in the literal sense. More economical than prose, it is corporeal and not actually written. The dancer's text is thus, he suggests, a poem that, paradoxically, is never inscribed (i.e., fixed or permanently recorded as is the poem on the page).[5]

> . . . la danseuse *n'est pas une femme qui danse,* pour ces motifs juxtaposés qu'elle *n'est pas une femme,* mais une métaphore résumant un des aspects élémentaires de notre forme, glaive, coupe, fleur, etc., et *qu'elle ne danse pas,* suggérant, par le prodige de raccourcis ou d'élans, avec une écriture corporelle ce qu'il faudrait des paragraphes en prose dialoguée autant que descriptive, pour exprimer, dans la rédaction: poëme dégagé de tout appareil du scribe. (304)

Mallarmé designates this articulation of the fundamental duality of dance—its combined poetic (or metaphorical) function and its corporeal, uninscribed nature—as "le jugement, ou l'axiome, à affirmer en fait de ballet!" In fact, his perception of the dual, oxymoronic character of dance (as an unwritten body writing) is already implicit in his designation of the dancer as a "metaphor" (a woman dancing who is not a woman dancing).[6] Like the ensemble of her text, the dancer acts, for the poet, as a negative poetic sign. The absence-in-presence of the dancing figure implies a presence-in-absence of the literary text.

If the ballerina writes like a poet, it is because her steps are generally

---

5. I do not think that Mallarmé ever considered the possibility of dance notation, which would, undoubtedly, have interested him from several points of view.

6. Mallarmé's presentation of the dual aspect of the dancer in the passage cited from "Ballets" is alluded to (and simplified) in the following passage from Valéry's *L'âme et la danse* (1957): "Elle [la danseuse] est une femme qui danse, et qui cesserait divinement d'être femme si le bond qu'elle a fait y pouvait obéir jusqu'aux nues. Mais comme nous ne pouvons pas aller à l'infini, ni dans le rêve, ni dans la veille, elle, pareillement redevient toujours elle-même: cesse d'être enfin tout ce qu'il plut à la flûte qu'elle fut car la même terre qui l'a envoyée, la rappelle, et la rend toute haletante à sa nature de femme, et à son ami" (151).

"emblematic," that is, abstractly representational, not mimetic. Mallarmé (unlike the father of dance theory, Jean-Georges Noverre) sees the dancer as different, in essence, from the mime.[7] He compares dance to hieroglyphs, not because its symbols are iconic but, rather, because this pictorial writing (like the musical score) has a mysterious and sacred quality and is difficult to decipher.

In "Ballets," after having described dance as a kind of (unwritten) poetic text, Mallarmé offers a guide to its proper reading:

> L'unique entraînement imaginatif consiste . . . patiemment et passivement à se demander devant tout pas, chaque attitude si étranges, ces pointes et taquetés, allongés ou ballons. "Que peut signifier ceci" ou mieux, d'inspiration, le lire. (307)

In order to read or interpret the dance poem, spectators must study the dancer's various attitudes and transpose what they see into the conceptual languages of their own imaginations. The spectators hold within themselves the key to the significance of the dance. They must surrender to the dancer's feet the flowers of their own "poetic instinct[s]," intangible flowers similar to the ideal "roses" that her pointe-shoes pick and offer for interpretation. As was the case with nonverbal music, it is only when the audience supplements dance steps with a metaphorical sense that the dancer attains a sign-function, and the dance becomes a poem:

> . . . (serais-tu perdu en une salle, spectateur très étranger, Ami) pour peu que tu déposes avec soumission à ses pieds d'inconsciente révélatrice ainsi que les roses qu'enlève et jette en la visibilité de régions supérieures un jeu de ses chaussons de satin pâle vertigineux, la Fleur d'abord *de ton poétique instinct,* n'attendant de rien autre la mise en évidence et sous le vrai jour des mille imaginations latentes: alors, par un commerce dont paraît son sourire verser le secret, sans tarder elle te livre à travers le voile dernier qui toujours reste, la nudité de tes concepts et silencieusement écrira ta vision à la façon d'un Signe, qu'elle est. (307)

---

7. Mallarmé was fascinated by pantomime and eloquently describes its essence in "Mimique." Relentless, however, in advocating the necessity for purity in genres, he resented the mixing of dance and pantomime. In "Ballets" he states that these two rival, silent art forms should be "allied" but not confused, and expresses his regret that "the dancer, who expresses herself through steps" understanding "no other eloquence, even gesture" should be required by some choreographers to mime (306).

In this description of dance's signifying process, the veil, which remains intact but across which the dancer transports the spectator's imagination, symbolizes that mysterious, transparent entity dividing the sign into two elements at once identical and contrary (i.e., equivalent and yet complementary in their opposition): the dance step (signifier) and its meaning (the signified).

Dance, then, is like poetry in that it constitutes a signifying system. However, insofar as it remains true to its symbolic nature—which is neither mimetic, nor arbitrarily prescribed by convention—dance is not, strictly speaking, a gestural form of language. Its symbolism does not develop, as that of poetry does, from a *codified* semiotic system. Dance movements may constitute signs for the spectator, but unlike most linguistic signs these are inherently open-ended. Only the signifier is given; the reader is free to choose the signified.

This explains in part why Mallarmé, who sought open-ended suggestiveness also in his poetry, views the dancer as constituting an ideal sign. His belief in the ideality of dance (underscored in the above-cited passage by the capitalization of the term *Sign*) is, however, also determined by his perception of the dance sign as being not only a representation but also a symbolic *embodiment* of whatever ideal form of beauty the spectator might interpret it to represent. Unlike linguistic signs, which, Mallarmé often stresses, can only name or refer to what is physically present in the world (or evoke, as in poetry, the affecting presence of things in their absence), dance signs seem generally to constitute their own referents; they do not merely name, copy, or suggest but actually materially incorporate what they signify. Moreover, Mallarmé (like one of his mentors, Théophile Gautier, who described the primary subject of dance as dancing) deems "the mobile synthesis" of the dancers' attitudes to be the ultimate signified of every dance and of the art of dance on the whole. He dismisses the plots of both *Viviane* (an allegorical battle between light and darkness) and *Les deux pigeons* (a fable about love, separation, and reconciliation) as pretexts, albeit charming, for the exposition of the signifying process of dance itself.

That which permits the completion of this ideal signifying process is, of course, the spectator's capacity to transpose form and movement into virtual poetry—in effect, into a not-yet-written poem. And it is this exchange between dance and poetry (like that between music and poetry), that Mallarmé views as expressing the Idea, the identity-in-difference of tangible forms and immaterial concepts.

We should recall that in "La musique et les lettres," to reveal the existence of the Idea was merely to present a human subject, or Self, with one or the other of its contrary manifestations—either tangible being (a dynamic vision or sound, as is set forth in dance or music) or its transposition in the realm of the imaginary (which the language of poetry transcribes). By virtue of participation in both these worlds of being, the Self holding either one of the Idea's manifestations inevitably supplies the other.

Thus, the reader/spectator of the poetic or balletic art work always already carries within, as it were, the art work's other half. The reader reacts to poetry sensorially, and the spectator, to dance intellectually. This does not mean that poetry is directly experienced as sensorial or dance as intellectual. Rather, the text appeals directly to the reader's intellect, which calls on his or her imagination to re-create the sensory impressions produced by the spectacle of dance. Conversely, when witnessing dance, the spectator's senses are appealed to directly, but in such a way as to provoke the intellectual process of meaning deciphering implicit in the reading of poetic texts.

Ballet (like nonverbal music) is an art especially well suited to this exchange, because in its bareness of meaning, or lack of particular signification, the dance form provides the imagining intellect with an ideal means of reflection and counterpart for its own "nudity," which (as opposed to the nudity of dance) consists in an inherent lack of tangible form. It is in the marriage or juxtaposition of these two nudities—the naked beauty of dance forms (metaphorically interpreted as "fleur, onde, nuée, et bijou") and that of concepts ("notre nudité spirituelle")—that the "rite" of the Idea consists. Since the dancer (as metaphor) herself appears dual—that is, as half a sign-object ("à demi l'élément en cause") and half an imagining subject, a human being who like the spectator interprets signs ("à demi humanité apte à s'y confondre, dans la flottaison de rêverie")—she is both the real and symbolic focal point of what Mallarmé calls the aesthetic "operation":[8]

> Le ballet ne donne que peu: c'est le genre imaginatif. Quand
> s'isole pour le regard un signe de l'éparse beauté générale, fleur,
> onde, nuée et bijou, etc., si, chez nous, le moyen exclusif de le
> savoir consiste à en juxtaposer l'aspect à notre nudité spirituelle

---

8. Thus, while Mallarmé discusses the dancer primarily from the point of view of the spectator, he is aware that she, too, is in a sense a reader interpreting in her choreographed role the innerworld of her own imagination as well as that of the spectator (which is indeed possible given the open-ended signification of dance signs). That is why he points to her as the center of the aesthetic "operation." We shall see further, however, that in the process of underscoring the physical quality of dance, he also characterizes the dancer as a not fully conscious artist, as one who (as opposed to the poet) acts "instinctively" through her body rather than through her mind.

afin qu'elle le sente analogue et se l'adapte dans quelque confu-
sion exquise d'elle avec cette forme envolée—rien qu'au travers
du rite, là, énoncé de l'Idée, est-ce que ne paraît pas la danseuse à
demi l'élément en cause, à demi humanité apte à s'y confondre,
dans la flottaison de rêverie? L'opération, ou poésie, par excel-
lence et le théâtre (295–96).

Dance, then, like poetry, produces semiosis, the integration of the
sign's initial, representational value into a higher, more complex level of
significance. But like the other performing arts, dance for Mallarmé is
more closely associated with the signifier (body and exteriority) than is
literature, which (although it, too, depends on a minimal amount of
material) is more closely associated with the signified, the immaterial
concept. Although he was undoubtedly aware of the weakness of this
dichotomy, his critical essays go far in the direction of establishing it.
Not only in his dance essays but also frequently elsewhere in his critical
prose, he presents dance as the superlative means of expression of tangi-
ble being—exteriority, materiality, and act—and the literary text as the
privileged expressive medium of the intangible reflection of being in
consciousness—interiority, immateriality, and thought.

Through the near (material) transparency of words the literary text
presents thought directly to the reader and, thus, the existence of an
imagined, immaterial world. But like the crystal chandelier, which hangs
above the audience exhibiting only its illuminated glasswork, dance pres-
ents nothing but a transparent, multifaceted form: a dynamic exteriority
illuminating only itself and the spectators' ephemeral, multifaceted vi-
sions. Indeed, the ceaselessly mobile dancer (in an unbroken chain of
pirouettes) demonstrates the axiomatic principle that everything repre-
sented in the theater should be (although concrete) as art itself com-
mands, "*fictif ou momentané*":[9]

> Seul principe! et ainsi que resplendit le lustre, c'est-à-dire lui-
> même, l'exhibition prompte, sous toutes les facettes, de quoi que
> ce soit et notre vue adamantine, une œuvre dramatique montre la

9. In "Le sacre du printemps" (1983, 115–23), Jacques Rivière draws a parallel between
two types of artifice in dance, which Nijinsky set out to destroy. The first is that of Fuller, in
which the dancer's body appears to become lost in her illuminated veils. The second occurs in
those ballets in which the lines of the body are lost in hazy, indefinite movements. In his untitled
essay on Fuller, Mallarmé comments on the same parallel without objecting to either type of
artifice. Indeed, he claims that a fundamental characteristic of dance is to fill itself out. While
the ballerina is too sparsely clothed, she (like Fuller) creates "imaginary wefts," but through
flight and movement alone (311).

succession des extériorités de l'acte sans qu'aucun moment garde de réalité et qu'il se passe, en fin de compte, rien. (296)

Though dance (and particularly ballet) clearly aspires to the immaterial realm of poetry, Mallarmé refers to it as the supremely material art form, as the visual and "plastic" (541) "incorporation of the Idea" (306). In order to reveal the Idea, the dancer uses her *body* as a vehicle or instrument (again, she is not just a woman but a "metaphor"). This instrument, which draws out form, is at once similar to and different from the writer's pen, the difference being that the latter directly (i.e., verbally) transcribes thought. Although the dancer does not articulate thoughts, she shares with the writer the common goal of establishing communication between the sensory and conceptual worlds: "avant un pas elle invite, avec deux doigts, un pli frémissant de sa jupe et simule une impatience de plumes vers l'idée" (306). We perceive the dancer's legs "sous quelque signification autre que personnelle, comme un instrument direct d'idée" (312). Thus, by contrast to the various genres of literary expression (whether poetic, fictional, or dramatic) dance actually requires not only a text form (which in and of itself evokes the inner theater of the mind) but also three-dimensional space within which to unfold:

> La danse seule, du fait de ses évolutions, avec le mime me paraît nécessiter un espace réel, ou la scène.

> A la rigueur un papier suffit pour évoquer toute pièce: aidé de sa personnalité multiple chacun pouvant se la jouer en dedans, ce qui n'est pas le cas quand il s'agit de pirouettes. (315)

Recognizing that dance, in contrast to literature, is a highly physical phenomenon, Mallarmé emphasizes that dancers are bound by the laws of nature. He appreciates that, try as they may, they cannot overcome their fundamental attachment to the earth. Indeed, he seems to delight in "cette espèce d'extatique impuissance à disparaître qui délicieusement attache aux planchers la danseuse" (305). The ballerina may appear to overcome gravity, but this illusion is the result of a difficult-to-maintain inner tension, a masterful control over the body.[10] "Ballets" opens with a description of Elena Cornalba, who seems, without even the help of a light, floating costume, to suspend herself in the air:

10. In *Feeling and Form* (1953, 193), Suzanne Langer presents dance as the manifestation of "virtual powers." Primary among these is the illusion of the conquest of gravity, which makes the ballerina seem like an apparition.

La Cornalba me ravit, qui danse comme dévêtue; c'est-à-dire que sans le semblant d'aide offert à un enlèvement ou à la chute par une présence volante et assoupie de gazes, elle paraît, appelée dans l'air, s'y soutenir, du fait italien d'une moelleuse tension de sa personne. (303)

In contrast to the tutu-clad ballerina, Fuller makes full use of her costume, but she, too, attempts to defy the laws of physics, filling the stage with yards of illuminated silks suspended in the air by the skillful manipulation of her body. Impressed at once by the aesthetic effect (produced in part by the lighting) and the technical difficulty of this feat, Mallarmé associates its production with both art and industry: "L'exercice, comme invention, sans l'emploi, comporte une ivresse d'art et, simultané un accomplissement industriel" (307). (In "La musique et les lettres" music was likewise compared to industry, while literature was compared to "finance.")

Being a highly physical mode of expression, dance is inherently tangible, or sensorially concrete. This is for Mallarmé an important factor distinguishing dance from literature. Literature, which presents itself in writing or print on paper, is, of course, also tangible (and we shall see that he focused with increasing intensity on its concrete aspects in such late works as *Un coup de dés* and *Le Livre*). But dance is certainly experienced by both dancers and spectators as being far more tangible than literature. Moreover, what is tangible in dance is generally more relevant to its aesthetic impact than are the concrete aspects of a text. This explains why a choreographic score (like its musical counterpart) is much less satisfying than a poetic "score": the former is clearly not the dance, while the latter (though it may also be read aloud) seems adequately enough to embody the poetry. The relative difference in the degree of concreteness of literature and dance also, somewhat paradoxically, explains why a literary work can be submitted to various types of radical formal transformation (e.g., translation) and still retain some measure of its original identity, while a dance cannot.[11]

Thus, despite his insistence on the semiotic character of dance, Mallarmé does not imply that the signifying function of the dancer presupposes a possible abstraction of her physical being. Though he sometimes describes the dancer as an apparition—the ballerina is an "être

---

11. What I wish to stress is that when a dance is rechoreographed or radically formally altered in a manner comparable to that required by a literary work's translation, the altered dance is neither necessarily perceived nor expected to faithfully reflect an earlier dance form. Rather, by virtue of its rechoreographing, the dance is felt to be a new and original work of art.

prestigieux reculé au-delà de toute vie possible" (307), and Fuller, "l'étranger, fantôme" (308)—he does not suggest that the dancer's presence can be itself illusory (e.g., imaginatively evoked as the mere effect of a written sign). On the contrary, it is owing to her concrete *physical presence* that the spectator can perform the theatrical "operation" of illusion, transforming her being into a ghost.

Contrary to what several critics have proclaimed, dance and poetry are not presented by Mallarmé as merely two variants of a single type of writing.[12] Rather, owing to dance's greater participation in matter and to the inherent duality of the dancer as both *interpreting subject* and *sign,* he considers it to be antithetical to poetry in some respects and to fulfill certain requirements of an ideal, all-encompassing art work that the poetic text cannot. If Mallarmé wished only to emphasize that poetry and dance are two forms of writing, two different manifestations of a general sign language, it would be pointless for him to stress as he does another distinguishing factor, the nonlinguistic, nonverbal character of dance.

While it is obvious that dance is a nonverbal form of expression and communication,[13] this fact is far from insignificant to Mallarmé, who underlines it on several occasions. The dancer, he insists, cannot express herself verbally; she is "mute," and her only eloquence is dancing (304,

---

12. Arguing (in my view incorrectly) that Mallarmé wished to achieve a literary synthesis of the arts comparable to Wagnerian music-drama, many critics have emphasized only the importance of his articulation of the similarities between poetry and dance (see, for example, Suzanne Bernard's *Mallarmé et la musique* [1959] and Guy Delfel's *L'esthétique de Stéphane Mallarmé* [1951]). In "La double séance" (1972, 273–75), Jacques Derrida underscores Mallarmé's articulation of differences among the arts. However, he, too, perhaps underplays the significance of a critical difference between literature and dance (the one being literally written, the other performed), suggesting that all differences among the arts are, for Mallarmé, less important than their collective demonstration of the general principle of writing as difference or differentiation. Derrida does not, for example, discuss the fact that Mallarmé sometimes presents literal and corporeal writing as not only different but also as partially contrary, or antithetical, modes.

13. Because dance is a means of expression and communication many dancers and theorists refer to it as a language. They do not, however, neglect the distinction between dance and literal language; rather they underscore the implications of dance's nonverbal character. In *The Language of Dance* (1966), Mary Wigman stresses the immediacy and directness with which dance conveys "man's innermost emotions and need for communication"; so does Rudolf von Laban in *The Language of Movement* (1974). In *To Dance is Human: A Theory of Non-verbal Communication* (1979), Judith Lynne Hanna analyzes dance as a form of communication similar to language except for its nonverbal aspect. In *The Dance* (1980), John Martin emphasizes the significance of this exception in describing dance as "the common impulse to resort to movement to externalize emotional states which cannot be externalized by rational means." For Martin, "rational means" are evidently those of language since he perceives dance as an "intuitive reaction which is too deep for words" (10).

306, 307). More strikingly (because it seems less generally relevant to an evaluation of dance), Mallarmé characterizes the dancer as illiterate. In "Ballets" the narrator instructs the spectator to follow attentively the configurations of "la ballerine illettrée se livrant aux jeux de sa profession" (307). In effect, he dramatically cuts the dancer off from every possible access to language.

Mallarmé's emphasis that the dancer does not communicate verbally, that dance is not linguistic, stems in part from his close association of language and consciousness, and he considers dance, in contrast to poetry, to be primarily unconscious and instinctive. This appraisal of dance (while it is far from unique to Mallarmé) is, of course, highly questionable. Dancers do not necessarily operate by instinct any more than poets do. It is important, however, to note Mallarmé's persistent implications that dancing does not involve any conscious, intellectual process, for it is partially on this basis that he posits the opposition and complementarity of dance and poetry.

Recall that in "Ballets" he tells the spectator to surrender their imagination not to the ballerina but to "ses pieds d'inconsciente révélatrice" (307). And though he credits Fuller with being an innovator, capable of teaching aesthetic lessons, he characterizes her, too, as a barely conscious source of revelation (her lesson is that dance ought not to be confined within the context of a fixed decor, i.e., immobile cardboard stage sets):

> . . . je dénonce . . . une erreur ordinaire à la mise en scène: aidé comme je suis, inespérément, soudain par la solution que déploie avec *l'émoi seul de sa robe ma très peu consciente* ou volontairement ici en cause inspiratrice. (Emphasis mine, 308)

It is in part because the dancer does not read, write, or speak that she is seen by Mallarmé as closer than other artists to nature. Dancers communicate directly through their bodies and operate, he says, "by instinct" (309). Hence, they portray animals better, for example, than actors do. The dancing characters of *Les deux pigeons* are well suited to represent lovebirds, being "plus instinctifs comme bondissants et muets que ceux à qui un conscient langage permet de s'énoncer dans la comédie" (304).

Yet Mallarmé describes the female lead of *Les deux pigeons* as both *animal-like* and *divine*: "l'émerveillante Mademoiselle [Rosita] Mauri résume le sujet par sa divination mêlée d'animalité trouble et pure" (305–6). The ballerina's "divination" clearly consists in the fact that without recourse to any form of human "sign" language, either gestural (she does not mime), written, or spoken, she nevertheless signifies, expresses, and communicates. Moreover, as earlier discussed, her body language does not seem to Mallarmé merely to represent. Rather (like the Word of God) it *embodies* its own referents and is thus a divine utterance ("parole divine").

Of crucial importance to Mallarmé is the capacity of dance *to be precisely what it signifies:* "Il est (tisonne-t-on), un art, l'unique ou pur qu'énoncer signifie produire: il hurle ses démonstrations par la pratique" (295). And what dance signifies most keenly is the physical dynamism of the human self. This is the particular virtue of dance for Mallarmé and what draws him to consider it as a superlative counterpart to the literary text.

Literature on its own constitutes the perfect monument to the human spirit, the solid binding of the book "offrant le miniscule tombeau, certes, de l'âme" (379).[14] And insofar as it maintains its distance from the sense-oriented world of theater, literature preserves also the secret of its own distinctive life and origin in the mind—an ever-hidden, intangible aspect of the self.

Yet literature, on its own, lacks an essential element testifying to the total fact of human being: it lacks the very aspects of the Self/Idea that dance and other performing arts provide in their presentation of a performing body. While the text can and should contain the author's image as a depersonalized origin of duality (as actor)—"L'écrivain . . . doit s'instituer, au texte, le spirituel histrion" (370)—it can do this only in an already dead, or (in Mallarmé's terms) "abolished" form—for example, through the narrative pronoun *I*. The advantage of dance and the performing arts generally is that in performance we perceive directly a depersonalized incorporation of the origin of the Idea. We behold the performer of the aesthetic *opération* through which this metaphysical principle is revealed, and we behold her live and in full action.

For Mallarmé, Fuller's seductive veil dances concretely exemplify that art is a process of self-transformation, of alternative self-projection and introjection. Art arises from the interaction and reciprocal influence between the mind and the body and between the self and the world. Mallarmé calls "emotion" the force or energy that permits this exchange: "Toute émotion sort de vous, élargit un milieu; ou sur vous fond et l'incorpore" (309). Emotion compels the innerself (imagination or

---

14. Mallarmé wrote a number of literary "tombeaux," three sonnets dedicated to the memory of Edgar Allan Poe, Charles Baudelaire, and Paul Verlaine, and *Pour un tombeau d'Anatole*, a heart-wrenching collection of notes commemorating the death of his own son, published posthumously by Jean-Pierre Richard (Mallarmé 1961).

spirit) to perform the act of becoming body or tangible form; and conversely it is emotion also, a sensorial reaction to the external world of tangible form (a "milieu"), that determines the creation of the imagining inner self.

Dance he thus views as a primary, fundamental form of art, its only "accessory" being "la présence humaine" (309), which extends itself into the world, reformalizing and therefore *depersonalizing* its own corporeal/spiritual nature:

> Une armature, qui n'est d'aucune femme en particulier, d'où instable, à travers le voile de généralité, attire sur tel fragment révélé de la forme et y boit l'éclair qui le divinise; ou exhale, de retour, par l'ondulation des tissus, flottante, palpitante, éparse cette extase. (311)

The dancer's veil is symbolically illuminated here as much from within as from without, as much by the dancer's as by the spectator's inner vision. In its trajectory toward the body (the "armature") the veil both draws from and attracts to that center a blinding light, "l'éclair qui le divinise." In its trajectory outward it becomes the figure of a palpable ecstasy, a being outside of itself. The veil is the optimal, symbolic extension of the dancing persona, because, like her, it embodies a mysterious, intermediate transparency that simultaneously separates and rejoins the real and the illusory, the sensory and the imagined: "Oui, le suspens de la Danse, crainte contradictoire ou souhait de voir trop et pas assez exige un prolongement transparent" (311). Like the dance itself, the veil is a vehicle rather than a barrier for the imagination; it epitomizes the nonrestrictive yet tangible presence that appealed to Mallarmé in all nonverbal performing arts.[15]

Like the "strange attitudes" of the ballerina, which deliver (across a veil) "mille imaginations latentes," Fuller's moving, illuminated veils reveal both her own and the spectators' fantasies (or naked concepts) (Figs. 2 and 3). The veils are a "fantasmagorie oxyhydrique" driven by "le vertige d'une âme comme mise à l'air par un artifice" (308). Fuller's only sets consist, miraculously, of this "fictional," ephemeral decor, which lies latent within yet another veil, the image-engendering music:

> Le décor gît, latent dans l'orchestre, trésor des imaginations; pour en sortir par éclat, selon la vue que dispense la représentante

---

15. In *L'univers imaginaire de Mallarmé* (1961a), Richard offers a comprehensive inventory of transparent or translucent things that held for Mallarmé a similar appeal, for example, "la fenêtre," "l'eau," "le nuage," "la chevelure."

> ça et là de l'idée à la rampe. Or cette transition de sonorités aux tissus (y a-t-il, mieux, à une gaze ressemblant que la Musique!) est, uniquement, le sortilège qu'opère la Loïe Fuller, par instinct, . . . instituant un lieu. (309)

Mallarmé thus describes her as one who both induces and exorcises visions: "L'enchanteresse fait l'ambiance, la tire de soi et l'y rentre, par un silence palpité de crêpes de Chine" (309). She draws forth and retracts the fantasy world of the spectators and is at the same time a "fontaine intarissable d'elle même" (311).

In the closing passage of his essay on Fuller, Mallarmé's prose emulates her exploitation of centrifugal force as his description alternates in focus between her central, rigid body and the surrounding expanse of whirling veils. The virtually inimitable, natural figures, which seem almost to detach themselves from her body—skies, sea, evening, perfume, and froth—suggest that, for Mallarmé, what Fuller exorcises and embodies is simply the imprint on the imagination of the sense-perceived beauty of the natural world.

> Ainsi ce dégagement multiple autour d'une nudité, grand des contradictoires vols où celle-ci l'ordonne, orageux, planant l'y magnifie jusqu'à la dissoudre: centrale, car tout obéit à une impulsion fugace en tourbillons, elle résume, par le vouloir aux extrémités éperdu de chaque aile et darde sa statuette, stricte, debout—morte de l'effort à condenser hors d'une libération presque d'elle des sursautements attardés décoratifs de cieux, de mer, de soirs, de parfum et d'écume. (309)

In *Crayonné au théâtre* dance is described on several occasions as ritual: it is called a "rite" (295), a "sacre" (296), a "sortilège" (309), and a "mystérieuse interprétation sacrée" (305). Dance is consistently associated with ritual, and not just from a strictly formal point of view (as a self-referential mode of expression consisting of gestures as opposed to words). Mallarmé clearly also perceives dance as performing a ritual function (as indeed it often does)—that is, as providing a means of public consecration of (and communion in) an absolute metaphysical principle.[16]

---

16. Dance, like music, plays an important part in many religious rites. In ethnological essays such as those collected by Franzisca Boas in *The Function of Dance in Human Society* (1944), we learn that dance has had a vital function in religious practice all over the world. In "Dance as a Rite of Transformation" (1981) Joann Kealiinohomoku explains concretely and in depth

Fig. 2.   Charles Maurin, *Loïe Fuller,* pastel, c. 1895. Courtesy Herbert and Ruth Schimmel Archives, The Jane Voorhees Zimmerli Art Museum, Rutgers, The State University of New Jersey.

Fig. 3. Charles Maurin, *Loïe Fuller,* pastel, c. 1895. Courtesy Herbert and Ruth Schimmel Archives, The Jane Voorhees Zimmerli Art Museum, Rutgers, The State University of New Jersey.

As we have seen, Mallarmé's absolute metaphysical principle, the Idea, is (as in many philosophies and religions) an abstract conceptualization of the unity-in-duality of mind and body on which human existence depends. Like music, dance within his critical texts is presented as an act confirming that duality as much as unity is intrinsic to the human condition. Though dance cannot repair the split separating mind and body, it can be a means of mediation. Like Rudolf von Laban and many other modern theorists of dance, Mallarmé views the mediation of the mind/body duality as one of dance's primary functions.[17] The stress he places on the mediative power of dance is evident in his persistent presentations of dance not only as allowing communication and exchange between mind and body and between the self and the world but also as mediating between a host of other contraries: in *Viviane*, between light and darkness (the stars and the night) and the one and the many (the prima ballerina and the corps de ballet); and in *Les deux pigeons*, between the natural and the supernatural (the woman who walks and the fairy who flies), the animal and the human (lovebirds and lovers), and male and female ("la différence sexuelle") (303–7).

Since dance has in its oxymoronic nature—as a pure (or nonlinguistic) body "language"—the capacity both to illustrate the duality inherent in the Idea and to mediate between its oppositions, Mallarmé considers it (along with music) a highly effective form of ritual.

In an important critical essay entitled "L'action restreinte" Mallarmé recommends that the writer perform a sacrificial rite of self-transformation, a dance whose description is uncannily similar to that of Fuller's veil dance. He also includes notes for a ritual ballet in the manuscript of his unfinished mystery play *Les noces d'Hérodiade, Mystère*, an earlier fragment of which inspired one of Martha Gra-

---

how religious ideas provide stimuli for dance behavior and how dance behavior functions, in turn, as "an agent for transforming religious ideas to religious emotions" (137). It is interesting to note that while in Western civilization the importance of dance to religious ritual has generally waned, its status as an art form has (since the seventeenth century) steadily increased. Thus, it is surprising to the contemporary reader that in a philosophical work devoted explicitly to analyzing the complete system of fine arts, first published in the 1830s, Hegel (1975) omits any discussion of dance on the ground that dance is (like gardening) an incomplete art.

17. In *The Language of Movement* (1974), Laban rationalizes the individual's need for movement (as body language) in the same manner that Lévi-Strauss rationalizes the human need for ritual. Dance, Laban suggests, is a means of coping with the fundamental duality inherent to the self for it integrates the attitudes of the body with those of the mind: "The integrating power of movement is perhaps its most important value for the individual" (12). In describing Mallarmé's conception of this process, I prefer to speak in terms of "mediation" rather than "integration," because he does not suggest that the mind/body duality either can or should be finally overcome.

ham's most important ritualistic dances, *Hérodiade* (1944).[18] Dance,
moreover, has an important place in the ceremonies of a future cult
whose program is set forth in *Le Livre*. Indeed, in the opening para-
graph of the essay "Parenthèse" (in which Mallarmé subtly compares
his vision of the temple of the art of the future to that of Wagner), the
dancer waiting in the wings is explicitly designated as the supreme
officiant of the rite:

> Cependant non loin, le lavage à grande eau musical du Temple,
> qu'effectue devant ma stupeur, l'orchestre avec ses déluges de
> gloire ou de tristesse versés, ne l'entendez-vous pas? dont la
> Danseuse restaurée mais encore invisible à des préparatoires céré-
> monies, semble la mouvante écume suprême. (322)

18. Mallarmé also inserts a ritual ballet into his very liberal translation of Mary Summer's
tale "Le mort vivant"—a ballet celebrating the marriage of the tale's principal characters,
Tchandra-Rajah and Lakshmi: "Un ballet merveilleux et unique s'inscrivit au cérémonial." The
dancers are a troup of "bayadères" whose veils are light on one side and dark on the other.
They disperse, presenting to the spectators first their light side (representing the flight of "les
jours du prince"); then, reconverging, they present "la moitié nocturne de leurs voiles et
simulent, en une rigidité de sommeil, les monotones nuits du tombeau." Finally, "elles
confondent, tel le mariage de chaque nuit avec son jour restauré, leur aspect double, sombre ou
clair, dans un tourbillon sur la pointe des pieds" (615).

CHAPTER FOUR

Theater:
"Le vrai culte moderne"

Mallarmé analyzes theater in most of the essays in *Crayonné au thé-âtre*.[1] As he does with music and dance, he often compares theater to literature and designates it as a quintessential art form: "Le Théâtre est d'essence supérieure" (312). Spectacle in general strongly appeals to him (even circuses, parades, and side shows), and he presents the physical site of theater as the perfect framework for the ultimate work of art:

> La scène est le foyer évident des plaisirs pris en commun, aussi et tout bien réfléchi, la majestueuse ouverture sur le mystère dont on est au monde pour envisager la grandeur. (314)

As is evident in this passage, Mallarmé defines theater both as a form of public entertainment and as an aperture onto metaphysical truth. We shall see further that he stresses the alienating effects of theater and the mutual estrangement of its constituent arts as well as its carthartic powers and sensorial concreteness. His theatrical criticism thus anticipates, and in a sense reconciles, important aspects of the two predominant theories of twentieth-century theater, those of Bertolt Brecht and Antonin Artaud.[2]

---

1. In a less serious vein, under the pseudonym Ix, he also reviewed a number of plays in *La dernière mode's* "Chronique de Paris."

2. In considering theater as both entertainment, "les plaisirs pris en commun," and ritual, Mallarmé is, for example closer to contemporary theorists of performance such as Richard Schechner who regard these two poles of theater as inseparable (see Chapter 1) than to either Brecht or Artaud. While Artaud completely identifies theater with its metaphysical function, Brecht sharply distinguishes theater from ritual on the basis that the former maintains its distance from the spectator and produces only "pleasure" (1977, 181).

Mallarmé's attitude toward the theater of his day was, however, extremely ambivalent. He described theater as a "monstre ou Mediocrité" (313), a crude provisionary machine offering the public not satisfaction but only an ever-deepening hunger. Owing especially to his own great expectations for a theater to come, he was frustrated by the ineptness of contemporary playwrights who filled:

> . . . mais des éléments de médiocre puisés dans leur spéciale notion du public, le trou magnifique ou l'attente qui, comme une faim, se creuse chaque soir, au moment où brille l'horizon, dans l'humanité—ouverture de gueule de la Chimère méconnue et frustrée à grand soin par l'arrangement social. (294)

There are three types of theater about which Mallarmé writes: drama (in the broad sense of the staging, or *mise en scène*, of a literary text); pantomime, the silent, gestural transcription of a text or *libretto;* and the Catholic Mass, whose performance he designates as the model for a modern theater both metaphysical and political in nature. The Mass he characterizes as "la mise en scène de la religion d'état, par nul cadre encore dépassée et qui . . . satisfait étrangement un souhait moderne philosophique et d'art" (396).

Mallarmé's paramount criticism of contemporary theater concerns its dramatic content. For the most part, he considers plays to be devoid of the fantasy and mystery of which poetry, music, and dance are made, offering a "marchandise différente de l'extase et du faste" (330). *Crayonné au théâtre* opens with a self-portrait of the poet/critic who has dragged himself to the theater and now sits before a typical play that leaves him bored and cold. He leans over the balcony "traits à l'avance fatigués du néant," suppressing a symbolic yawn: "un bâillement, qui est la suprême, presque ingénue et la plus solitaire protestation ou dont le lustre aux mille cris suspend comme un écho l'horreur radieuse et visible" (293).[3]

He is bored because the play is nothing but a realistic (i.e., verisimilar) representation of the events of everyday life, "une anecdote mise debout avec des airs insupportables de vraisemblance" (337). As briefly discussed in Chapter 1, for Mallarmé the mere representation of an extrinsic referent, (whether it be anecdote, legend, history, or a current event) cannot constitute an authentic artwork. He consistently labels prosaic

---

3. The yawn is provoked by an inane nothingness, the insignificance of the representation, but the *lustre* that echoes or reflects this yawn symbolizes a significant and therefore frightening metaphysical nothingness.

dramas with the negative term *simulacrum* and deems them unworthy of enthroning upon the stage.

As Haskell M. Block (1963) has shown, in underscoring the mediocrity of the theater of his time and in insisting on the necessity for restoring its magic, Mallarmé played a crucial role in the development of Symbolist theater. As early as 1874 (in *La dernière mode*), he called for a revolution in the theater: "l'art dramatique de notre Temps, vaste, sublime, presque religieux, est à trouver" (717). He was an active supporter of both Paul Fort's Théâtre d'Art and Lugné-Poe's Théâtre de L'Œuvre, whose most important playwrights, such as Maeterlinck, Jarry, and Claudel, were deeply influenced by his work. As we shall see, however, the Symbolist drama did not correspond to Mallarmé's vision of ideal theater. And the fundamental ambivalence he expresses toward contemporary theater in general suggests his dissatisfaction with "Symbolist" as well as "realist" plays.

It would be a great oversimplification, however, to view Mallarmé's dramatic criticism as rejecting theater outright. He underscores positive aspects not only of the detheatricalized poetic dramas of Banville and Maeterlinck but also of the realist and naturalist plays of the Goncourt brothers, Daudet, and Zola. Rather than lingering on the inappropriateness of the brand of fiction that some of these authors chose to stage, he isolates various good features in their theatrical productions and compliments certain qualities of their dramatic texts.

Mallarmé tends to discuss the literary value of his peers' works and avoid discussion of their theatrical value in part because no ordinary play can overcome what he perceives as a basic flaw inherent in the dramatic genre itself: its mixed, or hybrid, quality. For him, an effective verbal text is self-sufficient. It requires no performance (unless, as in *Le Livre*, it strives to be total, or all-encompassing, art). Similarly, an effective performance (of music or dance, for example) does not require the accompaniment of a verbal text; the listeners or spectators supply a verbal translation to what they hear or see. But drama (unlike music, dance, or literature) implies the necessary and explicit collaboration of verbal and nonverbal modes; it is thus not a "genre entier."[4]

4. Mallarmé's aversion to the hybrid quality of theater is clearly expressed in an 1876 letter to Anatole France. Since theater and poetry should not be mixed, Mallarmé implores France not to categorize his *Noces* (a version of *Hérodiade* that will be explored later) as a "poème dramatique," because an intrinsic necessity for staging implies a weakness in the literary power of the text: "Avant de parler des *Noces*, je tiens à exprimer à leur endroit une opinion qui fait loi pour moi, relativement au moule où vous les avez jetés: le poème dramatique me désespère car si j'ai un principe quelconque en critique, c'est qu'il faut avant tout rechercher la pureté des genres. Théâtre d'un côté ou poème de l'autre." The poem itself should be able to supplement

Throughout *Crayonné au théâtre,* and particularly in the essays "Planches et feuillets" and "Le genre ou des modernes," Mallarmé stresses the point that literature does not require the complement of real objects—things, people, or actions—in order to attain its full effect; words are the currency of the immaterial world. The intellect-oriented efficacy of a verbal text (even though it may have been originally destined for theatrical performance) is essentially different from the sense-oriented efficacy of dance or mime:[5] "A la rigueur un papier suffit pour évoquer toute pièce: aidé de sa personnalité multiple chacun pouvant se la jouer en dedans, ce qui n'est pas le cas quand il s'agit de pirouettes" (315). In fact, from Mallarmé's point of view, the effectiveness of a verbal text (be it dramatic or otherwise) is weakened or even destroyed by the concreteness of a supporting performance:

> Par une mentale opération et point d'autre, lecteur je m'adonne à abstraire la physionomie, sans le déplaisir d'un visage exact penché, hors la rampe, sur ma source ou âme. Ses traits réduits à des mots, un maintien le cédant à l'identique disposition de phrase, tout ce pur résultat atteint pour ma délectation noble, s'effarouche d'une interprète. (318)

The only theater appropriate for the staging of poetry, in particular, is the theater of the mind, whose curtain rises in confrontation with its instrument, the book:

> ... maintenant le livre essaiera de suffire, pour entr'ouvrir la scène intérieure et en chuchoter les échos. Un ensemble versifié convie à une idéale représentation. ... Un théâtre, inhérent à l'esprit, quiconque d'un œil certain regarda la nature le porte avec

---

the effect of theater (like the effect of music), to re-create a theatrical atmosphere by means of its internal structure: "A agir autrement, ne voyez-vous pas un inconvénient dans l'absence de ce va-et-vient des personnages parmi l'enchantement scénique, la lumière et le décor visibles du théâtre?" (Mallarmé 1953, 119).

5. I disagree with critics such as André Chastel who argue that, for Mallarmé, the power of theater and the power of literature are one and the same: "La poésie est la mise en scène des mêmes pouvoirs que le théâtre; comme l'attention sollicitée et conquise par le jeu de la scène, l'exercice mental appelle, chatoiement de merveilles, apparitions de personnages, dédoublements infinis, suggestions et rappels" (1948, 98). The obvious but crucial difference is that poetry calls upon a mental exercise to perform this "mise en scène" while theater immediately provides it, appealing directly to the senses.

soi, résumé de types et d'accords; ainsi que les confronte le vo-
lume ouvrant des pages parallèles. (328)

Paradoxically, on the rare occasion that Mallarmé has an especially
favorable reaction to a play, it is because the play does not dissimulate its
hybrid origins. Just as the text creates the impression of a performance,
the performance creates the impression of a text. He compliments
Daudet and Maeterlinck for achieving precisely these effects. Daudet's
theater offers an unusual charm for both spectators and readers, who
find themselves captivated by that which seems neither completely a
spectacle nor a text.

> Art qui inquiète, séduit comme vrai derrière une ambiguïté entre
> l'écrit et le joué, des deux aucun; elle verse, le volume presque
> omis, le charme inhabituel à la rampe. Si le présent perfide et cher
> d'un asservissement à la pensée d'autrui, plus! à une écriture—
> que le talisman de la page; on ne se croit, ici, d'autre part, captif
> du vieil enchantement redoré d'une salle, le spectacle impliquant
> je ne sais quoi de direct ou encore la qualité de provenir de
> chacun à la façon d'une vision libre. (319)

Akin to Daudet's art is "l'art de M. Maeterlinck," who brought the
pleasures of the text into the theater, "*Pelléas et Mélisande* sur une scène
exhale, de feuillets, le délice" (330) and "qui, aussi, inséra le théâtre au
livre!" (329).

It is not despite but *because of* his belief in the necessary purity, or
integrity, of genres that Mallarmé appreciates the generic ambiguity of
Daudet's and Maeterlinck's plays. Clearly exhibiting the contradiction
inherent to theater, these at least appeal to him as honest ("true") works
of art. Their performances do not play over the text, as though referring
directly to reality; nor do their texts render the world of theater into
oblivion. Rather (like the Ideal Book Mallarmé describes in "Solennité")
they call up this world and supplement it:

> Quelle représentation! le monde y tient; un livre, dans notre
> main, s'il énonce quelque idée auguste, supplée à tous les théâtres,
> non par l'oubli qu'il en cause mais les rappelant impérieusement,
> au contraire. (334)

But what is the nature of this theatrical world to which the book and
its imaginary theater act as supplements? It is not itself an imagined,
immaterial world, but a world of concrete presence. It is the physical

site, or context, in which man places himself (as both actor and speculator) in order to act and also to witness "le mystère dont on est au monde pour envisager la grandeur" (314).

Mallarmé appreciates Shakespeare's theater, and particularly *Hamlet*, because it exposes a central metaphysical issue, the antagonism between human dream and destiny. Hamlet's solitary existential drama "semble le spectacle même pourquoi existent la rampe ainsi que l'espace doré quasi moral qu'elle défend, car il n'est point d'autre sujet, sachez bien: l'antagonisme de rêve chez l'homme avec les fatalités à son existence départies par le malheur" (300). He also generally approves of the profounder types of drama: of classical French tragedy, whose intention was to "produire en un milieu nul ou à peu près les grandes poses humaines et comme notre plastique morale" (319), and even of certain contemporary dramas such as Zola's *Renée,* in which humanity's tragic revolt against its fate is also revealed, though in a less explicit way.

> Ce volontaire effacement extérieur qui particularise notre façon, toutefois, ne peut sans des éclats se prolonger et la succincte foudre qui servira de détente à tant de contrainte et d'inutiles précautions contre l'acte magnifique de vivre, marque d'un jour violent le malheureux comme pris en faute dans une telle interdiction de se montrer à même.
>
> Voilà une théorie tragique actuelle ou, pour mieux dire, la dernière: le drame, latent, ne se manifeste que par une déchirure affirmant l'irréductibilité de nos instincts. (321)

For Mallarmé, the tragedy of human existence consists not only in the inaccessibility of the ideal but also in the identity-in-difference of the real and the ideal. Thoroughly entrapped in a concrete and contingent world, humanity cannot let go of its dreams of the absolute, which are themselves the product of that world. Humanity thus continually experiences the conflict that Lévi-Strauss names in defining what creates the need for ritual, not simply the world's resistance to man but "la résistance, à l'homme de sa pensée" (1971, 609).

For Mallarmé as for Shakespeare, "all the world is a stage," every play a shadow of "la pièce écrite au folio du ciel et mimée avec le geste de ses passions par l'Homme" (294). Clearly, he views the tangible theater as a fabricated microcosm of the "universal theater," a reconstruction of the world similar to that of the poetic text, which, as Richard E. Goodkin (1984, 19) has shown, Mallarmé also recognizes as man's "home-away-from-home." The book, then, functions not only as a supplement to theater but also as a supplement to the world: "avec deux pages et leurs vers, je supplée, puis l'accompagnement de tout moi-même, au monde! où je perçois, discret, le drame" (328).

Though material and concrete, the theater has, for Mallarmé, as much an ideal status as the imaginary world reconstructed in the text. In "L'Action restreinte" he makes it clear that theater should aim directly at the representation of truth with a view toward its public celebration. Though he admits that the theater he envisages has yet to be born, he designates it as the only authentic form of action for the restless poet wishing to become engaged in events "en l'ordre réel" (370). The theater toward which he directs the poet is fictional (though not false), ephemeral, and thus Ideal:

> Ainsi l'Action, en le mode convenu, littéraire, ne transgresse pas le Théâtre; s'y limite, à la représentation—immédiat évanouissement de l'écrit. Finisse, dans la rue, autre part, cela, le masque choit, je n'ai pas à faire au poëte. (371)

In his "Notes sur le théâtre" Mallarmé stresses that it is essential to safeguard in theater the uncanny atmosphere embodied in the mask. This atmosphere can be variously created, of course, through lighting, makeup, and music (as, for example, in melodrama) and also, Mallarmé argues, by the placing of males in female roles (as in Shakespeare). Such inversions "prêtent à un cas trop rare où persiste chez nous l'impression d'étrangeté et de certain malaise qui ne doit jamais, quant à une esthétique primitive et saine, cesser tout à fait devant le déguisement, indice du théâtre, ou Masque" (339).

If theater is to retain its status as an art "d'essence supérieure," it is fundamental that it preserve its mysterious, enigmatic quality. Although Mallarmé considers his contemporaries to have ignored or abused the proper function of theater, he asserts that all of the elements necessary for the ultimate work of art are housed there:

> Notre seule magnificence, la scène, à qui le concours d'arts divers scellés par la poésie attribue selon moi quelque caractère religieux ou officiel, si l'un de ces mots a un sens, je constate que le siècle finissant n'en a cure, ainsi comprise; et que cet assemblage miraculeux de tout ce qu'il faut pour façonner de la divinité, sauf la clairvoyance de l'homme, sera pour rien. (313–14)

The drama of man in the world is concretely re-created in the theater, whose three essential elements are "la scène," the stage on which we find the physical presence of the actor; "la salle," the hall in which we also find the presence of humanity, here in the role of spectator; and "le lustre," which hangs overhead ignored, symbolizing "la clairvoyance." Though it does not actively constitute a part of the spectacle, the chandelier is, for Mallarmé, an important symbol in that it crystallizes the value of theater as illuminated, multifaceted form. As we saw in the preceding chapter, insofar as it symbolizes transparent being, or presence, the *lustre* is a more complex variant of the dancer's veil. Its suspended, ideal presence consists of a singular capacity to simultaneously be, illuminate, and reflect "quoi que ce soit et notre vue adamantine" (296). By virtue of its inner light and the transparency of its tiers of glass, the chandelier symbolizes what is at once interior (conscious) and exterior (corporeal) presence. By virtue of its location, the chandelier also symbolizes the paradoxical inaccessibility to humanity of what in fact constitutes its own modality of being—in short, the transposition of self-presence into an absent transcendence. Like the unattainable Idea, the chandelier hangs high above both spectators and actors; even its symbolic significance is beyond their reach. The spectators see only themselves "ainsi qu'ils se connaissent dans la rue ou à la maison" (315) and the reflection of themselves in the actors upon the stage: "rien n'existe qu'eux, demeurent sur la scène seulement des gens pareils aux spectateurs" (313). The actors have an equally limited perspective: "le théâtre institue des personnages agissant et en relief précisément pour qu'ils négligent la métaphysique, comme l'acteur omet *la présence du lustre*" (emphasis mine, 327).[6]

Paradoxically, for Mallarmé, it is just this lack of "clairvoyance" (on the part of the spectators and actors) that allows theater, like music and dance, to reign alongside literature as a superior art form "approaching" the Idea (a unity of the physical and the conceptual, which can never appear as such). While literature, we have seen, is closely identified in Mallarmé's criticism with the immaterial world of spiritual light (i.e., of concepts and understanding), theater, like music and dance, is primarily associated with the material world, with the body and the senses, and with unconscious feeling.

For Mallarmé as for Artaud (in *Le théâtre et son double*) the essence of theater does not reside in verbal language but, rather, as Artaud puts

---

6. In "Plaisir sacré" Mallarmé speculates that if the members of the audience were aware of the metaphysical truth symbolized by the *lustre* they would never come to the theater to seek it out: "Jamais ne tomberait l'archet souverain battant la première mesure, s'il fallait qu'à cet instant spécial de l'année, le lustre, dans la salle, représentât, par ses multiples facettes, une lucidité chez le public, relativement à ce qu'on vient faire" (388).

it, in a "langage physique et concret," a "poésie pour les sens," drawn from the various media of the stage (1964, 54).[7] The fact that Mallarmé designates not drama but "mimique, jonglerie, danse, et la simple acrobatie" as "les forces théâtrales exactes" (314) strongly suggests that he considers any explicit involvement of language in theater to be a contamination of the purity of theatrical expression. Thus, in spite of his rejection of the traditional ideal of art as mimesis, we should not be entirely surprised to find that he holds up pantomime as an exemplary model of theatrical form.

Mallarmé makes a number of brief references to pantomime throughout his discussion of performing arts, but his fullest analysis of the genre is to be found in a short piece entitled "Mimique." In spite of its brevity (two paragraphs) "Mimique" is one of the most difficult and elliptical of his critical texts. It is difficult because nearly every phrase is the expression of a paradox, and it is elliptical in that there are several important buried allusions to the particular history of the pantomime being discussed. As is the case with many of Mallarmé's essays, there is more than one version of "Mimique," and the textual references become progressively more obscure with time. In *La double séance*, Jacques Derrida has done the archaeological work necessary for the reader who seeks a full understanding of the complex intertextuality of "Mimique." Here I will be discussing primarily the 1897 *Divagations* version as reproduced in the *Œuvres complètes*.[8]

In the first paragraph Mallarmé equates the silence *engendered* by the blank spaces of poetry (following after each verse) with the silence experi-

---

7. In Artaud's work, as in Mallarmé's, there is a clear correlation between the favoring of nonverbal performative modes and the drive to restore to theater its ritual function. In *Le théâtre et son double* Artaud rejects the Western dramatists' traditional dependence on language—the dialogue or dramatic text. In so doing he claims to be restoring to theater its "metaphysical" aspect—described as "une sorte de démonstration expérimentale de l'identité profonde du concret et de l'abstrait . . . l'idée furtive du passage et de la transmutation des idées dans les choses" (1964, 164–65)—and to be following the example of oriental theater (which is ritual), where music, dance, and gesture have always played a very prominent role. "Faire cela, lier le théâtre aux possibilités de l'expression par les formes, et par tout ce qui est gestes, bruits, couleurs, plastiques, etc., c'est le rendre à sa destination primitive, c'est le replacer dans son aspect religieux et métaphysique, c'est le réconcilier avec l'univers" (1964, 106).

8. Derrida reprints the two anterior versions of the essay: one from *La Revue Indépendante* (1886) and the other from *Pages* (1891). He also digs up the pantomime libretto and its preface, as well as their intertexts (1972, 222–33). While I am indebted to his reading, my conclusions may be incompatible with his. As will become clear, I perceive "Mimique" as underscoring more the peculiar paradoxical relationship of gestural and literal writing in pantomime than the general principle of writing as difference per se.

enced *during* the performance of music and in front of the mime, Paul Margueritte:

> Le silence, seul luxe après les rimes, un orchestre ne faisant avec son or, ses frôlements de pensée et de soir, qu'en détailler la signification à l'égal d'une ode tue et que c'est au poëte, suscité par un défi, de traduire! le silence aux après-midi de musique; je le trouve, avec contentement, aussi, devant la réapparition toujours inédite de Pierrot ou du poignant et élégant mime Paul Margueritte. (310)

The silence in question is clearly not just what exists in the absence of noise but, rather, a silence or absence of language, which paradoxically is drawn out, or formalized, by the tangible presence of music or mime— a silence challenging the poet to attempt its linguistic translation. The silence of mime is thus the equivalent of the blankness of the page, a whiteness, whose presence is (as Mallarmé writes in "Le mystere dans les lettres") ideally *authenticated* (rendered true) through its contrary—the blackness, or presence, of a poem there inscribed:

> Lire—
>
> Cette pratique—
>
> Appuyer, selon la page, au blanc, qui l'inaugure son ingénuité, à soi, oublieuse même du titre qui parlerait trop haut: et, quand s'aligna, dans une brisure, la moindre, disséminée, le hasard vaincu mot par mot, indéfectiblement le blanc revient, tout à l'heure gratuit, certain maintenant, pour conclure que rien au-delà et authentiquer le silence—
>
> Virginité qui solitairement, devant une transparence du regard adéquat, elle-même s'est comme divisée en ses fragments de candeur, l'un et l'autre, preuves nuptiales de l'Idée.
>
> L'air ou chant sous le texte, conduisant la divination d'ici là, y applique son motif en fleuron et cul-de-lampe invisibles. (386–87)

Owing to its unwritten, nonverbal character, mime (like music and dance) consists, for Mallarmé, of a white or "negative" writing. But in the above-cited passage we must wonder what the corresponding "candeur" of black (literal) writing consists of. Doesn't its "virginity" reside in the fact that it represents the negation, or rendering absent, of things tangible such as are perceived in nature or in music, dance, or mime?

This interpretation may be difficult to accept, since writing is, after all, tangible. Yet in "Mimique," as we shall see, the absence of linguistic signs (literary whiteness/silence) is explicitly equated with the presence of performative, corporeal writing (which might seem more similar to the literary "black"), and conversely, the presence of a written libretto (the literary "black") is equated with the absence of performative writing. In "Mimique" (as in the above-cited passage from "Le mystère dans les lettres") we are clearly invited to recognize that ideal silence (or the Idea) results from the equation of such contraries as presence and absence, silence and nonsilence, and so forth.

The pantomime *Pierrot Assassin de sa Femme* (a composite of the gestural writing and libretto) establishes this ideal silence in three different ways. The first is the way in which the mime mimes, or represents. He offers a representation that is really not one, since his performance is said not to repeat anything that has gone before, either words or gestures; his "réapparition" is paradoxically ever new, "toujours inédite." The gestural pantomime (which, as Derrida has pointed out, did in fact historically precede the writing of the libretto) presents itself as a representation of something verbal, but of a speech unspoken and a still unwritten text, "soliloque muet que, tout du long à son âme tient et du visage et des gestes le fantôme blanc comme une page pas encore écrite" (310).

Second, an ideal silence results from the nature of the action that the mime represents—"l'assassin[at] de sa femme," Colombine. This is neither an effective murder (it is a tickling to death) nor any real action at all. Pierrot mimes only his anticipation of the murder and his memory of it. He mimes both of these as though they were taking place in the present, but in fact never mimes the "fatal" deed itself.

> "La scène n'illustre que l'idée, pas une action effective, dans un hymen (d'où procède le Rêve), vicieux mais sacré, entre le désir et l'accomplissement, la perpétration et son souvenir: ici devançant, là remémorant, au futur, au passé, *sous une apparence fausse de présent*. Tel opère le Mime, dont le jeu se borne à une allusion perpétuelle sans briser la glace: il installe, ainsi, un milieu, pur, de fiction." (310)[9]

---

9. Derrida points out that this is not a real quotation, that Mallarmé is simply using the effect of quotation to graft on another layer of representation to those already confused in the mime. One important aspect of this complexity (which cannot be easily inferred from "Mimique") is that Pierrot (playing both himself and Colombine) is at once the victim and perpetrator of his crime. After Colombine dies of laughter, Pierrot hallucinates that it is she,

Finally, the libretto, which verbally translates the gesturing of the mime, necessarily presents itself to the reader as an amputated discourse, a mute or silent theatrical text. Its words will never be spoken, nor will they, in fact, be mimed, for as the narrator emphasizes from the outset the mime's performance is ever original, "toujours inédite." By virtue of the fact that the libretto is not destined to be performed, its integrity is safeguarded along with that of the performance. Cut off from its performance, the text preserves its own aura of absence and silence (a performative silence equal to that of the mime's mute soliloquy), one which Mallarmé designates as necessary for the act of reading:

> Surprise, accompagnant l'artifice d'une notation de sentiments par phrases point proférées—que, dans le seul cas, peut-être, avec authenticité, entre les feuillets et le regard règne un silence encore, condition et délice de la lecture. (310)

Thus, the Ideal silence, established by both the pantomime performance and libretto (and reflected thematically within the content of each), depends not merely on their respective lacking of a verbal or gestural complement but, rather, on the reference to, and projection of, the possibility of these complements and their simultaneous denial.

The advantage that Mallarmé discerns in pantomime over ordinary drama is that it maintains an inviolable distance between the performative and textual modes. We might say that pantomime (as a disjunct composite of a nonverbal performance and a nonperformed text) pushes the Brechtian principle of the isolation and mutual alienation of theater's constituent arts to its radical extreme (Brecht 1977, 204). In accomplishing this, pantomime is able to coordinate two aesthetic principles that ordinary drama cannot. It presents to the spectator/reader all constituents of theater: the verbal and the gestural, the intellectual and the sensorial, the immaterial and the concrete, thereby providing a work of art capable of "representing" the totality of experience. But it also preserves the full effect and purity of these divergent aspects. Pantomime thus respects the fundamental principle of unity-in-duality, which dictates for Mallarmé that works of art remain eternally incomplete. The vision of totality that the theater presents is one in which each part can refer only to its supplement (that is, the latent or virtual exis-

---

reanimated in her portrait, who has the last laugh: "Pierrot est repris par la trépidation et le chatouillement, enfin il meurt aux pieds de sa 'victime peinte qui rit toujours' " (Derrida 1972, 229).

tence of its complement), which is not immediately present within it but which would (if present) render it complete.

For Mallarmé, therefore, although an important element of ideal theater may be verbal, this element is not paradoxically *parole,* but, rather, *écriture,* a silent literary text relating to gesture in the same manner that it relates to music. The presence of the gestural or musical performance implies the presence-in-absence of the verbal text. Thus (as we shall see further) in works where he represents the combination of literary and performative modes, these combinations do not function to create the impression of a synthetic, unified whole but, rather, to re-inforce our sense of these arts' reciprocal estrangement and of the work's wholeness-in-fragmentation.[10]

If pantomime is an exemplary model for theater in terms of form, the Catholic Mass provides the example that theater should follow in terms of ritual atmosphere and metaphysical ambition. In the essays grouped under the title "Offices," Mallarmé poses a triple association among religion, performing arts, and secular rituals celebrating the absolute principles around which the state organizes public life.

In the first essay, "Plaisir sacré," we saw that Mallarmé considered music to provide the public with a means of fulfilling both its ancient need for religion—a metaphysical cult—and its need for a social, secular event—"un culte humain." In "De même" he affirms that even when religion has lost its hold over people, a cult will remain necessary to sanction their devotion to the interests of the State.

> Quand le vieux vice religieux, si glorieux, qui fut de dévier vers l'incompréhensible les sentiments naturels, pour leur conférer une grandeur sombre, se sera dilué aux ondes de l'évidence et du jour, cela ne demeurera pas moins, que le dévouement à la Patrie, par exemple, s'il doit trouver une sanction autre qu'en le champ de bataille, dans quelque allégresse, requiert un culte: étant de piété. (397)

Mallarmé considers religion, like art, to be a means of masking the nothingness that humanity encounters, both outside of itself in the material world (395) and within—that emptiness which is felt physically as hunger and spiritually as an abhorrence of death (390–91). Humanity

10. In this regard it is interesting to note Brecht's call for "the literarization of theater" as a means of preventing the spectator from being "carried away" by the single track of the dramatic action. He explains the projection of scene titles on screens in his *Threepenny Opera* as a "primitive attempt" at achieving this (1977, 43–44).

projects its sense of nothingness and death into an eternal metaphysical abyss and then fills it up with a heavenly presence dictating absolute principles, which are nothing but the principles inherent to being human. Thus is inevitably created a self-deceiving transcendence, a chimerical God, or "Divinité, qui jamais n'est que Soi" (391). Mallarmé speculates that this dream of transcendence will always survive, if not in the form of religion as it has been known at least in the form of its secular or political corollaries, for example, in inviolable social principles: "Quand même survivrait, acceptation courante d'une entre les Chimères, la religion, en cette épreuve liminaire, la Justice" (392).

The question for Mallarmé, then, is not *whether* society should concern itself with transcendent principles and the absolute, but *how*. In "Catholicisme" and "De même" he describes his vision of "les fêtes futures" and shows how the essence of these anticipated secular ceremonies has already been created in the rudiments of the Catholic Mass.

In both these ceremonies the transcendent being is shown to be a presence-in-absence. The "Divinity" is not represented as an epiphany; rather it is actually configured as a void. It is enclosed in a grand theater where we find the essential elements of theater earlier discussed. There is communication between *la scène* and *la salle,* and *le lustre* (a symbol for the divine presence) is suspended high above. As in ordinary theater, here the *lustre* does not illuminate or clarify for the participants either the nature of what is being worshiped or the meaning of the worshiping event taking place, it merely reflects the various aspects of the ceremony and symbolizes it. Here is how Mallarmé's describes his crystal-ball entry into the theater, or temple, of future rites:

> L'intrusion dans les fêtes futures.
>
> Que doivent-elles être: tributaires, d'abord, du loisir dominical—
>
> Nul, à moins de suspendre, comme sa vision, le lourd lustre, évocateur multiple de motifs, n'éclairerait ici; mais on peut déduire, pourtant, des moyens et des nécessités en cause.
>
> A quelque amphithéâtre, comme une aile d'infinité humaine, bifurque la multitude, effarouchée devant le brusque abîme fait par le dieu, l'homme—ou Type.
>
> Représentation avec concert. (393)

As in "Plaisir sacré," in "Catholicisme" music is presented as a vehicle for reciprocal interaction between those present and he who is absent.

Through it the members of the audience commune in that nonpresence, which constitutes the divine Myth:

> Le miracle de la musique est cette pénétration, en réciprocité, du mythe et de la salle, par quoi se comble jusqu'à étinceler des arabesques et d'ors en traçant l'arrêt à la boîte sonore, l'espace vacant, face à la scène: absence d'aucun, où s'écarte l'assistance et que ne franchit le personnage.

The "représentation" is a "Mystère," a Passion play portraying (but more abstractly than the Christian version) the birth, life, death, and rebirth of Man, assimilated to the cycle of the seasons.

> Ici, reconnaissez, désormais, dans le drame, la Passion, pour élargir l'acception canoniale ou, comme ce fut l'esthétique fastueuse de l'Église, avec le feu tournant d'hymnes, une assimilation humaine à la tétralogie de l'An. (393)

The hero of the Mystery, in fact, lies latent in each member of the crowd, "protagoniste à son insu." Everyone is God:

> L'orchestre flotte, remplit et l'action, en cours, ne s'isole étrangère et nous ne demeurons des témoins: mais, de chaque place, à travers les affres et l'éclat, tour à tour, sommes circulairement le héros—douloureux de n'atteindre à lui-même que par des orages de sons et d'émotions déplacés sur son geste ou notre afflux invisible. Personne n'est-il, selon le bruissant, diaphane rideau de symboles, de rythmes, qu'il ouvre sur sa statue, à tous. (393)

To Mallarmé, it seems inevitable that humanity should respond to this portrayal of the central drama of life by performing a corresponding physical, concrete act. Our visions of the world are transposed into actions (and vice versa); the myth engenders the rite: "Sa hantise, au théâtre que l'esprit porte, grandira, en majesté de temple." An act of communion such as that of the sacrament—"la consécration de l'hostie"—would be a necessary element of the rite, "l'amateur que l'on est, maintenant, de quelque chose qui, au fond, soit ne saurait plus assister, comme passant, à la tragédie . . . tout de près, exige un fait." The act of Communion symbolizes the believers' faith (in Mallarmé's view also a literal reality) that the hero of the myth is a " 'Présence réelle': ou, que le dieu soit là, diffus, total, mimé de loin par l'acteur effacé, par nous su tremblants, en raison de toute gloire, latente si telle indue, qu'il assuma" (394).

What is striking in Mallarmé's references to the Mass is that beyond his association of the drama of man with Christ's Passion, there is no attention whatsoever to the content of Christian "mythology," which is, of course, expressed in the verbal messages or pronouncements of the officiant of the Mass. As he explains in "De même," his interest in the Mass is focused solely on the way in which it achieves its end, evoking the mysterious presence of the absolute:

> Je néglige tout aplanissement chuchoté par la doctrine et me tiens aux solutions que proclame l'éclat liturgique: non que j'écoute en amateur, peut-être soigneux, excepté pour admirer comment, dans la succession de ces antiennes, proses ou motets, la voix, celle de l'enfant et de l'homme, disjointe, mariée, nue ou exempte d'accompagnement autre qu'une touche au clavier posant l'intonation, évoque, à l'âme, l'existence d'une personnalité multiple et une, mystérieuse et rien que pure. Quelque chose comme le Génie, écho de soi, sans commencement ni chute, simultané, en le délire de son intuition supérieure: il se sert des exécutants, par quatuor, duo, etc., ainsi que des puissances d'un instrument unique, jouant la virtualité. (395–96)

Mallarmé contrasts liturgical music, in which the singers both respond to and evoke only a virtual presence, a "Génie, écho de soi," "personnalité multiple et une," to operatic music, in which the melody is hindered and broken by an effort toward the verisimilar representation of the way people actually communicate: "[l]'opéra, où tout afin de rompre la céleste liberté de la mélodie, seule condition et l'entraver par la vraisemblance du développement régulier humain" (396).

It is not the narrative or doctrine but the "agencement dramatique," the *mise en scène* and its effects, that Mallarmé would retain from the Catholic liturgy as a model for future rites:

> Une assimilation m'obsède, parmi le plaisir, d'effets extra-ordinaires retrouvés ici et de certain sens, pour nos fastes futurs, attribuable peut-être au théâtre, comme fut, au sanctuaire un agencement dramatique rare: séance ne le montra autre part, constituée pour l'objet. (396)

He sums up the three essential elements of this "agencement" that will survive in future ceremonies (sponsored by the state). The first element is the presence of "le peuple," who participate in the creation of the divinity but solely in a nonverbal, performative mode. Each member of the audience sings, but this constitutes primarily a nonsignifying gesture for them, since they do not understand the words they are singing:

> La nef avec un peuple je ne parle d'assistants, bien d'élus: quiconque y peut de la source la plus humble d'un gosier jeter aux voûtes le répons en latin *incompris,* mais exultant, participe entre tous et lui-même de la sublimité se reployant vers le chœur: car voici le miracle de chanter, on se projette, haut comme va le cri. Dites si artifice, préparé mieux et à beaucoup, égalitaire, que cette communion, d'abord esthétique, en le héros du Drame divin. (emphasis mine, 396)

The second element is the priest, or officiant of the rite, who manipulates the invisible "presence," not like an actor (who would strive to represent it), but like a magician:

> Le prêtre céans, n'ait qualité d'acteur, mais officie—désigne et recule la présence mythique avec qui on vient se confondre; loin de l'obstruer du même intermédiaire que le comédien, qui arrête la pensée à son encombrant personnage. (396)

The third element is the organ, which helps to define and then expand the limits of the ritual site. It is situated on the threshold. As long as the doors of the sanctuary are closed, the organ music expresses the infinite darkness outside it. But when the doors of the sanctuary are opened, these musical "ténèbres" spill themselves into the outside (which, within, they symbolized) transformed. They are tamed by their participation in the ritual and now extend the site of refuge into the whole world:

> Je finirai par l'orgue, relégué aux portes, il exprime le dehors, un balbutiement de ténèbres énorme, ou leur exclusion du refuge, avant de s'y déverser extasiées et pacifiées, l'approfondissant ainsi de l'univers entier et causant aux hôtes une plénitude de fierté et de sécurité. (396)

The dual structure of this rite recalls both the double silence of "Mimique" and the divided "virginity" of the poem giving rise to the Idea. In the Mass there is a presence of music, engendering an absence (the unknowable divinity). And the reverberation of these contraries extends itself into infinity, thus confirming or authenticating the fact of their existence as constituting an irreducible absolute:

> Telle, en l'authenticité de fragments distincts, la mise en scène de
> la religion d'état, par nul cadre encore dépassée et qui, selon une
> œuvre triple, invitation directe à l'essence du type (ici le Christ),
> puis invisibilité de celui-là, enfin élargissement du lieu par vibra-
> tions jusqu'à l'infini, satisfait étrangement un souhait moderne
> philosophique et d'art. (396)

Paradoxically, it is the construction of an ultramodern theater that
inspires Mallarmé's vision of how the Mass might be modified in order
to become a modern rite, for in the architecture of this theater, several
characteristics of the church are reconstructed:

> La première salle que possède la Foule, au Palais du Trocadéro,
> prématurée, mais intéressante avec sa scène réduite au plancher
> de l'estrade (tréteau et devant de chœur), son considérable buffet
> d'orgues et le public jubilant d'être là, indéniablement en un édi-
> fice voué aux fêtes, implique une vision d'avenir; or, on a repris à
> l'église plusieurs traits, insciemment. (396–97)

If Mallarmé felt this construction to be premature, it was because the
performance that he wished to take place there had yet to be designed, a
performance neither theatrical nor religious in the ordinary sense: "La
représentation, ou l'office, manque: deux termes, entre quoi, à distance
voulue, hésitera la pompe" (397). In fact, as we shall see further in
examining *Le Livre*, the rite that Mallarmé envisioned did conserve
certain aspects of the Mass. And it consisted not merely of a "representa-
tion" but of a solemn presentation of the Book.

It is ironic that Mallarmé should have expended so much effort in
driving the literary text out the back door of theater only to bring it in
again through the front, or rather to reinstate it literally on the stage at the
center of his ideal art work. This irony undoubtedly results from his
ambition to present the public with a "total" work of art (one including
text and performance) and yet also preserve the difficult presence/absence
relationship that, for him, bound literature to the performing arts.

In the discussion of opera in the chapter to follow we shall not yet
discover how Mallarmé attempts to realize this ambition. But the prob-
lems inherent in his project should become still clearer, for in his critique
of the Wagnerian music-drama he scrutinizes the form nearest in his time
to all-encompassing art.

■

CHAPTER FIVE

Opera:
"Le Monstre-Qui-ne-peut-Être"

In 1885 Mallarmé wrote his only piece of opera criticism: "Richard Wagner: Rêverie d'un poëte français."[1] The article was solicited by his friend Edouard Dujardin, editor of *La Revue Wagnérienne*. In a letter to Dujardin, Mallarmé explains that the writing of this piece, "moitié article—moitié poème en prose," was not a simple task, for at the time of its composition he had never seen a Wagnerian opera:

> Jamais rien ne m'a semblé plus difficile. Songez donc, je suis malade, plus que jamais esclave. Je n'ai jamais rien vu de Wagner et je veux faire quelque chose d'original et de juste et qui ne soit pas à côté. (1592)[2]

As might be expected, Mallarmé was indeed able to produce something original (both in concept and in style), and his discussion of Wagner is "juste" and to the point insofar as it focuses on the central issue of

1. Mallarmé also briefly discussed Wagner in the essay "Parenthèse," expressing his regret that public scandal and reactionary attitudes had caused a premature closing of *Lohengrin* at the Eden Theater in Paris. He also mentioned Wagner in other critical essays and composed an "Hommage" to him (published in 1885 in *La Revue Wagnérienne*). In " 'Le principal pilier': Mallarmé, Victor Hugo, et Richard Wagner," L. J. Austin argues that the "Hommage" heralded Wagner as the rightful successor to Victor Hugo (1951, 154–80). In "Hommage ou contre-hommage à Richard Wagner," Anne-Marie Amiot demonstrates that the ambivalence articulated in Mallarmé's essay on Wagner is also prevalent in this poem (Amiot 1974).

2. Mallarmé's familiarity with Wagnerian aesthetics was undoubtedly derived partially from the reading of contemporary appraisals of Wagner's work such as Baudelaire's 1861 article "Richard Wagner et Tannhäuser à Paris" and partially from conversations with friends such as Dujardin, Villiers de l'Isle Adam, and Catulle Mendès, who were avid connoisseurs of Wagner.

Wagner's aesthetic theory: the possibility of achieving in opera a perfect synthesis of the arts.

There are two interwoven parts, or movements, to Mallarmé's critique. One is the description of Wagner's aesthetic and of the shortcomings that Mallarmé considers inherent to it; the other is the description of his own conception of what the ideal combination of music and drama would be. Though his appraisal of Wagner is, overall, more negative than positive, his criticisms are interspersed with many compliments. And it is clear that if he does not find his aesthetic Ideal attained in Wagnerian art, he does find there an important source of inspiration.[3]

Indeed, as Mallarmé indicates from the beginning of the essay, if he, a poet, has dared to speculate on the nature of future theatrical rites, "Cérémonies d'un jour qui gît au sein, inconscient, de la foule: presque un Culte" (541), it is owing in part to the pioneering example of Wagner. In the opening paragraphs he lays claim to private and solitary reflections on the nature of this Ideal: "il [le poète] accepte pour exploit de considérer seul, dans l'orgueilleux repli des conséquences, le Monstre-Qui-ne-peut-Être!" Yet he quickly admits that Wagner has inevitably influenced his thoughts: "cet amateur, s'il envisage l'apport de la Musique au Théâtre faite pour en mobiliser la merveille, ne songe pas longtemps à part soi . . . déjà, de quels bonds que parte sa pensée, elle ressent la colossale approche d'une Initiation" (541). In fact, as we shall see, Wagner's influence over Mallarmé was mostly contrary in its effect, for in constructing his own vision of "le Spectacle futur," he proceeded by negating the fundamental principles informing Wagner's works.

Mallarmé's commentary addresses three aspects of Wagner's art. The first is Wagner's ambition to create not just an artwork but, rather, the *Gesamtkunstwerk,* a work striving to represent the totality of human experience by including the widest possible variety of aesthetic modes. The second is Wagner's attempt to restore to theater its sociopolitical importance as the optimal vehicle and framework for the celebration of public life. The third aspect is Wagner's aim to reveal metaphysical truth through art. Paradoxically, while Mallarmé's highest praise of Wagner is for his efforts in these three directions, it is also in relation to them that he considers Wagnerian opera unsuccessful.

With respect to Wagner's ambition to produce the total artwork, Mallarmé appreciates his attempt to coordinate the effects of music and

---

3. It seems that Mallarmé long continued to seek inspiration from Wagner. In his *Vie de Mallarmé* (1941, 802), Henri Mondor recounts that a translation of Wagner's *Beethoven* was found near his body at the time of his death.

drama, yet he feels that the composer is going about accomplishing this in the wrong way. Wagner allies an incongruous form of theater (personal drama) with music, which is "Ideal":

> Allant au plus pressé, il concilia toute une tradition, intacte, dans la désuétude prochaine, avec ce que de vierge et d'occulte il devinait sourdre, en ses partitions. Hors une perspicacité ou suicide stérile, si vivace abonda l'étrange don d'assimilation en ce créateur quand même, que des deux éléments de beauté qui s'excluent et, tout au moins, l'un l'autre, s'ignorent, le drame personnel et la musique idéale, il effectua l'hymen. (543)

Mallarmé considers this an inauspicious marriage. Rather than recognizing the identity-in-difference that implicitly binds music to drama as a virtual presence, Wagner eagerly proceeds to actually wed these disparate arts and produces not so much a perfect synthesis as a "compromise," a hybrid in which neither music nor drama retains integrally its special quality and effect.

Mallarmé articulates this criticism in a rather delicate and ambiguous way. First he suggests that Wagner's synthesis is never, strictly speaking, achieved: "Quoique philosophiquement elle ne fasse là encore que *se juxtaposer,* la Musique . . . pénètre et enveloppe le Drame de par l'éblouissante volonté et s'y allie" (emphasis mine, 543). Then he suggests that in order to fuse music and drama, Wagner has, in fact, significantly altered the nature of each so as to transform it (although not completely) into something else: "Le tact est prodige qui, sans totalement en transformer aucune, opère, sur la scène et dans la symphonie, la fusion de ces formes de plaisir disparates" (543). Finally, he suggests (albeit in an innocent and inoffensive way) that Wagner's music is hardly music in the ordinary sense. Forcing music to signify through leitmotifs, he makes it defy its own most basic principle—the abstraction that makes its meaning impossible to specifically encode in signs: "pas d'ingénuité ou de profondeur qu'avec un éveil enthousiaste elle [l'éblouissante volonté de Wagner] ne prodigue dans ce dessein, sauf que son principe même, à la Musique échappe" (543). And further, Mallarmé describes Wagner's compositions as conserving more the rules than the spirit of music:

> Maintenant, en effet, une musique qui n'a de cet art que l'observance des lois très complexes, seulement d'abord le flottant et l'infus, confond les couleurs et les lignes du personnage avec les

timbres et les thèmes en une ambiance plus riche de Rêverie que
tout air d'ici-bas. (543–45).

In "Solennité" Mallarmé again emphasizes that Wagnerian opera is,
strictly speaking, neither music nor drama (though here, too, he is care-
ful not to denigrate the composer's work, designating it as a special,
complex form of Poetry nonetheless):

> Chez Wagner, même, qu'un poëte, le plus superbement fran-
> çais, console de n'invoquer au long ici, je ne perçois, dans
> l'acception stricte, le théâtre (sans conteste on retrouvera plus, au
> point de vue dramatique, dans la Grèce ou Shakespeare), mais la
> vision légendaire qui suffit sous le voile des sonorités et s'y mêle;
> ni sa partition du reste, comparée à du Beethoven ou du Bach,
> n'est, seulement, la musique. Quelque chose de spécial et com-
> plexe résulte: aux convergences des autres arts située, issue d'eux
> et les gouvernant, la Fiction ou Poésie. (335)

The criticism that Wagner's music suffers from its subordination to
theater (and vice versa) is of course far from particular to Mallarmé. It is
also expressed, in far stronger terms, by Nietzsche, for example, in *The
Case of Wagner* (1967, 173):

> Wagner was *not* a musician by instinct. He showed this by aban-
> doning all lawfulness and, more precisely, all style in music in
> order to turn it into what he required, theatrical rhetoric, a means
> of expression, of underscoring gestures, of suggestion, of the psy-
> chologically picturesque. Here we may consider Wagner an inven-
> tor and innovator of the first rank—*he has increased music's
> capacity for language to the point of making it immeasurable:* he
> is the Victor Hugo of music as language. Always presupposing
> that one first allows that under certain circumstances music may
> be not music but language, instrument, *ancilla dramaturgica.*

Mallarmé rejects Wagner's synthesis of music and drama not only,
however, because it compromises the integrity, or purity, of each genre.
He also does not accept the principle that duality and diversity can be at
last overcome or transcended in art. For Mallarmé, unlike Wagner and
others of his contemporaries such as Baudelaire, the universe is not
ultimately a synthetic, undivided whole. To portray it as such, as Wagne-
rian opera does, is to presuppose and aesthetically reflect the existence of

a transcendent, synthesizing agent and thus to perpetuate a worldview that is false.[4]

So while Mallarmé compliments Wagner for the scope of his ambition and for his effort to combine the pleasures of music and drama, in constructing his own vision of "le Spectacle futur," he suggests an alternative (and more partial) approach, limiting the number and nature of arts that can successfully be allied. In this theater, music and drama complement each other but only insofar as *the nature of drama is radically transformed,* that is, rendered impersonal, with its verbal, or narrative, aspect being annulled. The Wagnerian hero, whose medium of expression is "song-speech," is replaced here by a purely gestural performer, whose expressive medium seems to be mime! Wagner's innovating techniques (such as the leitmotif), which involve music in narrative, are then also rejected as superfluous and counterproductive, since the telling of a story is itself deemed unnecessary. The relationship between the music and the actor's performance is simple as opposed to complex: music is merely the animating force that compels the hero to move and to render the music's meaning through pure gesticulation. Without the orchestra, the mime becomes immobile, a "statue" (which is to say, symbolically silent):

> Une simple adjonction orchestrale change du tout au tout, annulant son principe même, l'ancien théâtre, et c'est comme strictement allégorique, que l'acte scénique maintenant, vide et abstrait en soi, impersonnel, a besoin, pour s'ébranler avec vraisemblance, de l'emploi du vivifiant effluve qu'épand la Musique.

> Sa présence, rien de plus! à la Musique, est un triomphe, pour peu qu'elle ne s'applique point, même comme leur élargissement sublime, à d'antiques conditions, mais éclate la génératrice de

---

4. Wagner's theater generally suggests the existence of God and of a coherent, unified world order. In *Tannhäuser,* for example, the hero finds redemption as his inner conflict between sensual and spiritual love is ultimately resolved. While Baudelaire is, on the surface, a dualist, he fundamentally shares Wagner's synthetic worldview. In "Richard Wagner et Tannhäuser à Paris," in fact, he presents Wagnerian opera as substantiating his own theory of "correspondances." For him the fusion of music and drama, "ces formes de plaisir disparates," is a great achievement requiring no *a posteriori* justification, "les choses s'étant toujours exprimées par une analogie réciproque, depuis le jour ou Dieu a proféré le monde comme une complexe et indivisible totalité" (Baudelaire 1925, 206). Mallarmé does not accept this romantic worldview or its expression in Wagnerian terms, for his own beliefs are not unambivalently in God, unity, and order. Rather, he believes in the contrary principles that difference is intrinsic to Being and that the world is governed by Chance.

toute vitalité: un auditoire éprouvera cette impression que, si l'orchestre cessait de déverser son influence, le mime resterait, aussitôt, statue. (542–43)

As is already becoming apparent, Mallarmé finds Wagner's music-drama unsatisfactory from more than the structural point of view. He also apprehends that it misleads the public in its search for common values and enduring truths. Mallarmé and Wagner agree that this quest (though it may not be fully conscious) is what brings people to the theater in the first place. Theater is entertainment, but it is also a "solemnity." People converge there in order to celebrate and commune in a sanctified image of themselves and their origins, to contemplate an Ideal that defines the essence of their lives. Wagner's theater strives to provide the public with this Ideal, but in Mallarmé's view his effort is at the same time only half-successful and too successful. He intimates that the self-image with which Wagner provides the people is not, in fact, a portrayal of their essence and that the "truths" that his works so effectively proclaim are falsehoods.

We have seen that Mallarmé primarily faults the kind of fiction that Wagner is bringing to the stage. While his music is modern and innovative, his drama, crudely representational, belongs to a bygone era:

> Il surgit au temps d'un théâtre, le seul qu'on peut appeler caduc, tant la Fiction en est fabriquée d'un élément grossier: puisqu'elle s'impose à même et tout d'un coup, commandant de croire à l'existence du personnage et de l'aventure—de croire, simplement, rien de plus. (542)

Wagner's theater resembles this decadent form of theater insofar as it implies no invention on the part of the spectators and is geared toward a passive audience. While nineteenth-century audiences still seem satisfied with this form of entertainment, Mallarmé speculates that audiences of the future will have a different demand. Wanting to participate in the creation of new and original images of their own, they will reject this form of fiction that revives ready-made images from the past:

> Son jeu reste inhérent au passé ou tel que le répudierait, à cause de cet intellectuel despotisme, une représentation populaire: la foule y voulant, selon la suggestion des arts, être maîtresse de sa créance. (542)

Unfortunately, Wagner ignores the possibility of this new mandate. His music casts a spell that compels the spectators to believe in the reality of what they see represented, and the contents of his music-dramas are the myths and legends appertaining to his own Germanic past. Thus, he provides a particular audience with a tangible image of itself and its past, but one that is extracted, midstream, in the course of its cultural history. He does not portray an authentic and universal image of humanity drawn at the source:

> Voici à la rampe intronisée la Légende.
>
> Avec une piété antérieure, un public pour la seconde fois depuis les temps, hellénique d'abord, maintenant germain, considère le secret, représenté, d'origines. Quelque singulier bonheur, neuf et barbare, l'asseoit: devant le voile mouvant la subtilité de l'orchestration, à une magnificence qui décore sa genèse.
>
> Tout se retrempe au ruisseau primitif: pas jusqu'à la source. (544)

While German audiences may remain content with Wagner's revival of ancient legend, Mallarmé asserts, the French public (in accordance with its cultural characteristics) will inevitably reject it:

> Si l'esprit français, strictement imaginatif et abstrait, donc poétique, jette un éclat, ce ne sera pas ainsi: il répugne, en cela d'accord avec l'Art dans son intégrité, qui est inventeur, à la Légende. Voyez-les, des jours abolis ne garder aucune anecdote énorme et fruste, comme une prescience de ce qu'elle apporterait d'anachronisme dans une représentation théâtrale, Sacre d'un des actes de la Civilisation. (544)[5]

The French have evolved to the point at which they will no longer believe in ancient myths: "Quoi! le siècle ou notre pays, qui l'exalte, ont

---

5. Wagner's theatrical revivals of legend are for Mallarmé necessarily anachronistic, both historically and in terms of their attempt to constitute ritual. They are historically anachronistic because they present the stuff of old theater as though it were new (thus, Mallarmé's oxymoronic characterization of his aesthetic as "neuf et barbare," as proceeding from that which is primitive but not original: "Tout se retrempe au ruisseau primitif: pas jusqu'à la source"). The anachronism of Wagner's theater with respect to ritual (as discussed in Chapter 1) lies in the fact that its representations refer to an extrinsic referent—"Sacre d'un des actes de la Civilisation"—to a reality that precedes the performance rather than being constituted by it.

dissous par la pensée les Mythes, pour en refaire!" In their place, the
French will accept a new kind of myth devoid of specific historical
content, one whose meaning will be borrowed from the consciousness of
the community of spectators, "la Fable, vierge de tout, lieu, temps et
personne sus, . . . empruntée au sens latent en le concours de tous, celle
inscrite sur la page des Cieux et dont l'Histoire même n'est qu'une
interprétation, vaine" (544–45). Modern myth will not be tied to any
predetermined narrative context. Its hero will be an impersonal, ab-
stract, human "Type" in which members of the audience can invest their
own identity, which naturally divides itself into gesture and dream:

> Le Théâtre les appelle [les mythes], non: pas de fixes, ni de
> séculaires et de notoires, mais un, dégagé de personnalité, car il
> compose notre aspect multiple: que, de prestiges correspondant
> au fonctionnement national, évoque l'Art, pour le mirer en nous.
> Type sans dénomination préalable, pour qu'émane la surprise:
> son geste résume vers soi nos rêves de sites ou de paradis,
> qu'engouffre l'antique scène avec une prétention vide à les
> contenir ou à les peindre. (545)

Music will not collaborate (as it does in Wagner's opera) with words
and gestures to tell false and antiquated stories. Rather, containing latent
within it the seed of the spectator's poetic dream world, it will simply
cause, on the part of the actor, a gestural reaction whose symbolism will
be interpreted and rendered real by the audience.[6] The music engenders
simultaneously this gestural performance and its (poetic) interpretation.
And through the exchange between these elements, there arises the Fig-
ure of a nonexistent Ideal, which the actor paradoxically incarnates by
virtue of his own unity-in-duality—"la Figure que Nul n'est":

> Alors y aboutissent, dans quelque éclair suprême, d'où s'éveille la
> Figure que Nul n'est, chaque attitude mimique prise par elle à un
> rythme inclus dans la symphonie, et le délivrant! alors viennent
> expirer comme aux pieds de l'incarnation, pas sans qu'un lien
> certain les apparente ainsi à son humanité, ces raréfactions et ces
> sommités naturelles que la Musique rend, arrière prolongement
> vibratoire de tout comme la Vie. (545)

6. Thus, in Mallarmé's theatrical Ideal the role of the actor becomes indistinguishable from
that of the dancer. Indeed, at the beginning of his essay on Wagner, Mallarmé suggests that
dance constitutes in and of itself the ultimate theatrical spectacle: "en sa perfection de rendu, la
Danse seule capable, par son écriture sommaire, de traduire le fugace et le soudain jusqu'à
l'Idée—pareille vision comprend tout, absolument tout le Spectacle futur" (541).

The actor/hero thus stands as the intermediary between "le fictif foyer de vision dardé par le regard d'une foule" (the imaginary theater of the crowd) and the music that engenders it. The crowd's latent poetic images, "ces raréfactions et ces sommités naturelles que la musique rend," expire at his feet, while the music is represented as a vibration extending behind him. For Mallarmé then, as for theorists of theater as different as Jerzy Grotowski and Denis Diderot, the actor is simply Man, the dual Being, whose life renders the contradiction of his psychophysical aspects authentic—a life divided between actions and thoughts, between physical gestures and dreams:[7] "L'Homme, puis son authentique séjour terrestre, échangent une réciprocité de preuves" (545).

The identity of Mallarmé's theatrical hero brings us to his final and perhaps most insurmountable objection to Wagner's art. This objection concerns the fact that his music-dramas glorify, and persuade the audience to believe in, the existence of (other-than-human) supreme beings. As in the case of his feelings toward the Catholic Mass, Mallarmé appreciates both the ritual character and metaphysical purpose of Wagner's work, yet he cannot adhere to what he perceives as its "religious" doctrine. In Wagnerian opera the hero is often presented as a demigod:

> Toujours le héros, qui foule une brume autant que notre sol, se montrera dans un lointain que comble la vapeur des plaintes, des gloires, et de la joie émises par l'instrumentation, reculé ainsi à des commencements. (544)

Tannhäuser, Parsifal, The Ring Cycle, and other works testify to the existence of God or gods, which for Mallarmé do not exist:

> cette orchestration, de qui, tout à l'heure, sortit l'évidence du dieu, ne synthétise jamais autre chose que les délicatesses et les magnificences, immortelles, innées, qui sont à l'insu de tous dans le concours d'une muette assistance. (545)

Wagner's art excites the crowds into believing that through opera they can gain access to a transcendent, metaphysical Ideal: "il exalte des

---

7. In Grotowski's theater the actor comes to represent (as he does in the above-cited text of Mallarmé) the site and origin of the myth of total Being as well as the executant of a rite (Borie 1981, 137). Although Mallarmé divests the actor of language, the position he assigns him is also similar to that described in Diderot's *Paradoxe sur le comédien* (written in the 1770s). The actor is a hypothetical combination of "l'homme de la nature," "l'être sensible" (who acts and feels), and the poet (who thinks) (Diderot 1967, 186–87).

fervents jusqu'à la certitude: pour eux ce n'est pas l'étape la plus grande jamais ordonnée par un signe humain, qu'ils parcourent avec toi comme conducteur, mais le voyage fini de l'humanité vers un Idéal" (546). For Mallarmé this Ideal (though it is rooted in man) is by definition unreachable. The undivided heavenly presence that opera represents is a "chimera," "le Monstre-Qui-ne-peut-Être": "cette cime menaçante d'absolu, devinée dans le départ des nuées là-haut, fulgurante, nue, seule: au-delà et que personne ne semble devoir atteindre" (546). Wagner's revelation of the Ideal is thus inevitably false, for while the actor can stand as a symbol of the origin of the transcendent Ideal, this is itself necessarily a nothingness, "la Figure que Nul n'est."

An analysis of Mallarmé's essay leads one to conclude that if he and Wagner agreed on anything, it was on the dominion that art should hold over all other aspects of human life. Where they did not agree was on the art form most suitable to occupy this lofty position. While Wagner perceived the music-drama as the obvious candidate, Mallarmé was obstinate in assigning this place to literature. He did not mean ordinary literature, however, but literature capable of proving itself to be the identical yet contrary face of what it does not incorporate—music, dance, and theater. Mallarmé believed that the universe was destined to find its highest expression in the form of a Book that would constitute the culmination of the world: "le monde est fait pour aboutir à un beau livre" (872). Like Wagner, Mallarmé believed that artistic events would take the place of both religious and political rites, but these would be literary/theatrical rather than synthetic operatic events: "Je crois que la Littérature, reprise à sa source, qui est l'Art et la Science, nous fournira un Théâtre dont les représentations seront le vrai culte moderne" (875). Finally, like the aim of the Wagnerian *Gesamtkunstwerk*, the ultimate purpose of Mallarmé's ideal Book was to reveal metaphysical truth. It would provide an explication or unfolding of the world, which, musical and mysterious, would also be its nonexplanation: "L'explication orphique de la Terre, qui est le seul devoir du poëte et le jeu littéraire par excellence" (663).

For Wagner and Wagnerites, past and present, Wagner's music-drama constituted the ultimate aesthetic revolution; the construction of its temple at Bayreuth symbolized the dawn of an eternal utopian era. For Mallarmé, Wagnerian opera represented a stopping point rather than a beginning. "Un repos," "un isolement," it marked the closing of the Romantic era, a significant phase in the process of Art.[8]

8. For a thorough discussion of Wagner's place in relation to both romanticism and modernity see Jacques Barzun's *Darwin, Marx, and Wagner* (1958).

CHAPTER SIX

"La fausse entrée des sorcières dans *Macbeth*"

In the previous chapters we saw that Mallarmé consistently describes music, dance, and theater as presences-in-absence supplementing the literary text and describes the literary text, in turn, as supplementing music, dance, and theater. We also saw that he presents the capacity of literature and the performing arts to supplement each other as dependent on their identity-in-difference as verbal and corporeal languages, a relationship reflecting the unity-in-duality of the signified and the signifier and of the mind and body within the human Self. Thus, in Mallarmé's critical essays, we find the complete exposition of an original and paradoxical aesthetic theory; however, we do not find this theory put into practice. Although these essays persistently refer to performance, they contain no signs suggesting their own relation to an exterior performative corollary that might simultaneously replace their representations and add concreteness to them. Clearly complete in their literariness, these essays do not evoke or require supplementary performances, either imaginary or real.

This is not the case in the poetic texts I shall be examining in the next four chapters: *Hérodiade*, *L'après-midi d'un faune*, *Igitur*, and *Un coup de dés*. In these texts we find, rather, a disquieting rupture of literary closure, one that curiously mirrors a break, or rupture, in theatrical performance that Mallarmé himself found in Shakespeare's *Macbeth*.

In *Hérodiade*, *Igitur*, and *L'après-midi d'un faune* there is a troubling presence of references to the performing arts appearing at once extraneous (unnecessary to the signifying process of the text) and intrusive (detrimental to the text's self-sufficiency, its literary closure). In *Un coup de dés* the performing arts reference affects the textual structure in a manner more radical still. The entire text presents itself as a structural syllepsis in which we find the previously differentiated performative and literary modes coexisting, but as contraries, in a symbiotic relationship.

In my examination of these works I shall be focusing primarily on these references to performance. Critics have generally dismissed such references as insignificant details, as historical accidents having no bearing on the general meaning of these texts. My analysis will show, to the contrary, that we cannot grasp the broadest significance of these texts if we overlook their references to performance and attempt to read them as the pure and self-sufficient literary monuments that without these references they would be.

To support my own focus on detail and persuade my readers of the value of reading what previous exegetes have shrugged off as the meaningless vestiges of Mallarmé's misguided preoccupation with theater—as vestiges, in effect, of his literary mistakes—I offer as a bridge between his theory and practice the closing essay of *Crayonné au théâtre*, "La fausse entrée des sorcières dans Macbeth" (1897). Here Mallarmé comments at length on the significance of one of Shakespeare's theatrical "mistakes." The essay presents itself as having been triggered by a recent rereading of *Macbeth*, a rereading itself inspired by a reading of Thomas de Quincey's "Essai sur le heurt à la porte, dans Macbeth." De Quincey has, in Mallarmé's view, brilliantly elucidated the significance of the knock on the door following Duncan's murder. The knock underlines the "horror" of a preceding pause in the action, a moment of suspense, by breaking it in a forceful, tangible way and abruptly returning our attention to the ensuing action:

> ". . . le pouls de la vie commence à battre encore: et le rétablissement des faits communs au monde dans lequel nous vivons, soudain nous rend sensibles profondément à la terrible parenthèse qui les avait suspendus." (348)

De Quincey's elucidation of this detail encourages Mallarmé to follow suit, to comment on another detail in the same play that he claims to have forgotten but to have thought about previously very hard and for a very long time:

> Oubli—voici des années quand l'influence shakespearienne, souverainement, dominait tout projet de jeunesse relatif au théâtre, certaine vision, d'un détail, s'imposa et pourquoi résistai-je, par quelle hésitation, à l'écrire? elle me semble, maintenant, empreinte de sublimité. Toute filiation, de concept ou dans les

moyens, interrompue avec l'art éternel de la Renaissance,—pour
cette cause, peut-être, l'opportunité vient, de réparer un manque-
ment: et, ma réminiscence poussée à l'obsession, de la délivrer
mieux qu'à part moi. . . . L'aperçu que je signale, me hanta
depuis son illumination lointaine. (346)

Clearly, the detail in question has had an enormous impact on Mal-
larmé's perception of theater, as well as on his own creative productivity.
In his youth he was dominated by the influence of Shakespeare's theater.
Then for a time he distanced himself from this influence—"toute
filiation interrompue." This distance allows him to articulate the impact
on him of a detail in Shakespeare's text. The renewed contact with
Shakespeare that he owes to De Quincey's essay finally allows him, as it
were, to admit that he, too, has read *Macbeth* in an extraordinary,
unprecedented way:

Je ne me défends pas, tout à coup, à propos d'un poëme élargi, en
sa magnificence, parmi les mémoires séculaires, de crier à quelque
nouveauté—d'éclat si soudain qu'il ne rencontra de regard sauf le
mien, certes et indéfectiblement: n'était qu'une observation se
révéla aussi, quant à un passage différent de la tragédie, souvenez-
vous, pour Thomas de Quincey qui composa le rare et persuasif
Essai sur le heurt à la porte, dans Macbeth. (346)

An uncomfortable suspense is created as Mallarmé proceeds to sum-
marize and quote from De Quincey's critical observation before articulat-
ing his own. When we finally come to Mallarmé's observation, it is
presented as the contrary of the "knock," as a subtle disappearance, one
that escapes or deceives curiosity: "Rien, en intensité, comparable aux
coups à la porte répercutés dans la terreur; mais ici, au contraire, un
évanouissement, furtif, décevant la curiosité" (348).
    The point at issue is how, in *Macbeth*, should the witches be pre-
sented? How will the invisible, or the supernatural, be represented in the
play? Mallarmé argues that the witches, insofar as they paradoxically
incorporate the immaterial world, should not be present to the audience
on stage:

Introduire le funeste Chœur, par quel moyen? je lis bien, sous le
titre, après

"Un lieu vide, tonnerre et éclairs."

(*Entrent trois sorcières*) (349)

To support his argument he begins by questioning the authenticity of this stage direction: "pure indication courante et peut-être apocryphe: les sœurs vieilles n'entrent pas, sont là, en tant que le destin qui préexiste." He proceeds to quote the witches' prologue and another stage direction following it, "(*Les Sorcières s'évanouissent*)." It is this last stage direction that has led him to question whether the first is authentic: "il n'est pas inscrit sortent, comme elles sont *apparues,* et non d'après la teneur, *entrées.*" The witches' chorus, he concludes, should not have been presented as an integral part of the play: "Les présenter, insisté-je, comment? Au seuil et qu'elles y règnent; même pas en prologue participant de la pièce: *extra-scéniquement*" (emphasis mine). For Mallarmé, the "évasif morceau" is not and should not have been a theatrical scene, because it expresses something that never actually takes place:

> La tragédie commence de plain-pied. . . . Le prodige, antérieur—que de bizarres artisanes tissent de leurs chuchotements le sort! plane et s'isole; n'eut lieu, du moins régulièrement ou quant à la pièce: on en fut témoin, tant pis, on le devait ignorer, comme primordiaux antécédents obscurs ne concernant personne.

He then proceeds to justify and explain the fact of their presentation in Shakespeare's play—owing to the incongruence of "(*Entrent trois sorcières*)" and "(*Les Sorcières s'évanouissent*)"—as the effect of a brilliant maneuver on the part of the playwright, who intentionally sets out to expose, or reveal, a theatrical accident. In short, Mallarmé reads Shakespeare as pretending to hide what should remain hidden (on stage) even as he lets it be seen:

> Shakespeare qui ne pouvait pas poser, en tant qu'auteur, sciemment, sans la réduire au degré théâtral ordinaire, l'irruption du fantastique, feint, plutôt, de dissimuler insuffisamment et laisser voir, dans un coup de vent.
> Le public apprécie une découverte par lui faite indûment.
> Artifice extraordinaire ou infraction aux usages jusqu'à présent, mettant dans le jeu, comme qui dirait, *l'accident.* (Emphasis mine, 350)

And he describes this artificially accidental ambiguity in stage directions (partially revealing and partially obfuscating witches who are not intentionally present in his play) as the revelation of a Mystery, an opening onto and within a great work of art:

Ouverture sur un chef-d'oeuvre: comme, en le chef d'œuvre, le rideau simplement s'est levé, une minute, trop tôt, trahissant des menées fatidiques.

Cette toile qui sépare du mystère, a, selon de l'impatience, prématurément cédé, . . . exposé, dans une violation comme fortuite, pour multiplier l'angoisse, cela même qui paraissait devoir rester caché, tel que *cela* se lie par derrière et effectivement à l'invisible. (351)

The veil separating the visible from the invisible, or what is performed from what is merely imagined, has been penetrated, "as though fortuitously," in Shakespeare's *Macbeth*.

This, we shall see, is also the case in the four poetic texts to be discussed in the pages that follow. The model of Shakespeare's theatrical mistake is simply inverted. In these works the reader is constantly directed toward a tangible theatrical "scene," toward performances that curiously ought to have remained hidden in these nontheatrical works. Thus, it is not surprising that Mallarmé's public has long treated these theatrical references as a "découverte faite par lui indûment," as an anxiety-producing manifestation of performances that do not belong in his self-referential, autonomous texts. How indeed can we read these absent performances that mar the purity of his texts "as though by accident" and "extratextuellement." We cannot, in fact, read them, for as performances they belong to the realm of what must be seen or heard. We shall see, however, that the literary representations of performance in *Hérodiade, L'après-midi d'un faune, Igitur,* and *Un coup de dés* point to the same reciprocally authenticating, supplementary text-performance relationship described throughout Mallarmé's critical prose.

CHAPTER SEVEN

Hérodiade

Hérodiade holds a position of preeminence in Mallarmé's poetic corpus. Begun in 1864 and on the verge of completion at the time of his death in 1898, the work reflects the evolution of an entire literary career. The chronology of the text is significant, because it reveals an enormous investment on the part of the author. Clearly, he viewed *Hérodiade* as one of his major works.

The extent to which *Hérodiade* represents Mallarmé's artistic ambition is amply documented in the poet's correspondence.[1] In an 1864 letter to Henri Cazalis we find that for this text Mallarmé felt himself obliged to invent a new poetic language; a language in which the referential value of words would become subordinate to the value of their effect:

> Pour moi, me voici résolument à l'œuvre. J'ai enfin commencé mon *Hérodiade*. Avec terreur car j'invente une langue qui doit nécessairement jaillir d'une poétique très nouvelle, que je pourrais définir en ces deux mots: *Peindre, non la chose, mais l'effet qu'elle produit.* Le vers ne doit donc pas, là, se composer de mots; mais d'intentions, et toutes les paroles s'effacer devant les sensations. (Mallarmé 1959, 137)

In my analyses of the various versions of *Hérodiade*, I shall examine this new poetics where language appears "to efface itself in front of

---

1. Comments in various letters testify to the degree of Mallarmé's commitment to this particular text. In one letter he realizes that his entire being has been invested in the poem: "*Hérodiade*, où je m'étais mis tout entier sans le savoir" (1953, 68). In another, he claims that the page containing its title constitutes the culmination of his work: "La plus belle page de mon œuvre sera celle qui ne contiendra que ce nom divin *Hérodiade*. Le peu d'inspiration que j'ai eu, je le dois à ce nom, et je crois que si mon héroïne s'était appelée Salomé, j'eusse inventé ce mot sombre, et rouge comme une grenade ouverte, *Hérodiade*" (1959, 154).

sensations," a poetics whose predominant characteristics are the cancellation of referentiality and the evocation of sensory impressions that seem to fill up or complete lacunas within the text.

The texts resulting from Mallarmé's early period of work on the project are the "Scène"—a dialogue between the heroine and her nurse (first published in 1871 in *Le Parnasse Contemporain*) and the "Ouverture ancienne" (first published posthumously in *La Nouvelle Revue Française* in 1926). Though Mallarmé continues to refer intermittently to his work on *Hérodiade,* it seems that most of the texts that were to make up the last version of the work, *Les noces d'Hérodiade, Mystère,* were composed during the last years of his life. In his *Vie de Mallarmé* (1941, 801), Henri Mondor relates a note that shows Mallarmé engaged in the completion of *Hérodiade* between the attacks of epiglottal suffocation that brought on his death: "Je ne laisse pas un papier inédit excepté quelques bribes imprimées que vous trouverez puis le *Coup de Dés* et *Hérodiade* terminée s'il plaît au sort."

Unfortunately, *Hérodiade* was to remain incomplete. The modern reader who has gained access to posthumously published texts will never be in a position to determine their status from the perspective of the creator. This being the case, I shall focus my attention on the relationship between the reader and the text in the versions available, rather than on speculation about what the final product, or definitive text, might have become. Without arguing for the greater validity or importance of any version of a text over any other, I shall merely state from the outset which texts are the objects of my analysis. My discussion of *Hérodiade* will pertain primarily to the notes and manuscripts published by Gardner Davies in 1959—entitled *Les noces d'Hérodiade, Mystère*—since these texts best represent the ensemble of the work as it has come into the public domain.

As my study concerns chiefly the role of references to performance in *Hérodiade,* I should mention the record of Mallarmé's position with regard to whether or not the work was destined to be performed (though as a general matter I am not concerned with intentionality except inasmuch as it is recorded in the text).

Insofar as we can determine this from the poet's correspondence, *Hérodiade* was originally conceived as a performance piece. In 1864 Mallarme referred to it repeatedly as his "tragédie" and envisaged submitting it to Théodore de Banville and Constant Coquelin for production at the Théâtre Français. Subsequently, it seems, he abandoned this ambition and planned to rework the piece as a poem. In so doing, he alone would acquire full responsibility for its production; he implies that the text will somehow provide for its theatrical supplement: "Je commence *Hérodiade,* non plus tragédie, mais poëme . . . je gagne ainsi l'attitude, les vêtements, le décor, et l'ameublement, sans parler du mystère" (Mallarmé 1959, 174). It is difficult to determine whether the final version, *Les noces,* was destined for theatrical performance and, if so, what kind. Notes accompanying the text have the appearance of stage directions; yet for the most part these are not integrated within the body of the text. Though Mallarmé refers to the piece as a poem, he entitles it according to a theatrical genre: *mystère.*[2] The work is not structured in the conventional manner of theatrical works; nevertheless, it has many elements of a theatrical structure. There are no letters to prove that Mallarmé sought to have *Les noces* performed, but there is an 1898 letter from Geneviève Mallarmé to her father, testifying to the desire of a well-known actress to perform it: "Alors *Hérodiade* est commencée. Mlle. Moreno a l'idée fixe de la jouer un jour, elle sent qu'elle y sera parfaite" (Mallarmé 1945, 1443).

From the perspective of our analysis it is just this ambiguity "entre l'écrit et le joué" that provides the most interest.[3] Though the question of Mallarmé's actual intentions concerning the relationship between text and performance must remain ultimately unresolved, the presence of performing arts signs or references within the text strongly suggests that performance played a crucial role, for him, albeit virtual or latent, in this text's incompletion. The references to performing arts around the perimeters of the poetic text—in its structuring, in titles and subtitles, and in disparate but related notes—serve paradoxically to undermine the closure of the work as a whole, even while the verse retains its integrity, not being contaminated by the explicit presence or accompaniment of any other art form.

Before analyzing this poetic purity and the juxtaposition to it of references to performance, it might be useful to sum up the "argument," or narrative sequence, of the mystery play.[4] The thematic content of the work is highly relevant to its form.

The characters of the *mystère* are three, listed (according to a theatri-

---

2. The theatrical definition of *mystère* is: "Au moyen âge, genre théâtral qui mettait en scène des sujets religieux." Beyond this genre marker, the presence of *mystère* in the title of *Hérodiade* also denotes the broader meanings of the term: "rite, culte, savoir réservé à des initiés . . . chose cachée, secrète . . . énigme" (*Petit Robert* 1979, 1250).

3. In this regard the reader should recall the discussion (in Chapter 4) of Mallarmé's favorable reaction in "Le genre ou des modernes" and "Planches et feuillets" to theatrical works that reveal this very ambiguity.

4. For a more detailed summary of *Les noces* see Paul Schwartz's article "*Les Noces d'Hérodiade*" (1972, 33–42). For a discussion of its relationship to psychoanalysis, see Mary Ellen Wolf's *Eros under Glass: Psychoanalysis and Mallarmé's Hérodiade* (1987).

cal convention) on the title page as "Hérodiade," "La Nourrice," and "La tête de Saint Jean." The plot is related (but only distantly) to the biblical story of King Herod, his wife Herodias, and her daughter Salomé, who as a reward for her seductive veil dance demanded John the Baptist's head on a platter.[5] Saint John's accusations of adultery and incest (directed at Herodias) are thereby both silenced and avenged. Though Mallarmé's text conforms in few ways with its biblical intertext, it seems safe to assume (as several critics have suggested) that Mallarmé's heroine represents a fusion of the characteristics of Herodias and her daughter. Hérodiade inherits the mother's coldness and desire for vengeance and the seductive body and perfect beauty of Salomé. The nurse plays the role of servant, frustrated confidante, and oracle. The Baptist's head plays the role of Hérodiade's spouse in the strange wedding that occurs in the last section of the text. The head is presented as a symbol of pure spirit, "le génie."

Les noces consists of four major sections: a "Prélude," a "Scène," a "Scène intermédiaire," and a "Finale." The "Prélude" reworks many of the images of the 1864 "Ouverture," designated as the nurse's "incantation." It establishes the atmosphere of the play, prepares the reader for the "Scènes" between Hérodiade and the nurse, and foreshadows the events to take place in the "Finale."

The "Prélude" is divided into three parts. In the first part the primary images are those of the setting sun and its reflection on a golden platter set on a dresser in Hérodiade's chamber. The sun is compared to the halo that will crown the Baptist's head. There are also allusions to the wedding, which will take place in the "Finale," in the fusion of the reflections reverberating off the "aiguière bossuée et le tors candélabre" (55).[6] Further, it is suggested that this wedding will be an unusual celebration;

---

5. The story is in Matthew 14:1–11. The reader of Les noces does not have to be very well acquainted with the biblical narrative, for except that it offers a clue to the identity of "Hérodiade" (Salomé is called simply the daughter of Hérodias), it offers no relevant details (to Mallarmé's text) inaccessible through the many other versions of the story of Salomé. Beyond the biblical narrative, critics have associated Mallarmé's text with a number of nineteenth-century artworks: Flaubert's story Herodias and novel Salammbô, an untitled sonnet of Baudelaire, Banville's Diane au bois, Heine's Atta Troll, Oscar Wilde's Salome (performed by Sarah Bernhardt in 1893) and Richard Strauss's opera based on it, and two portraits of Salomé, one by Henri Regnault and one by Gustave Moreau, exhibited in Paris in 1870 and 1874, respectively.

6. Unless otherwise specified all quotation references are to Gardner Davies's edition of Les noces. The reader will note further that several of the lines are incomplete. I have reproduced the gaps in the verse as they appear in this edition (Mallarmé 1959).

the platter will not serve to contain "Le délice attendu du nuptial repas" (56). As this section closes, the nurse questions the future as to the symbolic significance of the platter:

> Alors, dis ô futur taciturne, pourquoi
> Ici demeure-t-il et s'éternise coi . . .
> Cette vacuité louche et muette d'un plat?
> (56)

The second part of the "Prélude" is the "Cantique de Saint Jean." Here, too, we find the image of the setting sun. John describes its trajectory and that of his head at the moment of decapitation. Freed at last from his body, his head rises for a moment and then falls back down to earth; his gaze strives to follow his pure vision into the cold glaciers of eternity.

In the third part of the "Prélude" the scene returns to Hérodiade's chamber, in which we find a personified echo of John's canticle "psaume de nul antique antiphonaire" (59). The "Fantôme"/echo is merged with the "Ombre" of the nurse. Hérodiade's bed is described as a vain or negative symbol of union.[7] Again the golden platter is referred to, this time as a "placide ambassadeur," an unambiguous symbol or carrier of fate. Toward the end of this section the corporeal or "authentique" presence of the nurse (as opposed to her "shadow") is also evoked.

Following the "Prélude" is the "Scène." This section is the only traditionally theatrical portion of the play; it is structured like a conventional dialogue. Hérodiade has just returned from an early morning walk. The nurse engages her in conversation as she assists her with her *toilette*. The nurse tries to play the role of confidante and is anxious to know Hérodiade's innermost feelings. She attempts to embrace her, to touch her hair, and to offer her perfumes, but Hérodiade rejects all these advances, keeping the nurse at a physical and emotional distance. When the nurse refers to her nubile state, suggesting that the princess must be waiting for a future spouse, she abruptly cuts her off: "c'est pour moi, pour moi, que je fleuris déserte" (68). Yet at the end of the "Scène," Hérodiade admits to herself that she is experiencing an inner transformation:

---

7. In *Mallarmé et le rêve d'Hérodiade* (1978), Davies draws interesting parallels between the negative images of union and birth in the "Prélude" and those of Mallarmé's 1887 trilogy of sonnets: "Tout Orgueil fume-t-il du soir," "Surgi de la croupe et du bond," and "Une dentelle s'abolit" (78–79).

>   Vous mentez, ô fleur nue
> De mes lèvres!
>   J'attends une chose inconnue
> Ou peut-être, ignorant le mystère et vos cris,
> Jetez-vous les sanglots suprêmes et meurtris
> D'une enfance sentant parmi les rêveries
> Se séparer enfin ses froides pierreries.

(70)

The "Scène intermédiaire" which follows is designated in related notes as a "dialogue muet." Here we find that the nurse is still lingering in Hérodiade's chamber, though in the last passage of the preceding scene it seemed that she had left. Hérodiade recognizes that it is the nurse who holds the key to the mystery. The secret of her destiny, the identity of her future spouse, seems to cling to the nurse's clothing: "autour de son sachet de vieille faille / Rôde, tourne et défaille / Le message . . . de traits / Du fiancé" (73).[8] She bids her then to go and bring her fiancé, to fetch Saint John's head on a golden platter.

The "Finale" consists of Hérodiade's monologue and two other brief passages in which the meaning of Hérodiade's wedding to the saint is summed up. In her monologue Hérodiade expresses her perception of the event, addressing her words to the Baptist's head. She alludes to his spiritual asceticism and his quest for purity. She refers to a garden that might have been the site of their love scene. She then beseeches the head to tell her the true meaning of their union: "Hymen froid d'une enfance avec l'affreux génie" (78). The head is silent, but the princess proceeds to consecrate or seal their marriage with erotic gestures in verses emphasizing that through this act she is losing her virginity. She kisses the head, pours its blood ("L'inexplicable sang déshonorant le lys") all over her body ("ma tige"), and then throws it out the window toward the sun and crimson skies:

> Tien et précipité de quelque altier vertige
> Ensuite pour couler tout le long de ma tige
> Vers quelque ciel portant mes destins avilis
> L'inexplicable sang déshonorant le lys
> A jamais renversé de l'une ou l'autre jambe . . .
> Le métal commandé précieux du bassin

---

8. In the preceding chapters we saw several instances in which clothing and accessories acquired the function of withholding and symbolizing a mystery, for example, in Mallarmé's description of the apparel of the crowd, "gardienne du Mystère," earlier cited in the context of my analysis of "Plaisir sacré."

Naguère où reposât un trop inerte reste
Peut selon le suspens encore par mon geste
Changeant   en   nonchaloir
Verser son fardeau   avant de choir.
(78)⁹

As her monologue closes, Hérodiade reveals that she was in need of the Baptist's head in order to "open herself up," to become mature and triumphant as a queen:

Comme soufflant le lustre absent pour le ballet
Abstraite intrusion en ma vie, il fallait
La hantise soudain quelconque d'une face
Pour que je m'entr'ouvrisse et reine triomphasse.
(79)

The head is compared to the theatrical "lustre" by virtue of its illuminating, self-reflecting quality, its self-cognitive function for Hérodiade. It is important to recognize that she rids herself of the head, or blows out the light, at the moment when she performs the ballet. Thus, a distance is maintained between the acts of the body and those of the mind, which both the chandelier and head symbolize. As was explained earlier, for Mallarmé, the chandelier is never, strictly speaking, a part of the theatrical show; "le théâtre institue des personnages agissant et en relief précisément pour qu'ils négligent la métaphysique, comme l'acteur omet la présence du lustre" (327).

The other brief passages pertaining to the "Finale" again recount the conditions and significance of this strange marriage. One explains that the virginity of the princess has been broken through, but not in the usual way. The child has come to know herself by merely *recognizing* the existence of the saint. It is through the knowledge of his spirit that she has been liberated or has come to know the mystery of her body. This newfound discovery of the duality of her person is expressed in the oxymoron "mystère éclairé":

9. In Mallarmé's texts we find a very frequent usage of the conventional floral metaphor for the woman's body. In his 1864 poem entitled "Les fleurs" we also find an explicit reference to a bloodied rose/Hérodiade: "L'hyacinthe, le myrte à l'adorable éclair / Et, pareille à la chair de la femme, la rose / Cruelle, Hérodiade en fleur du jardin clair, / Celle qu'un sang farouche et radieux arrose!" (Mallarmé 1945, 34).

> Une enfant   de l'heure a voulu
> Attentive au mystère éclairé de son être
>
>   connaître . . .
> Sous les gouffres   pubère
>   libère
> Sa chair   de s'offrir en festin
> Pour avoir reconnu le seigneur clandestin
>   (80–81)

In the other passage it is explained that the heroine has lost her inno-
cence without blame or remorse. She has willingly exchanged her pure
body, "une virginité," for John the Baptist's pure mind, or "génie" (83).

As Davies points out, the union of Hérodiade's body with John's head
undoubtedly represents a kind of mutual self-fulfillment.[10] By his decapi-
tation John experiences an end to his ordinary human condition. The
blade puts a clean end to his hybrid existence as body and spirit:

> Comme rupture franche
> Plutôt refoule ou tranche
> Les anciens désaccords
>   Avec le corps
>   (58)

By means of this definitive separation John's spirit becomes pure spirit
(by joining with nothingness), and his body, pure matter—as his heaven-
borne head returns to earth. In death his duality comes to a close.

Conversely, by John's decapitation, Hérodiade becomes dual, at last
fully alive. She symbolically joins his head to her body in order to inherit
his now pure spirit, which, according to an ancient religious tradition, is
conveyed through the blood of sacrifice; the saint's consciousness, or
Idea, bleeds onto her body. In notes rendering this exchange explicit, we
find the cutting sword and resulting blood functioning as syllepses, signify-
ing both the sacrifice of the martyr and the loss of virginity of Hérodiade:

---

10. Davies (1959) interprets the significance of their union as follows: "Pour saint Jean, le
supplice a été la réalisation de son Idée, que symbolise la virginité de l'héroïne. . . . Le martyre a
libéré saint Jean des entraves de la vie humaine, en l'unissant sous un aspect impersonnel à la
beauté idéale représentée par Hérodiade. Pour que la princesse elle-même se réalisât com-
plètement, il fallait que sa beauté vierge arrivât à la pleine conscience de soi en traversant cette
révolte de la chair" (41–42).

le glaive qui trancha ta tête a déchiré mon voile

    sur la dalle couchée
    jusqu'au col
mon corps aveu de l'homme
    nécessaire
féconde de la splendeur par ta mort
           précoce
   Tu me possèdes, tu m'es . . .

              (136)

—idée

      saigne—sang sur ses cuisses
        pourpre des cuisses
          et leur royauté
           (138)

Thus, it is through her inheritance of John's genius that Hérodiade achieves full awareness of herself. The mirror to which she is so attached during the "Scène" becomes interiorized in the "Finale," as the heroine is enabled to see herself through the eyes of another. Hérodiade achieves womanhood and royalty as she comes to understand her own ambiguity: the duality of human existence as being in flesh and in spirit (that is, consciousness of being or ideality):

   l'ambiguïté d'Hé-
   rodiade et de sa
   danse . . .
      elle maîtrise cette
  tête révoltée
    qui a voulu
     penser plus haut—
  où s'éteint l'idée
     inouïe et [   ]

      dont elle bénéficie
  couverte de diamants
       et mourante
     évoque la beauté
     humaine de la vie—
     qu'on ne dépasse
    en même temps qu'elle
    représente la vieille
    chair

       (111–12)

The central theme of *Les noces* is thus (as the title suggests) Hérodiade's discovery of her unity-in-duality. The simultaneous unity and duality of body and spirit within the human subject constitutes the central mystery that Hérodiade through her marriage to the Baptist's head comes to know.

This duality is reflected, for Mallarmé, even within the name of his heroine: he associates it with a cutting, a wound, an "ouverture," as is evident both in the earlier-cited passage from his correspondence, "ce mot sombre et rouge comme une grenade ouverte" and in the earlier-cited passage from "Les fleurs," in which the flower Hérodiade is described as bathed in blood: "Hérodiade en fleur du jardin clair / celle qu'un sang farouche et radieux arrose." This opening, or cutting, within the heroine may well have been suggested to Mallarmé by her name, since in it the suffix "diade" (very close to the Greek "dyad") is attached to "Héro." In any case the morpheme "dia" suggests the division of a unity.[11]

We shall see that the body/spirit dichotomy fundamental to the narrative content of *Les noces* is equally fundamental to its formal arrangement. The mind/body duality of the heroine and Saint John is *formally* extended in the ambivalent relationship between text and theatrical performance that informs the global structure of *Les noces*.

As mentioned earlier, *Les noces* does not have the character of an ordinary theatrical text. Among other things, it is missing a strong narrative action or anecdotal element, which the theatergoer of Mallarmé's time was still in a position to expect.[12] In his notes for the "Préface" Mallarmé states that his omission of the well-known anecdote of Salomé's dance is deliberate: a dance is referred to in the "Préface" and in the "Finale" but "pas anecdotique" (94). His purpose is not to tell a story that everyone already knows but, rather, to isolate the heroine in a moment of confrontation between herself and the Baptist's head and express her innermost feelings: "l'isoler comme l'ont fait des tableaux solitaires dans le fait même terrible, mystérieux—et faire miroiter ce qui probablement hanta, en apparue avec son attribut—le chef du saint" (51). This ambition to create a psychological portrait of the hero seems more in keeping with the conventions of lyric poetry (which strives to express the intimate emotions of the subject) than with those of theater in Mallarmé's time.

---

11. *Dia-*, élément, du gr. *dia-* signifiant "séparation, distinction" (ex.: *diacritique*) ou à travers" (ex.: *dialyse*) (*Petit Robert* 1979, 533).

12. When Mallarmé decided to rewrite his "tragédie" as a poem, he wrote that this was because (like "L'après-midi d'un faune") *Hérodiade* lacked any anecdote, which (Banville had assured him) was necessary in order to provide an "intérêt dramatique."

Indeed, with the exception of the "Scène," which constitutes the cen-
terpiece of the work, most of the poetry of *Les noces* does not resemble
dramatic verse but, rather, the autotelic and nonrepresentational type of
poetry typical of Mallarmé's shorter poems.

While *Les noces* partially complies with certain fundamental rules of
tragedy—Aristotle's unities of action, time, and place—it also works
constantly to subvert them. The text marks itself as a theatrical genre by
setting up the unities as an integral part of its structure, but it also denies
this identification because within the textual process the action, time,
and place are also (to use Mallarmé's phrase) "littérairement aboli[s]"
(Mallarmé 1945, 379).

The unity of action (prescribing that in the evolution of the play a single
important event will take place) is undermined from the outset, in the first
word of the play—the hypothetical "Si . . ." —which introduces the "Pré-
lude." The "Prélude" presents symbols of the main events (the decapita-
tion and wedding) as though signifying that they *might* take place yet also,
paradoxically, that they already have. To forewarn the audience (or
reader) in the prologue of events that are about to take place is to comply
with a theatrical convention. This happens, for example, in the witches'
prologue in *Macbeth*. But to present these future events as hypothetical, to
state that their symbolic preparation may be in vain, thereby implying that
they might not take place (as the "Prélude" does), and later to deny that
they did (as the notes in the "Finale" do, e.g., "rien de tout cela est-il
arrivé" [139]) is to interfere with all learned expectations of the theater.
Tragedy, we know, is supposed to be the exposition of an action that
constitutes a crisis and not the exposition of something that is possibly
nothing after all.

The unity of time (prescribing that the dramatic action will evolve
within a brief and clearly determined time scheme) is equally subverted
by *Les noces*. The canticle of Saint John is sung (in the present) at the
moment of decapitation in the "Prélude," yet in the following "Scène" it
appears as though this event has not yet occurred. In the "Scène" we are
prepared for events that may or may not have happened in the "Pré-
lude," as Hérodiade's character is drawn out and possible motivations
are established for her desire both to execute and marry John. In the
"Finale" as in the "Prélude" the reader has difficulty in grasping a
cyclical rather than chronological order of events; the wedding is de-
scribed in three subsequent passages that repeat rather than follow one
another.[13] We also find here references to what appear to be prior scenes

13. This synchronic approach to time is less familiar in the context of theater than in that of
music, which may explain why the first and last sections of the work are entitled not "Scènes"
but "Prélude" and "Finale."

(e.g., a meeting between Hérodiade and John) but to which, in fact, there are no previous allusions in the play. Furthermore, the notes indicate that the central dramatic action, the wedding, occurs at an undecidable time of day, twilight or daybreak:

> moment d'évanouissement vespéral ou
> matinal—on ne saura jamais
>
> (139)[14]

Our sense of place in *Les noces* is as unsure as our sense of time. Hérodiade's chamber is an illusive house of mirrors. In the "Prélude" every image is perceived through its double: the sun on the horizon reflects the platter on the wall; the "divers monstres nuls" are reflections of "L'aiguière bossuée et le tors candélabre." In the "Cantique de Saint Jean" the central image of the sun is not perceived directly but through its reflection in the sword blade hanging over the Baptist's head. In the last passage of the "Prélude" Saint John's song is heard as a phantom echo, and the nurse is portrayed first as her shadow. Even in the "Scène" (in which the stability of our ordinary perception of reality is least disturbed), the central figure is not presented directly; we do not see Hérodiade but her reflection in the looking glass.

In the "Finale" any remaining sense of security that readers might have, believing themselves in front of a text portraying a conventionally tragic world—that is, one that represents a particular time and place in which an action takes place—is definitively destroyed by Hérodiade's ballet. Her dance is terrifying ("effrayante") because its performance allows the heroine to be in two places at the same time ("à la fois ici là") without ever moving ("sur place, sans bouger"). As the notes pertaining to the dance clearly indicate, it has the magical function of eradicating, or effacing, the reality of all that has happened and of tangibly re-creating a virginal empty space:

> elle se réveille—
> *(rien de tout cela est-il arrivé)
>
> et danse un moment
> pour elle seule**—afin d'être
> à la fois ici là—et que
> rien de cela ne soit arrivé
>
> (139)

14. Cf. Baudelaire's "Crépuscule du matin" as symbolic expansion on the reversibility of dawn and dusk (Baudelaire 1982, 286).

                    une sorte de danse
                    effrayante   esquisse
                    —et sur place, sans
                    bouger
                                —lieu nul
                                  (114)

The offering and subsequent denial of representation forms perhaps the most striking characteristic of this text. In *Hérodiade* the "abolition," or subversion, of mimesis is not coextensive with the text as it is in several of Mallarmé's shorter poems (i.e., "Le sonnet en yx," "Sainte," and "Une dentelle s'abolit"), but it is perceivable in many passages—in their systematic cancellation of images—as well as in the overall structure of the work discussed above.

The "Prélude" and the "Ouverture ancienne" well demonstrate this point. The following are the first verses of the "Prélude":

            Si . . .
                    Génuflexion comme à l'éblouissant
                    Nimbe là-bas très glorieux arrondissant
                    En le manque du saint à la langue roidie
                    Son   et vacant incendie
                    Aussi peut-être hors la fusion entre eux
                    Immobilisés par un choc malencontreux
                    Des divers monstres nuls dont l'abandon délabre
                    L'aiguière bossuée et le tors candélabre
                    A jamais sans léguer de souvenir au soir
                    Que cette pièce héréditaire de dressoir
                                                            (55)

Clearly, this passage is in part representational. It evokes several images: the sun and its reflections in Saint John's halo and the golden platter; the water pitcher and the candelabra and their reflections in the "divers monstres." But accompanying the evocation of each object or image is (as already mentioned) a sign evoking its reverse image, or reflection, which functions as a negation. The fact that these various reflections constitute negative signs is confirmed by the addition of a negative qualifying word for each. The halo is an outline, empty at its center "en le *manque* du saint à la langue roidie." Similarly the sunset is vacant, "son *vacant* incendie," and further on this vacancy is attributed to the symbolic platter, which oddly refuses to signify: "cette *vacuité* louche et muette d'un plat." The images of the water pitcher and candelabra are negated, or "abolished," in advance—"*l'abandon délabre* / L'aiguière bossuée et le tors candelabre"—as are their reflections in the "divers monstres *nuls*" (emphases mine).

We find a similar cancellation of mimesis in the negation of images that prevails throughout the opening passage of an earlier version of the "Prélude," the "Ouverture ancienne":

> Abolie, et son aile affreuse dans les larmes
> Du bassin, aboli, qui mire les alarmes,
> Des ors nus fustigeant l'espace cramoisi,
> Une Aurore a, plumage héraldique, choisi
> Notre tour cinéraire et sacrificatrice,
> Lourde tombe qu'a fuie un bel oiseau, caprice
> Solitaire d'aurore au vain plumage noir . . .
> Ah! des pays déchus et tristes le manoir!
> Pas de clapotement! L'eau morne se résigne
> Que ne visite plus la plume ni le cygne
> Inoubliable: l'eau reflète l'abandon
> De l'automne éteignant en elle son brandon:
> Du cygne quand parmi le pâle mausolée
> Ou la plume plongea la tête, désolée
> Par le diamant pur de quelque étoile, mais
> Antérieure, qui ne scintilla jamais.
>
> (Mallarmé 1945, 41)

Given the denial of mimesis in passages such as those cited above and the subversion of theatrical convention in the structure of the piece, we might be tempted to understand *Hérodiade* as a pure, or self-sufficient, poetic work with no more reference to the world of theater than to that of "reality." This reasoning, however, does not account for the unfinished quality of the text. Clearly the text appears in some way fundamentally incomplete (not in the sense that many of the verses are unfinished). We find the key to this incompleteness in the many references to performing arts that are located, for the most part, outside the body of the text. In these references the text seems to create for itself a special performance context.

This performance context is established first by means of titles and subheadings which invariably pertain to the nomenclature of the performing arts. As mentioned earlier, the *mystère* in the title indicates that the text is theatrical in genre, as do the subheadings "Scène" and "Scène intermédiaire," which precede the two central sections of the piece. Mallarmé refers to both these sections as dialogues, though the "Scène intermédiaire" is designated in the notes as a "dialogue muet." The first and last sections of the play are also named according to performing arts terminology: "Prélude" and "Finale."

How can the reader understand these references to performing arts genres in the titles and subtitles of the poem? We might read them as metaphorical (as in Mallarmé's essay "Symphonie littéraire"), but this does not fully explain their function. These titles can be more fully understood if we look to Mallarmé's commentary on the nature and function of titles in general.

For Mallarmé, the title functions as the germ from which the entire work would ideally disseminate; we saw this with regard to his consideration of the name Hérodiade. Central as the title may be to the development of the poem, however, he does not consider it to be an *integral* part of the text. On the contrary, the title serves to delineate the white space surrounding the poem, "ce grand espace blanc laissé à dessein au haut de la page," to separate the poem from all that is other, and to create for it the "virginal" atmosphere in which it should be read.[15] In a previously cited passage from "Le mystère dans les lettres" the function of the title in relation to the text is clearly defined. The title must be relegated to oblivion, to the white space—that region of absence that it helps to define—and precisely because it says too much about the origin or secret matrix of the text. The matrix should not be simply given away from the start but rediscovered through the act of reading:

> Lire—
>
> Cette pratique—
>
> Appuyer, selon la page, au blanc, qui l'inaugure son ingénuité, à soi, oublieuse même du titre qui parlerait trop haut: et, quand s'aligna, dans une brisure, la moindre, disséminée, le hasard vaincu mot par mot, indéfectiblement le blanc revient, tout à l'heure gratuit, certain maintenant, pour conclure que rien au-delà et authentiquer le silence—
>
> Virginité qui solitairement, devant une transparence du regard adéquat, elle-même s'est comme divisée en ses fragments de candeur, l'un et l'autre, preuves nuptiales de l'Idée.

---

15. This description of the function of the title is taken from a letter to Maurice Guillemot: "Si l'on obéit à l'invitation de ce grand espace blanc laissé à dessein au haut de la page comme pour séparer de tout, le déjà lu ailleurs, si l'on arrive avec une âme vierge on s'aperçoit que je suis scrupuleusement syntaxier, que mon écriture est dépourvue d'obscurité, que ma phrase est ce qu'elle doit être et être pour toujours" (Scherer 1947, 79).

This second virginity or silence that the text acquires through its reading is (as we have often seen) not homogeneous but one that has divided itself into presence and absence, being and nothingness, text and context. In the passage following the one cited above Mallarmé clearly designates this space of absence surrounding the text as the space of music—a performing art—which leaves its final mark, like its initial mark, in the domain of the invisible:

> L'air ou chant sous le texte, conduisant la divination d'ici là, y applique son motif en fleuron et cul-de-lampe invisibles.
>
> (Mallarmé 1945, 386–87)

It is the "air or song under the text" that guides the discovery of its meaning, a music that is paradoxically present in a textually "invisible" space, the white space of absence surrounding the poem.[16]

Thus, like the overall structuring of *Les noces,* the genre-marking title and subtitles help to ensure that the reader will reconstitute a presence-in-absence of the performing arts and receive the text within a performing arts context.

A still more striking and ambiguous presence of the performing arts is evoked, however, in the notes accompanying the manuscript. These notes are found generally on separate sheets of paper and occasionally in the margins of the text. In many cases the notes appear preparatory—to outline the development of the text. But in other cases they are not assimilated within the body of the verse. Rather, they appear to add to the verses a performative, or theatrical, supplement. Among these notes we find theatrical asides, descriptions of characters and decor, and, in general, a kind of "mise en scène" referring to specific objects and gestures.

Though the marginal notes are few in number, they do recall (if in an unconventional manner) the pattern of stage directions. In the manuscript of the "Ouverture ancienne," for example, we find the following comments: "faisons le lit"; "pour échauffer"; "Plus de rougeur aux cieux—qu'un pâle tremblement de jour qui ne sera jamais—et que . . . perle enfouie en l'étang." Characters and objects are evoked: the "héros" and the "mandore" (232).

---

16. This passage from "Le mystère dans les lettres" recalls the one quoted earlier in "La musique et les lettres," by virtue of its presentation of music and letters as the "preuves nuptiales de l'Idée": "la Musique et les Lettres sont la face alternative ici élargie vers l'obscur; scintillante là, avec certitude, d'un phénomène, le seul, je l'appelai, l'Idée" (Mallarmé 1945, 649).

More copious and interesting than these marginal notes are those we
find in two series, not integrated within the manuscripts themselves.
Many of these notes have the appearance of theatrical asides. In one
(undoubtedly pertaining to the "Scène intermédiaire") Hérodiade ad-
dresses her nurse as if casting a magical spell to make her disappear:

> disparais toi
> ma hantise
> de ce que je ne
> serai pas et
> bannis
> la femme
> nourrice je crois
> t'appela-t-on
>
> vain fantôme
> de moi-même
> celle que je ne
> serai
> pas
> —qui tournes
> tout autour
> évanouis-toi
> (97–98)

In others Hérodiade addresses the Baptist's head, explaining to the
reader (or spectator?) various motivations for her actions that are kept
secret in the text:

> C'est toi cruel
> qui m'as blessée
> en dessous
> par la tête*—
> heurtant
> l'au-delà
>
> *par le bond de la pensée
> que tu ne connais pas—
> laisse-moi à ta place y
> verser regards vous
> pierreries nuit d'été—

—mais ouverts épa-
nouis   joaillerie—
              étoile
                     étoile et chair
       mariée
       et resplendissant de
       la vie qui s'éteint en
       tes yeux

              de l'un et l'autre
                     doigt

          c'était—baiser
       pour te fermer les
       yeux—
                 vous pouvez
       vous fermer beaux
                     yeux
              sur votre ouvrage
       qui coule en pliant les mains
       ____

       moi, non plus l'enfant
       capricieuse de tout
       à l'heure
                     (115–17)[17]

Other notes do not add theatrical discourse. They are purely descrip-
tive. For example, the following describe the appearance and gestures of
Hérodiade and Saint John's head:

              H. elle, sans
       attendre—
                 mains tendues
       renie
                 traits—
       de face effarante
              ____

____

17. Notice that Hérodiade refers to herself as John the Baptist's "ouvrage." Given the
emphasis on duality in these notes, "de l'un et de l'autre doigt," and on the fact that the Saint
has wounded her—"tu m'as blessée en dessous"—as well as rendered her eyes "ouverts," the
term is probably a pun signifying that Hérodiade is at once his finished product and an
"ouverture," that which has opened him and which he has opened.

```
                  glace des yeux qui
                  ne voient pas—
                     ce qu'ils ont
                        évoqué
                     qu'ils ne verront
                     jamais—
                        (102–3)
```

Several notes are generally descriptive of the scene (such as those cited earlier in which the time of day is designated as indeterminable and the scene or place as a "lieu nul"). And others describe even the diction of the words of the "Scène intermédiaire," those words of the "dialogue muet" that, perhaps, will never be uttered:

```
        ces mots négligemment
                              dits
                        ou sourdement
                           avec un
                        [        ]
                     ou méchamment
                     ce peut être—ou—
        Nul ne saura jamais
                  pas même elle évanouie
        mais a-t-elle entendu?—évanouie en
                  car furent-ils dits
        va me chercher le chef du saint sur un plat d'or
                     ces mots—rigides comme une épée
        ils le furent—car effroi de la pauvre vision
        qui s'en fut
                  non par une fente des tapisseries
        mais évanouie en sa trame usée.
                              (127–28)
```

One note seems to summarize the way in which the poetic discourse and the performing arts are combined within the text:

```
                     pensé
              monologue—
           silence et danse—
                     attitudes
              seul monologue
           éclat intérieur
                  (118)
```

The text, like the heroine, is a unity-in-duality. *Les noces* appears to comprise two contrary worlds: the world of thought, expressed in poetic discourse ("monologue"), and that of gesture ("attitudes"), expressed in various notes and, particularly, in those pertaining to Hérodiade's ballet. Only the "éclat intérieur" (of thought) is expressed in the body of the verse. The world of gesture and dance is referred to but is relegated to an invisible world, the silence surrounding the text.

The nature and function of the text's gestural, performative supplement is most clearly revealed in the notes describing Hérodiade's dance. The process of mirroring and negation that creates nothingness in a verbal or discursive mode is *performatively repeated* in the gestures of the dance. She juxtaposes various twin members of her body—her breasts and feet—creating a kind of hall of mirrors, or corporeal *mise en abîme,* of her own unity matching the ubiquitous unity-splitting reflections of images in the verse. Her identical yet contrary gestures and body parts function as if to cancel each other out so that in the end she is performing a kind of pure, or virginal, dance, the dance equivalent of the textual "virginité" attained through the reading of a page of poetry "divisée en ses fragments de candeur" (387). Through her bizarre dance she is enabled to re-create and illustrate (with no accessory other than her own body) a nothingness, "lieu nul," and in a paradoxically concrete or physical way:

> se penche-t-elle d'un
> côté—de l'autre—
> montrant un
> sein*—l'autre—
>
> et surprise
> sans gaze
> *selon ce sein, celui-là
> identité
> et cela fait—sur
> un pied l'autre,
> eux-mêmes
> sur les pieds
> seins
>
> une sorte de danse
> effrayante   esquisse
> —et sur place, sans
> bouger
> —lieu nul
> (113–14)[18]

It is by means of the gestural equivalent, this supplement, to the text—
the dance—that the central mystery of duality-of-self becomes fully re-
vealed both to the heroine and to the reader of the work:

> elle se réveille—
> *(rien de tout cela est-il arrivé)
>
>   et danse un moment
> pour elle seule **—afin d'être
> à la fois ici là—et que
> rien de cela ne soit arrivé
>
>   **pour la première fois
>   yeux ouverts—
>   (139)

This does not mean, however, that the mind/body dichotomy (the
duality referred to so persistently in the text) is ultimately reconciled or
resolved. Although the dance does repeat in a performative mode the
poetic process of autonegation (occurring throughout the body of the
verse), it is not integrated, absorbed, or described in the poetry that
constitutes the text. The purpose of the representation of performance is
thus not to accompany or support the poetry of the text but to cancel
this poetry out, by presenting itself as the text's mirror image or negative
sign.

For Mallarmé, the text is necessarily effaced, or abolished, in front of
the apprehension of that which is tangible—for example, those theatri-
cal performances directly expressive of the sensory effects that the poetic
text seeks indirectly to create: "Ainsi l'Action, en le mode convenu,
littéraire, ne transgresse pas le Théâtre; s'y limite, à la représentation—
immédiat évanouissement de l'écrit" (371). *Les noces* can thus be under-
stood as the perhaps still imperfect fruit of Mallarmé's long labor to-
ward a "très nouvelle poétique" portraying nothing but its sensory ef-
fects, a poetics in which the intention of the transfiguration of language
into something other is somehow recorded within the text—"Le vers ne
doit donc pas se composer de mots; mais d'intentions"—and in which
"toutes les paroles s'effacent devant la sensation" (Mallarmé 1959,
137).

---

18. It is important to note that in this minimal dance of duality, Hérodiade is represented
(unlike Salomé and all of the previously cited dancers in Mallarmé's texts) as dancing without a
veil, "et surprise sans gaze." This is a very significant differentiation, as the veil, for Mallarmé,
is a symbol of that nothingness-in-between that keeps the mystery of the duality of self intact.

The displacement of Hérodiade's dance—its extraction from the self-destructive narrative representation, which constitutes the body of text, and its transplantation into a supplementary "hors texte"—illustrates for the reader this point, as well as clarifying Mallarmé's ambiguous references to the dance in his notes for the "Préface." We understand why he removes all traces of a description of Salomé's erotic veil dance from his verse ("légende dépouillée de danse)" only to reinject a transfigured representation of this dance in its periphery—the white space of absence surrounding the text: "aujourd'hui je retrouverais la danse—déplacement de la danse—ici—et pas anecdotique" (93–94). The mind/body duality of self that constitutes the central mystery of the play is thus textually and structurally signified as the performative act is reinstated within the work, not as an integral part of the text, however, but "exposé, dans une violation fortuite, pour multiplier l'angoisse" (351) and, according to Mallarmé's previously explicated inversion of Shakespeare's text/performance model, "extra-textuellement."

CHAPTER EIGHT

L'après-midi d'un faune

In many ways the history of *L'après-midi d'un faune* runs parallel to that of *Hérodiade*. The work was begun at approximately the same time (1865), and though several versions of the poem were published in Mallarmé's lifetime, he envisaged reworking it as late as 1891, seven years before his death. The two works also share the theme of a mind/body duality within the hero and the formal manifestation of this theme in the juxtaposition of two contrary but related modes of expression: poetry and performing arts.

As in *Hérodiade* the several versions of the *Faune* reveal the presence of theater to a varying degree. The first version of the work, entitled *Le faune, intermède héroïque*, was explicitly conceived and written as a theatrical text, a "poème dramatique."[1] Integrated within the body of the text are a set of stage directions indicating gestures performed by the Faune. Insofar as we can deduce this from the unfinished manuscript, the *Intermède* was to include three scenes: the initial "Monologue d'un faune," the "Dialogue des nymphes," and a second monologue entitled "Le réveil du faune." Of these three scenes only the first appears complete.[2] This was undoubtedly the fragment that Mallarmé submitted in 1865 to Théodore de Banville and Constant Coquelin in hopes of having it produced at the Théâtre Français.[3]

1. Banville's *Diane au Bois*, with which Mallarmé's *Faune* is often associated, is an example of this genre, which consisted of "une scène poétique à un ou à plusieurs personnages, et comportant un seul récitant" (Mallarmé 1945, 1448).

2. We know of this first version because of an autographed manuscript dated 1873–74, which Mallarmé copied for Philippe Burty. The manuscripts for this version and all others to which I will refer are published in *Œuvres complètes de Stéphane Mallarmé: Poesies*, ed. Carl Paul Barbier and Charles Gordon Millan (Paris: Flammarion, 1983). Unless otherwise specified, all page number references are to this edition.

3. In an 1865 letter to Aubanel we learn that the manuscript was rejected on the ground that it lacked dramatic interest: "Les vers de mon *Faune* ont plu infiniment, mais de Banville et Coquelin n'y ont pas rencontré l'anecdote nécessaire que demande le public et m'ont affirmé

A second version of the work is a revision of the "Monologue" entitled *Improvisation d'un faune*.[4] Here the stage directions have disappeared but there appears a more indirect and subtle allusion to performance in the typographical disposition of the poem. The absent gestures leave their mark in the form of blank spaces that interrupt the alexandrine in the initial lines of the poem, and two segments of the text are set within quotation marks, each prefaced by the Faune's invocation of nature to speak. As I shall further demonstrate, these quoted passages cannot be understood other than as ironical, for within them nature is in fact represented as refusing to speak. By virtue of ironical typographical marks of a passage from indirect to direct discourse (ironical because incongruous with an otherwise clearly signified failure to textually represent nature's speech), the text signifies an unsuccessful passage from narrative to recitation, or from the mode of text to that of performance.

The third version of the *Faune* is *L'après-midi d'un faune, églogue*—the form in which the poem is best known today. The *Eglogue* was originally published in 1876 in a luxurious *plaquette* with illustrations by Manet. As in the *Improvisation,* in this version the original stage directions have disappeared, but the ironical juxtaposition of uncited and cited discourse survives, and it is underscored by a change from roman to italic type.

Though the *Eglogue* proved an immediate success and several editions of it were published, it seems that Mallarmé remained unsatisfied with the work. A bibliographical note in *Pages* (1891) reveals his intention to reincorporate stage directions and revise the work for the theater: "*L'après-midi d'un faune,* édition nouvelle définitive pour la lecture et pour la scène, avec notes, indications, etc. (sous presse)" (269).

Mallarmé's correspondence indicates that in 1890 he was encouraged by Paul Fort, director of the Théâtre d'Art, to undertake a staging of his poem, in collaboration with Claude Debussy. This project was undoubtedly the impetus for Debussy's composition of the celebrated "Prélude à l'après-midi d'un faune." The poem was to be recited, not sung; the music was to constitute a "gloss" (that is, an exegetical musical commentary) rather than an accompaniment. We see that even as Mallarmé envisaged a theatrical collaboration of music and poetry, he resisted the idea of their union, or synthesis. Though the program was announced, he in the end

---

que cela n'intéresserait que les poètes. J'abandonne mon sujet pendant quelques mois dans un tiroir, pour le refaire librement plus tard" (185).

4. In 1875 this text was submitted for publication in the *Troisième Parnasse Contemporain* and rejected by the jury: Théodore de Banville, Anatole France, and François Coppée.

defaulted, replacing the *Faune* with another poem, "Le Guignon," unrelated to Debussy's music. The various sections of Debussy's "glose musicale,"—consisting originally of a "Prélude," "Interludes," and "Paraphrases Finales," were fused into the celebrated "Prélude."[5]

Literary history records that throughout the poem's genesis, Mallarmé viewed the *Faune* as an ambiguously theatrical text; that is, he viewed it as simultaneously theatrical and nontheatrical in genre. This ambiguity is perhaps best summed up in an 1865 letter to Henri Cazalis:

> je rime un intermède héroïque dont le héros est un Faune. Ce poème renferme une très haute et très belle idée, mais les vers sont terriblements difficiles à faire, car je le fais absolument scénique, non *possible au théâtre* mais *exigeant le théâtre*. (184)

The ambiguity can be explained by the fact that in the *Faune* (as in *Hérodiade*) Mallarmé wished to produce the effect of theater (and also, as we shall see, the effect of music) without the loss of poetic integrity implied by the actual collaboration of a performing art. We shall see that all versions of the text indeed attempt to create for themselves, not so much a performative complement as a performative supplement, a performing arts context, by their structural and thematic references to these arts.

My analysis will begin with a summary of the argument of the text. The poem is a narrative of the *rêveries* of a faun who has just awakened from an afternoon nap. The Faune tells of a sexual encounter: his attempted rape of two nymphs. But he is unsure whether this event actually occurred or whether he is remembering a dream. Throughout the poem his attention vacillates between the real (or natural) world and the dream world of his fantasies. The narration of his pursuit of the nymphs is complete in the first section of the *Intermède,* the "Monologue," and it is primarily the "Monologue" that Mallarmé revised in the second and third versions of the text.

The depiction of a faun in amorous revelry with nymphs is typical of

5. In an 1890 letter to Edmond Deman, Mallarmé comments on this project: "On me propose de monter au théâtre *L'Après-midi d'un Faune,* qui est, en effet, écrit comme intermède scénique à l'origine. La façon très rare et curieuse dont je compte produire cela vaudra à cet opuscule quelque retentissement nouveau. . . . Je prépare une re-publication définitive, avec quelques reflexions de moi sur la poésie et le théâtre, la récitation de ce poème et le point de vue exact d'une mise en scène. Un dessin colorié représentant cela, au besoin; et peut-être quelques indications sur le rien d'ouverture musicale. Bref, une brochure présentant le tout comme un monologue en vers et qui ait chance de s'enlever, par cette fureur qui sévit de tableaux vivants et de morceaux dits, dans les salons" (269).

pastoral poetry, and the "Eglogue" of the title indicates that the text belongs to this genre. (Leconte de Lisle's 1864 translation, *Idylles de Théocrite et odes anacréontiques,* testifies to the fact that the classical genre was very much in vogue.) In Victor Hugo's "Le satyre" we find many of Mallarmé's *Faune's* allusions to Greek and Latin mythology—e.g., to the volcano Etna, to the uprising of Pan, or the Faunus, and to the ensuing anger of the gods expressed in a "foudroyement" (Hugo 1972, 92–101). And the choice of the faun as hero is hardly original to Mallarmé; the mythic animal-immortal appears in many other artworks in very distinct types of poetry such as Musset's *Rolla,* Rimbaud's "Antique," and Banville's dramatic *Diane au Bois,* and in paintings, such as Boucher's depicting a faun and nymphs, exhibited in London at the National Gallery in 1862.[6]

In spite of the many conventional aspects of this text, Mallarmé's treatment of the theme is quite original. What separates his *Faune* from many others is the emphasis on the Faune's duality. So central is the problem of duality to the thematics of the *Faune* that we might interpret the choice of hero itself as an economical means of expressing the simultaneous unity and discord of the mind and body within the self. Even more strikingly than in *Hérodiade,* the hero of this text is explicitly dual, divided between the world of his senses and the imaginative world of the mind. The hybrid creature symbolizes the two contrary but related aspects of human experience. As half-animal and half-god he participates equally, and to a hyperbolic degree, in the natural and the supernatural, the real and the imaginary, the earthly and the divine. The faun is thus a concrete image of the relationship between these contraries as it is developed throughout the poem.

This duality of the Faune's person is extended into the world as he attempts to fuse his natural environment, "les bois," with his illusions, merging his perceptions of both and expressing them simultaneously in his poetic discourse. The fusion of the two is presented, however, as impossible. Metaphors that appear at first to combine them are constantly unraveled or undercut. The Faune's perception of nature appears paradoxically to evoke but exclude the perception of his dream, and vice versa, so that throughout his monologue he slips back and forth, now confusing nature and illusion and now setting them apart.

The Faune's entanglement in these two worlds is clearly expressed in each version of the text. I shall analyze the relationship between dream and reality—the imagination and the senses—in the "Monologue" and

6. The most complete list of works associated with this text is to be found in H. Mondor's *Histoire d'un Faune* (1948).

reserve analysis of the "Improvisation" and the "Eglogue" for a more specific discussion of the formal extension of this relationship in the text's combination of poetry and performing arts (although this formal relationship, we shall see, is also suggested in several portions of the initial version of the text).

The Faune's oscillation between the natural world and the dream world begins with the opening lines of the text, for the nymphs disappear as the Faune begins to tell their story. The first stage direction emphasizes their recent departure. It is this absence that compels the Faune to speak:

> (*Un faune, assis, laisse et de l'un
> et de l'autre de ses bras s'enfuir deux nymphes.
> Il se lève.*)
>
> J'avais des nymphes!
>   Est-ce un songe? Non: le clair
> Rubis des seins levés embrase encore l'air
> Immobile,
>
>   (*Respirant*)
>
>   et je bois les soupirs.
>
>   (*Frappant du pied*)
>
>   Où sont elles?
>
>   (*Invoquant le décor*)
>
>   O feuillage, si tu protèges ces mortelles,
> 5   Rends-les-moi, par Avril qui gonfla tes rameaux
>   Nubiles (je languis encore de tels maux!)
>   Et par la nudité des roses, ô feuillage!
>   Rien.
>
>   (*A grands pas*)
>
>   Je les veux!
>
>   (*S'arrêtant*)
>   (252)

In the first stage direction the reader will notice the emphasis on duality; the reference to two nymphs is underscored by the stress on the twoness of the Faune's arms in *"de l'un et de l'autre* de ses bras" ("de ses bras" would have been sufficient to indicate the manner of their departure). This emphasis symbolically foreshadows the Faune's central dilemma, which will be repeatedly articulated in the text: the impossibility of embracing and retaining a duality.

The gestures in this opening passage are the most active of the entire poem. This is appropriate in that the Faune is not yet resigned to a purely poetic or imaginative re-creation of the nymphs; he wants to get them back in the flesh. He stands (as if to recapture them), breathes the burning air in which their presence is lingering, and stamps his feet as though this physical manifestation of his frustration at having lost them would compel them to reappear. This direct appeal failing, the Faune *invokes* nature to return *her* ward to him. The Faune's confusion of the nymphs with his natural habitat is presaged as he orders nature to give them back. Nature is characterized as nearly inseparable from the nymphs. The images of April in line 5 (freshness and youth), nature in full blossom (nubility), and the "nudité de roses" (sensual feminine beauty) in line 7 make the greenery the perfect asylum and camouflage for the nymphs. They are thus perceived as natural ("mortelles") and not supernatural creatures.

The refusal of nature to surrender the nymphs to the Faune, summarized in "Rien," brings his active, gestural search for them to a halt: "*(S'arrêtant)*." At this point he begins to question whether his encounter with the nymphs was real (that is, sensorial) or illusory:

> Mais si ce beau couple au pillage
> 9   N'était qu'illusion de mes sens fabuleux?
>
> (252)

In lines 10–18 the relationship between nature and illusion—the sensorial and the imaginative worlds—is examined. The Faune's propensity to combine these contraries is economically expressed in line 9 in the oxymoron "sens fabuleux." And this oxymoronic relationship is developed in the following verses as the Faune attempts but fails to fuse nature and illusion, first in a simile and then in a metaphor. His failure or refusal to accept the two as identical—as essentially one and the same thing—is expressed in the emphatic denial ("Non, non") and in the subsequent negation of the similarity previously suggested:

> 10   L'illusion, sylvain, a-t-elle les yeux bleus
> Et verts, comme les fleurs des eaux, de la plus chaste?

Et celle . . . qu'éprenait la douceur du contraste,
Fut le vent de Sicile allant par ta toison?
Non, non: le vent des mers versant la pâmoison
Aux lèvres pâlissant de soif vers les calices,
N'a pour les rafraîchir, ni ces contours si lisses
A toucher, ni ces creux mystères où tu bois
Des fraîcheurs que jamais pour toi n'eurent les bois

Paradoxically, illusion is presented as making a stronger appeal to the
senses than the natural world itself. The Faune feels his illusions more
tangibly than reality. The articulation of this paradox (which is a con-
stant of fantasy) merely expands on the oxymoron "sens fabuleux."
Nature and illusion are shown to be inextricably bound, but this interde-
pendence does not reconcile their opposition, since this opposition is
simultaneously stressed.

In the following lines of the poem, as though abandoning his attempt
to fuse nature and illusion (that is, his effort to get his illusion back in a
tangible form), the Faune appeals to *nature* to re-create his nymphs for
him in the next best mode—that is, in the form of a representational
narrative supplied by nature's voice. But this, too, results in failure:

Cependant!

(Au décor)

O glaïeuls séchés d'un marécage
20   Qu'à l'égal du soleil ma passion saccage,
Joncs tremblants avec des étincelles, contez
Que je venais casser les grands roseaux, domptés
Par ma lèvre: quand sur l'or glauque de lointaines
Verdures inondant le marbre des fontaines,
25   Ondoie une blancheur éparse de troupeau:
Et qu'au bruit de ma flûte où j'ajuste un pipeau
Ce vol . . . de cygnes? non, de naïades, se sauve
Je suis . . .
            Mais vous brûlez dans la lumière fauve,
Sans un murmure et sans dire que s'envola
30   La troupe par ma flûte effarouchée . . .

(Le front dans les mains)

(252–53)

As though realizing his failure to make the natural world comply with his desire (to re-create the nymphs *for* him in the form of a representation), the Faune interrupts *his* narrative (which should have been that of "les bords siciliens") to comment on just this lack of complicity, the refusal of nature to produce poetry, or to speak. The Faune's confusion of nature with illusion is again underscored in the text when an element in nature (the flight of swans) is again momentarily confused with the nymphs: "Ce vol . . . de cygnes? non, de naïades, se sauve."

The Faune's inability either to metaphorically combine or to clearly distinguish nature and illusion once again causes him a moment of self-doubt. The stage direction "(*Le front dans les mains*)" emphasizes his turning away from the exterior "(*Le décor*)" for a moment of introspection. All questions are now clearly addressed to himself:

> Hola!
> Tout ceci m'interdit: et suis-je donc la proie
> De mon désir torride, et si trouble qu'il croie
> Aux ivresses de sa sève?
> Serais-je pur?
> Je ne sais pas, moi! Tout, sur la terre, est obscur:
35 Et ceci mieux que tout encore: car les preuves
> D'une femme, où faut-il, mon sein, que tu les treuves?
> Si les baisers avaient leur blessure: du moins,
> On saurait!
> Mais je sais!
> O Pan, vois les témoins
> De l'ébat! A ces doigts admire une morsure
40 Féminine, qui dit les dents et qui mesure
> Le bonheur de la bouche où fleurissent les dents.

Nature is now qualified as obscure, not only refusing to speak but prohibitive of speech—"tout ceci *m'interdit*" (emphasis mine). The Faune thus abandons his search in the exterior world for any evidence of his encounter with the nymphs, but still seeks a tangible proof of its reality, not satisfied to accept the nymphs' existence as illusory. And he finds the evidence, "les preuves d'une femme," "une morsure féminine" in a physical mark on his body.

In the ensuing lines, which constitute the Faune's final address to nature ("le décor), the antagonistic relationship between him and his natural surroundings recalls (but inverts) the poet's dilemma in "L'Azur": nature is described as the treacherous cause for the poet's vain search for his illusions:[7]

(Au décor)

Donc, mes bois de lauriers remués, confidents
Des fuites, et vous, lys, au pudique silence,
Vous conspiriez? Merci. Ma main à ravir lance
45 En l'éternel sommeil des jaunes nénuphars
La pierre qui noiera leurs grands lambeaux épars:
Comme je sais aussi brouter sa verte pousse
A la vigne alanguie et demain sur la mousse
Vaine!
           Mais dédaignons de vils traîtres!

(253)

The Faune's antagonistic relationship with nature (the asylum of the nymphs) is underscored in his treatment of the *bois* and the *lys* as "conspirateurs" and "vils traîtres" and in his plan to wreak vengeance on nature by drowning the "nénuphars" and destroying the "vigne." The war between the Faune and nature had been suggested earlier: "O glaieuls séchés d'un grand marécage / qu'à l'égal du soleil ma passion *saccage*" (emphasis mine, 19–20), as had the violent nature of his intercourse with the nymphs, "ce beau couple au pillage" (line 8). The similarity between the two relationships is also underscored by the rhyme.

In the lines that follow (in a parallel movement to lines 30–41), the Faune turns his attention away from nature—abandoning his initial plan for vengeance in favor of reliving his ravishment of the nymphs (the dream figures), who are as "perfidious" as nature herself. Once again, he attempts to re-create the experience in the form of a representation. And this time he succeeds, for he assumes the role of the speaker/narrator in the absence of nature's corroboration. That is, he resigns himself to re-creating the presence of the nymphs as illusion, in the form of an artificial narrative representation of his own:

7. In "L'azur" nature is treacherous because she deceives the poet and makes him believe vainly in his dreams, even as he beseeches her to help him to forget them:

      . . .   —Vers toi! j'accours! donne, ô matière,
      L'oubli de l'Idéal cruel . . .

      En vain! l'Azur triomphe, et je l'entends qui chante
      Dans les cloches. Mon âme, il se fait voix pour plus
      Nous faire peur avec sa victoire méchante,
      Et du métal vivant sort en bleus angelus!

Serein,
50　　Sur ce socle déchu je veux parler sans frein
　　　Des perfides et par d'idolâtres peintures
　　　A leur ombre arracher encore des ceintures.

(253)[8]

The nymphs finally return to the faun as a presence-in-absence. Their
status is clearly expressed in an analogy: the nymphs return as memories,
just as by virtue of its translucency the hollowed grape allows the percep-
tion of the dream of the absent fruit:

Ainsi, quand des raisins j'ai sucé la clarté,
Pour que mon regret soit par le rêve écarté,
Rieur, j'élève au ciel d'été la grappe vide,
Et soufflant dans ses peaux lumineuses, avide
D'ivresse, jusqu'au soir je regarde au travers!

(253–54)[9]

This solution, or means of recovery, having been discovered, the
Faune returns to the position in which we found him at the opening of
the poem. He blows into the hollow grape ("regonflous") and recaptures
the nymphs as he returns to the world of dreams:

(Il s'assied)
Naïades, regonflons des souvenirs divers!

The attempted capture of the two nymphs that the Faune narrates is
an allegorical condensation of the central dream/nature duality. It is
introduced by several lines in which the natural and supernatural images
are constantly changing places; the "troupe" of nymphs both arises out
of and disappears into the landscape:

Mes yeux, trouant les joncs, suivaient une encolure
60　　Immortelle, qui noie en l'onde la brûlure
　　　Avec un cri de rage au ciel de la forêt:
　　　Et la troupe, du bain ruisselant, disparaît
　　　Dans les cygnes et les frissons, ô pierreries!

(254)

8. The representation of the Faune on a pedestal suggests that he is a statue; this is also how
the faun is portrayed in Rimbaud's "Antique" (Rimbaud 1960, 262). He is thus represented to
be as artificial as the nymphs of which he will speak in his "idolâtres peintures."
9. This creation of a poetic presence in the absence of a reality is a motif of many of
Mallarmé's poems such as "A la nue accablante tu" or "Mes bouquins refermés sur le nom de
Paphos."

The two nymphs whom the Faune tries to capture are themselves a symbolic variant of the oxymoron "sens fabuleux." Iane and Ianthé are a joined pair of opposites: Iane, "la plus chaste," and Ianthé, "celle qu'éprenait la douceur du contraste" (lines 11 and 12), are found enlaced in each other's arms.[10] The text simultaneously emphasizes their *union* and their separation, the fact that they are two as one, an inextricable couple:

> J'allais, quand à mes pieds s'entremêlent, fleuries
> 65 De la pudeur d'aimer en ce lit hasardeux,
> Deux dormeuses parmi l'extase d'être deux.
> Je les saisis, sans les désenlacer, et vole
> A des jardins, haïs par l'ombrage frivole,
> De roses tisonnant d'impudeur au soleil,
> 70 Où notre amour à l'air consumé soit pareil!

The narrative is interrupted as the Faune arises to declare (in the present) his feelings toward the nymphs, which are as antithetical as the object of his passion. His feelings are expressed in terms of oxymorons connoting the union of desire and revulsion, love and hate:

> *(Se levant)*
>
> Je t'adore fureur des femmes, ô délice
> Farouche de ce blanc fardeau nu qui se glisse
> Sous ma lèvre de feu buvant, dans un éclair
> De haines! la frayeur secrète de la chair,
> 75 Des pieds de la mauvaise au dos de la timide,
> Sur une peau cruelle et parfumée, humide
> Peut-être des marais aux splendides vapeurs.

---

10. The opposition between the nymphs is further emphasized in the "Dialogue des nymphes." At the end of their dialogue, Ianthé beseeches her sister to join her:

> Ianthé
> O folle, viens! Ne tarde
> Plus! Ma soeur, l'ennemi s'éveille, et tu me suis
> Dans les glaïeuls vermeils.
> Iane
> Non, pars seule! je suis
> Celle qui dois errer sous l'épaisse ramure
> Des forêts!
> *(elle s'en va du côté opposé)*
> (182)

Ultimately, the act of love (whose consummation would mean fusion since it could produce a synthesis) is characterized as both criminal and impossible. The Faune's crime, and failure, is his attempt to alter the oxymoronic status of the object of his desire: he can neither separate the couple (which he must do to in order to possess fully either one) nor possess them simultaneously. Like the impossible simultaneous apprehension of the natural world and the dream world, the Faune's taking of one nymph implies his loss of the other, and he loses both by attempting to have both:

> Mon crime fut d'avoir, sans épuiser ces peurs
> Malignes, divisé la touffe échevelée
> 80   De baisers que les dieux avaient si bien mêlée:
> Car à peine j'allais cacher un rire ardent
> Sous les replis heureux d'une seule, et gardant
> Par un doigt frêle afin que sa blancheur de plume
> Se teignît aux éclats d'une sœur qui s'allume,
> La petite, candide et ne rougissant pas,
> Que, de mes bras défaits par de lascifs trépas
> Cette proie, à jamais ingrate, se délivre,
> Sans pitié des sanglots dont j'étais encore ivre!

Thus, in the *Faune,* love (like poetry) operates according to a dialectic of presence and absence. It strives toward but cannot achieve the fusion of opposites, the reconciliation of duality. The text is engendered and extended by the alternating presence of the natural world and the dream world evoking each other as a desired complement in absence. The Faune's evocations (or invocations) of nature are inspired by the initial absence of the nymphs (who were present in his dream). Similarly, his evocation of the memory, or fantasy, of the sexual encounter is paradoxically made possible by the refusal of nature to reproduce the object of his desire.[11] This dialectic prolongs the text, for in the final movement of the poem the entire cycle is repeated as the Faune's desire for a real sexual experience is renewed by his failure to hold on to his dream: "Cette proie . . . se délivre" (line 87).

As this cycle begins, the Faune (now standing, as though fully awake), puts his dream behind him to think of future conquests:

---

11. In *The Death of Stéphane Mallarmé*, Leo Bersani describes this as a poetics of sublimation; the inaccessibility of the love object causes not a suppression but a kindling of desire and, therefore, greater poetic productivity (Bersani 1982, 80–83).

(Debout)

Oublions-les! Assez d'autres me vengeront
90   Par leurs cheveux mêlés aux cornes de mon front!

And a new fantasy emerges as he turns his attention to the surrounding landscape:

Je suis content! Tout s'offre ici: de la grenade
Ouverte, à l'eau qui va nue en sa promenade.
Mon corps, que dans l'enfance Eros illumina,
Répand presque les feux rouges du vieil Etna!
95   Par ce bois qui, le soir, des cendres a la teinte,
La chair passe et s'allume en la feuillée éteinte:

The Faune's erotic desire is rekindled on "la feuillée éteinte." It is the image of night falling on the greenery that provokes another fantasy, a second sexual encounter with the Goddess of love herself:

On dit même tout bas que la grande Vénus
Dessèche les torrents en allant les pieds nus,
Aux soirs ensanglantés par sa bouche de roses!
(255)

The realization of this dream, which the Faune begins to recount (and which implies his conquest of Venus), would constitute an even greater crime or blasphemy than the rape of the nymphs. To have his desire consummated by Venus would mean at the same time ultimate gratification and death: "être foudroyé." This end, or resolution, to his internal conflict the faun both desires and fears. This contradiction is verbally articulated in the "Si" and "Non" that frame the question "Mais ne-suis je pas foudroyé?" and symbolized theatrically in his gestures. He joins his hands in the air as if to seize Venus:

(Les mains jointes en l'air)
100   Si!...
(255)

and then wards off the thunderbolt he imagines as the consequence:

(Comme parant de ses mains disjointes une foudre imaginaire)

Mais ne suis-je pas foudroyé?

Non: ces closes

(Se laissant choeir)

Paupières et mon corps de plaisir alourdi
Succombent à la sieste antique de midi.

(255)

In an antithetical movement to the opening passage of the poem, the Faune falls back down to earth, bidding an ambiguous farewell to the objects of his desire:

Dormons . . .

(Etendu)
Dormons: je puis rêver à mon blasphème
Sans crime, dans la mousse aride, et comme j'aime
Ouvrir la bouche au grand soleil, père des vins.

(Avec un dernier geste)

Adieu, femmes: duo de vierges quand je vins.

(255)

The illusion/reality conflict seems at first to be put to rest as the Faune resolves to sleep and relive his blasphemous representations, (a variant in this context of the earlier "idolâtres peintures" [line 51]) by wholly reentering the dream world. But the conflict reemerges in the final verse of the text as the nymphs are represented neither as nymphs nor as virgins but as "real," or present, women whom the Faune may indeed have assaulted and whom (in a movement contrary to that of the first line "J'avais des nymphes! / Est-ce un songe?") he will lose in his dream.

In my exegesis of the "Monologue" I have dwelled on the Faune's dream/reality conflict and on the oxymoronic relationship between the imagination and the senses because these themes are central to the way in which poetry and performed arts are combined within the *Faune*. The relationship between these two modes of human experience is expressed or formally extended into the relationship between literature and performed arts in two ways.

One is in the inability of the Faune to merge nature's music, or sounds, with his own discourse. He fails to make music and poetry converge (as they should) through his instrument of expression (poetry), which is paradoxically symbolized by a musical instrument, the flute. The music of nature and that of poetry are presented as mutually exclusive; they never accompany each other. In order to make poetry, the Faune must violate the instrument of nature, the reed. He has to cut it, so that it can be transformed into his flute. Thus, when the Faune plays his flute, nature is inevitably silent, and in several instances, in a kind of role reversal, it attempts to silence him:

> Joncs tremblants avec des étincelles, contez
> Que je venais casser les grands roseaux, domptés
> Par ma lèvre: [. . .]
> Et qu'au bruit de ma flûte où j'ajuste un pipeau
> Ce vol . . . de cygnes? non, de naïades, se sauve
> Je suis . . .
> 　　　　Mais vous brûlez dans la lumière fauve
> Sans un murmure et sans dire que s'envola
30　　La troupe par ma flûte effarouchée . . .
>
> 　　　*(Le front dans les mains)*
>
> 　　　　　　　　　Hola!
> Tout ceci m'interdit:
>
> 　　　　　　　　　　　　(253)

We will examine this conflict between music (as the voice of nature) and poetry (as the voice of the Faune) in greater detail in the *Eglogue* and in the "Réveil du faune," where it is most fully developed.

In the *Eglogue* the first appearance of this conflict is in lines 16–22, where the Faune, in his attempt to disentangle his dream (the nymphs) from his natural surroundings, recognizes the difference or lack of complicity between his music (the artificial sound emitted by his flute) and the natural music of the water and the wind in the woods—"bosquet arrosé d'accords." Here, in contrast to the Romantic tradition (and also that of Baudelaire), the music of nature and that of poetry are characterized as incompatible:

> Ne murmure point d'eau que ne verse ma flûte
> Au bosquet arrosé d'accords; et le seul vent
> Hors des deux tuyaux prompt à s'exhaler avant
> Qu'il disperse le son dans une pluie aride,
20　　C'est, à l'horizon pas remué d'une ride,
> Le visible et serein souffle artificiel
> De l'inspiration, qui regagne le ciel.
>
> 　　　　　　　　　　　　(264)

In lines 26–27 the Faune's violation of nature in order to make poetry is expressed (as it was in the "Monologue"): *". . . je coupais ici les creux roseaux domptés / Par le talent."* And in the lines that follow (31–32) we see that it is just this violation, the Faune's seizure of nature's instrument to create his own music (the symbolic birth of pastoral poetry of which the "pipeau" is a symbol), that causes nature and her ward (the nymphs or swans) to flee him: *". . . au prélude lent où naissent les pipeaux, / Ce vol de cygnes, non! de naïades se sauve."*

The refusal of nature to comply with the Faune's ambition—his design to marry music and poetry—is clearly expressed in lines 32–34:

> Inerte, tout brûle dans l'heure fauve
> Sans marquer par quel art ensemble détala
> Trop d'hymen souhaité de qui cherche le *la*

The *"la"* is obviously an allusion to the sixth note in the musical scale ("premier degré de l'échelle fondamentale" [*Petit Robert* 1979, 1063]). As the expression "donner le la" also means to strike the tuning fork and, more generally in figurative language, "to set the tone," these lines express both the Faune's desire and his inability to make music and poetry converge in one art, his failure to find the right music for his verse.

Thus, like the fusion of illusion and reality, the *hymen* of music and poetry remains an inviting but impossible ambition. The two arts are interrelated but in an antagonistic mode. Like dream and reality they can be confused but not fused, as the one appears to appropriate the attributes of the other.

One instance of such confusion occurs in lines 43–51 of the *Eglogue* where, in a striking role reversal, nature's instrument, the rushes, takes on the ambition of the poet and dreams of making the "music" of his verse (the "sonore, vaine et monotone ligne") disappear. The role reversals are underscored by the word *confusions* in line 46:

> Le jonc vaste et jumeau dont sous l'azur on joue:
> Qui, détournant à soi le trouble de la joue
> 45 Rêve, dans un solo long, que nous amusions
> La beauté d'alentour par des confusions
> Fausses entre elle-même et notre chant crédule;
> Et de faire aussi haut que l'amour se module
> Evanouir du songe ordinaire de dos

> Ou de flanc pur suivis avec mes regards clos,
> Une sonore, vaine et monotone ligne.

In the subsequent lines (52–53), the Faune's attachment to and yet antagonism toward nature's instrument (the rushes) is expressed through yet another confusion. The reference to the "maligne Syrinx" (undoubtedly an allusion to Ianthé, the sensual "inhuman" nymph) is placed in apposition to the rushes, which must reflower for the Faune only to be recut:

> Tâche donc, instrument des fuites, ô maligne
> Syrinx, de refleurir aux lacs où tu m'attends!

In the "Réveil du faune" the close association between music, nature, sensuality, and the nymphs is still more clearly drawn. All these are the necessary antagonists of the Faune in his struggle to recapture his dream through poetry. Though the source of the Faune's illusions (his poetry) is clearly the music of nature—"mélodie, ô ruisseau de jeunesse qui coule" (182)—along with his love of nature and the nymphs, the rules of Art dictate that he must distance himself from these in order to create pure poetry:

> L'art, quand il désigna l'un des faunes élus,
> 　　　　　　　　　　　ne le déserte plus.
> 55　A des sons, dans le vice inutile, il recule.
> Et, l'impuissant fuyant dans un vil crépuscule,
> Le remords sur sa lèvre amènera, fatal
> Les stériles lambeaux du poème natal.
> Et la voix part des joncs unis, que nous n'osâmes
> Briser, pour demander le reste de nos âmes.
> 　　　　　　　　　　　　　　(182–83)

Here, the Faune's ambivalence toward the source of his poetry, nature and its music, is clearly expressed. In the grammatical anomaly ("Il recule à des sons," instead of "devant les sons") his flight from the source is qualified simultaneously as purposeful—in the paronomastic echo of the expression "reculer à dessein"—and vain—in the designation of his form of love (poetic fusion) as "le vice inutile." This articulation of the necessary backing off from the source of inspiration (recalling also the expression "reculer pour mieux sauter") underlines the point that the Faune must bypass the true object of his desire in order to safeguard it, to keep nature untouched so that it can function indefinitely to prolong his desire. It is the Faune's failure to actually take possession of nature (her sounds and her instruments: "la voix part des joncs unis, que nous n'osâmes briser") and his "remords" that enable him to create his own pure song: "Les stériles lambeaux du poème natal."

In the closing passages of the "Réveil du faune" the Faune again articulates the nature of the relationship between himself and the antagonists of his poetry: water, music, and women. In the final verses he prepares himself for a plunge into the "sources." He imagines that through a lustral rite he will absolve his duality and regain the lost unity of origins as an "être primitif." In fact, such an absolution would result only in the drowning of his art, as it does for the hero of Mallarmé's sonnet "Le pitre châtié": "Rance nuit de la peau quand sur moi vous passiez, / Ne sachant pas, ingrat! que c'était tout mon sacre, / Ce fard noyé dans l'eau perfide des glaciers" (1945, 31). But in the *Faune* no such punishment is incurred, for the consummation of desire, or fusion, never takes place:

> Je veux, dans vos clartés limpides, innover
> Une âme de cristal pur que jette la flûte,
> Et, natif, je fuirai, vainqueur de cette lutte
> Les femmes qui pour charme ont aussi de beaux pleurs.
>
> N'est-ce pas moi qui veux seul, et sans tes douleurs
> Amères, Idéal limpide?
>
> (183)

Even as the Faune prepares himself for this purgation (his plunge into the sources), he prepares simultaneously for his flight: "Et, natif, je fuirai, vainqueur de cette lutte." The result is that the Faune's battle will have been both won and lost (lost because he will not achieve the desired fusion and won because in this way his poetic productivity will be prolonged). The rejuvenation of his "âme de cristal pur" is made possible by situating the fusion of poetry and music—the expression of his soul and that of his sources—in an ever-inviting but never-to-arrive future:

> A la piscine
> 80   Des sources, à l'horreur lustrale qui fascine
> L'azur, je vais déjà tremper l'être furtif
> Qui de leur glace va renaître, primitif!
>
> (183)

In the preceding analyses we have noted how the relationship between illusion and reality extends itself thematically into the Faune's ambivalent desire to combine his poetry with music (the pure sounds of nature) and yet to keep it separate. In the evolution of the *Eglogue* we shall see that there is a parallel manifestation of the illusion/reality dichotomy in a poetry/theater dichotomy that extends itself into the structure of the text. The reader senses both the drive toward and the ultimate impossibility of the fusion of a text (a poetic representation) with its performance (a theatrical representation).

The text's failure to support itself with a theatrical representation is evident, as mentioned earlier, even in the first version, the *Intermède héroïque*. This text does seem to offer the minimum necessary references to performance. Though the gestures given in the stage directions are minimal, they are credible stage directions, at least at first. But as the text progresses and as the Faune's inability to act (to break through the *hymen* separating illusion and reality)[12] becomes more clear, the stage directions become more and more ineffectual. They finally appear ironical, for they no longer indicate anything that could be readily translated into gesture or into the concrete language of theater in any way. In the "Réveil du faune," for example, just as the Faune recognizes the need to steer clear of the source of his inspiration—the natural world, music, and women—his gestures come to a halt. And the stage directions become correspondingly impossible to convey by means of a theatrical representation. They interrupt the text to indicate nothing but the slightest nuances in the Faune's increasingly poetic mood:

> *(avec ravissement)*
> . . .
> *(doublant de ravissement)*
> . . .
> *(rêvant)*
> . . .
> *(rêvant plus)*
> . . .
> *(rêvant plus)*
> . . .
> *(commençant à être charmé)*
> (182)

---

12. In "La double séance" Derrida clarifies the symbolic value for Mallarmé of the term *hymen*. The hymen does not have to be ruptured, because it signifies both union and separation (1972, 237–42).

In the second and third versions of the *Faune,* the *Improvisation* and *Eglogue,* these stage directions, which have become increasingly less possible to direct or put into play, have disappeared. But in spite of this loss of explicit references to theater and the text's greater conformity to what we think of as a proper poem, it still seems that something is missing. The *absence* of a theatrical representation is underscored in several ways.

Initially, this absence is felt in the Faune's failure to express himself in the classical poetic way. The alexandrines of the opening passage are interrupted by white spaces, which seem as though they ought to be filled:

LE FAUNE

Ces nymphes, je les veux perpétuer.

Si clair,
Leur incarnat léger, qu'il voltige dans l'air
Assoupi de sommeils touffus.

Aimai-je un rêve?

Mon doute, amas de nuit ancienne, s'achève
5   En maint rameau subtil, qui, demeuré les vrais
Bois mêmes, prouve, hélas! que bien seul je m'offrais
Pour triomphe la faute idéale de roses.
Réfléchissons . . .

ou si les femmes dont tu gloses
Figurent un souhait de tes sens fabuleux!

(264)

To what can we attribute these white spaces, this breaking up of the initial Alexandrines of the poem? Readers familiar with the earlier versions of the text might see this disposition of the verse as marking the absence of the original stage directions. Or we might explain the faltering disposition of the Alexandrines as Mallarmé did, as a means of evoking for the text its own "musical accompaniment": "J'y essayais, en effet, de mettre, à côté de l'alexandrin dans toute sa tenue, une sorte de jeu courant pianoté autour, comme qui dirait d'un accompagnement musical fait par le poëte lui-même" (Mallarmé 1945, 870).

Whether or not the reader is aware of the absence of some sort of performative complement from the beginning, this absence and its origins will be felt further on in several changes of typography that constitute a frustrating surprise. In the *Eglogue* there are changes in typography at three points. Roman type becomes italicized and enclosed in quotation marks as the Faune narrates his illusion, the attempted rape of the nymphs. Generally, such a change in type indicates a change from indirect to direct discourse. This would normally imply that the Faune was relating words spoken at some preceding time, quoting himself or someone else. But as we shall now see, this is clearly not the case.

The first change in type occurs in lines 26–32, and it is prefaced and underscored by the boldfaced "CONTEZ." Here the Faune invokes nature to speak, to tell what happened between himself and the nymphs. Nature, however, refuses to participate in the narrative representation, and it is the Faune who continues to speak, as though *reciting* lines of indirect discourse that it would seem (like the script of the mime in "Mimique") had never before been spoken:

> O bords siciliens . . .
>   . . . CONTEZ
> *"Que je coupais ici les creux roseaux domptés*
> *"Par le talent. . . ."*
>   (264)

The cited italicized type continues into line 32 (which is itself interrupted), when the Faune suddenly recognizes that nature is not performing:

> *"Ou plonge . . ."*
>   Inerte, tout brûle dans l'heure fauve
> Sans marquer par quel art ensemble détala
> Trop d'hymen souhaité de qui cherche le *la*

The musical reference, *la,* is the only italicized word outside the passages in quotations; the italic functions to associate it with those cited passages as well as to lay stress on what the *la* (in this context) signifies: the Faune's inability to merge the music of nature with his poetic representation. Thus, the change in typography helps to underscore that the text is in some way deficient. The narrative presents itself as lacking, along with the support of nature, the functional collaboration of another art (which would better represent nature), a musical or theatrical accompaniment with a sensorial element that would make the representation complete.

The second change to cited discourse occurs as the Faune resumes his tale (lines 63–74). He now invokes the nymphs (rather than nature) as though abandoning his first hope that nature might back him up in the narration of his illusion. The change in type is again prefaced and underscored by the boldfacing of "SOUVENIRS." Here the change in type seems less surprising and inappropriate than in the first case. Though it is not the nymphs and Faune but the Faune alone who continues to speak, it appears at first that he is at least speaking in a different way, for we are brought closer to the moment of the event, witnessing the representation of his memories:

> O nymphes, regonflons des SOUVENIRS divers.
> *"Mon œil, trouant les joncs, dardait chaque encolure*
> *"Immortelle, qui noie en l'onde sa brûlure*
> 65   *"Avec un cri de rage au ciel de la forêt;*
> *"Et le splendide bain de cheveux disparaît*
>
>   (265)

However, no sooner does the reader come to associate the cited italicized type with the Faune's narrative and descriptive reconstruction of the event than the text undermines this identification. For the representation is interrupted by a typographical change (back to roman, uncited type at line 75) in a passage that paradoxically brings us still more closely into the immediacy of the event than does the preceding quoted and italicized narrative representation. The Faune's declaration of love to the nymphs (whom he addresses in the present) might have been appropriately enclosed in quotation marks in an ordinary poem but is printed here in roman, uncited type:

> 75   Je t'adore, courroux des vierges, ô délice
>   Farouche du sacré fardeau nu qui se glisse

The reader comes to recognize that this change in type represents something other than a mere inversion of the ordinary relationship between direct and indirect discourse (the past narrative is *direct* here, and the present address or declaration *indirect*), for in the lines following the declaration there is reversion to an indirect, descriptive, narrative mode without the now expected accompanying reversions to the past tense, and to cited, italicized type. (In the earlier "Improvisation" these lines [75–81] with slight variations remain within quotation marks.)

> Pour fuir ma lèvre en feu buvant, comme un éclair
> Tressaille! la frayeur secrète de la chair:
> Des pieds de l'inhumaine au coeur de la timide
> 80   Que délaisse à la fois une innocence, humide
> De larmes folles ou de moins tristes vapeurs.

In line 82 there is a reversion to the cited italicized type and to the past tense, but without any other radical change in the Faune's mode of speaking. He simply completes the narrative by explaining the nature of his crime and failure:

> *"Mon crime, c'est d'avoir, gai de vaincre ces peurs*
> *"Traîtresses, divisé la touffe échevelée*
> *"De baisers que les dieux gardaient si bien mêlée;*

Now the attentive reader cannot help wondering whether or how these striking variations in typography are expressive of a change in register or mode of speaking. The changes in type are troubling because they upset our understanding of the norms of citation in poetry and because they do not constitute a consistent system of transgressive reversals of these norms. For example, toward the end of the text we are led to associate verbs in the past tense with the cited, italicized discourse and verbs in the present tense with the uncited, unitalicized discourse, but several verbs in the past and present tense occur in both. The reader may seek the motivation behind this bizarre typographical interplay or dismiss it as fortuitous; in any case, it is quite visible. And insofar as it is effective, its general effect will undoubtedly be confusion.

We have seen that this formal, or structural, confusion has an important thematic analogue. The text formally confuses direct and indirect discourse in the same way that it confuses reality and illusion, presentation and representation, music and poetry. Our inability to understand the passages in quotations in terms of the usual poetic device of citation greatly emphasizes the alterity of cited discourse in relation to the narrative that constitutes the body of this poetic text. Herein lies the key to the role that the typography plays: it functions as a signal to the reader that within the text there is an only partially successful attempt at representing by definition a "direct" form of language with which the Faune's more indirect poetic narrative is literally confused. By virtue of the typographical interplay, both forms of language are represented, but in an oxymoronic relationship. Within the context of a poem that articulates a constant confusion between that which is merely represented and that which is actually performed, the proximity of citation to recitation, and of direct discourse to speech, is significant.[13] The Faune's inability to master the technique of poetic citation, that is, to represent through his

13. As Antoine Compagnon points out in *La seconde main ou le travail de la citation*, citation implies repetition of the act of speaking as well as the repetition of a statement (1979, 55).

poetry a living form of discourse, is very similar to his incapacity to incorporate music (as the voice of nature) into his verse.[14] The cited passages can thus be understood as indicating the impossibility of textually assimilating another variant of performed language—theatrical discourse—which consists of the *recitation* of a verbal text. The typographical anomalies make the point that while the text can represent the languages of performance (since it is related to these as an identity-in-difference), it cannot represent them fully without losing its own integrity. Therefore, the language of the text presents itself as ambiguously self-sufficient, yet theatrical, that is, as independent from any performative complement, whose absence it nevertheless makes felt.

The juxtaposition of cited and uncited verse in the *Faune* recalls the isolated *recitation* of the sonnet "La chevelure vol d'une flamme . . ." in the prose poem "La déclaration foraine." The poet has his lady friend stand up on the table so that he may perform his sonnet for a group of spectators at a country fair. As Barbara Johnson points out in "Poetry and Performative Language" (1981), the prose poem begins in silence, but the ubiquitous interjection of words denoting speech, the reference to speech acts, and the performance of the sonnet (which is itself represented as a speech act) together warn the reader that the central question in the text is "to speak or not to speak" (143). The sonnet is motivated by a theatrical context and by the violent physical need on the part of the spectators to have something performed:

> . . . ceci jaillit, forcé, sous le coup de poing brutal à l'estomac, que cause une impatience de gens auxquels coûte que coûte et soudain il faut proclamer quelque chose fût-ce la rêverie. . . . (Mallarmé 1945, 283)

Similarly, it is properly received by the lady whom it honors, owing to the fact of its public performance:

> Comme vous, Madame, ne l'auriez entendu si irréfutablement, malgré sa réduplication sur une rime du trait final, mon boniment d'après un mode primitif du sonnet, je le gage, si chaque terme ne s'en était répercuté jusqu'à vous par de variés tympans, pour

14. In "Toward the Poetics of Juxtaposition: L'Après-midi d'un Faune" (1977, 41–42), Roseline Crowley argues that the confusion between Speech and Writing (apparent in the typographical interplay) is intensified by constant punning and paronomasis. In the discourse framing the italicized portions (which she calls the fable) Crowley demonstrates how the motifs of music and writing are also ambivalently combined.

charmer un esprit ouvert à la compréhension multiple. (Mallarmé
1945, 283)

Like the unadorned woman whose ideal beauty is paradoxically cele-
brated by an allusion to the absence of adorning jewels, the unadorned
recitation of the sonnet "sans supplément de danse ou de chant" (281)
constitutes the most minimal or naked performance. But the very allu-
sion to the absence of any theatrical mode of expression (which ordi-
narily supports the performance of a text), and the very designation of
music and dance as *supplementary* indicates that the poem does indeed
imply a corresponding sense-oriented (visual or musical) performance.
Thus, while the sonnet seems autonomous or self-sufficient (lacking any
theatrical support) it in fact depends on a theatrical context for its very
existence and allusively evokes the concrete languages of theater as its
absent supplement.

This ambiguous relationship between the text and its performance is
similar to the one we have examined in the *Faune*. The poem refers to a
performative complement as a presence-in-absence by various structural
and thematic references to performed modes of expression that are inex-
tricably related to but cannot be reconciled with the language of the text.
Thus, the duality of performance and text functions as an extension of
the central duality of the hero. The Faune's inability either to fuse or
distinguish clearly between music and poetry and between dramatic (di-
rect) and narrative (indirect) discourse—in short, his entanglement in
the "ambiguïté entre l'écrit et le joué"—is a clear manifestation of his
entrapment in the duality so strikingly symbolized by the hybridity of his
person. The ambiguity of genre merely expands on the mind/body dichot-
omy intrinsic to the Faune, as well as constituting a formal expression of
his failure to possess simultaneously the several thematic oppositions:
nature and the dream world; the sexual fantasy and the sexual act; Iane
and Ianthé. The text thus globally reveals the hybrid nature of its creator
and conveys even within its structure the oxymoron that is its matrix:
the double Faune and his "sens fabuleux."

—■—

CHAPTER NINE

Igitur

Igitur was written during the late 1860s, at approximately the same time as the initial versions of *Hérodiade* and *L'après-midi d'un faune*. It resembles these works both thematically, in its exploration of various oppositions linked to the mind/body duality of the Self, and formally, in its incorporation of a theatrical code that breaks up the logical coherence and structural unity of the text. The first mention of the text occurs in an 1869 letter to Henri Cazalis in which Mallarmé refers to the *conte* as a kind of therapy, a cure for his feeling of "impuissance": "C'est un conte, par lequel je veux terrasser le vieux monstre de l'impuissance, son sujet, du reste, afin de me cloîtrer dans mon grand labeur déjà réétudié. S'il est fait, je suis guéri. *Similia similibus*" (Mallarmé 1959, 313).[1]

It is ironic that Mallarmé felt the need to overcome infecundity during this period of his life (the late 1860s), for as C. P. Barbier and C. G. Millan's recent edition of his poems (Mallarmé 1983) strikingly demonstrates, nearly every poem he wrote is a reworking of a text from this period. Thus, his "impotence" probably pertains less to his literary productivity than to a feeling of personal and spiritual incompleteness. He recounted the metaphysical and psychological crisis of this period in a series of well-known letters. Principally, he lost faith in any transcendent Ideal, replacing his belief in God and cosmic order with a belief in Nothingness and chance determinism, "le hasard." His loss of faith in a supreme being was accompanied by a loss of the sense of his personal identity ("je suis maintenant impersonnel et non plus Stéphane que tu as

---

1. The great labor to which Mallarmé refers probably pertains to his first conception of the "Grand Œuvre," the book on "Nothingness and Beauty" of which *Hérodiade* was to make up one part. It is possible that *Igitur* would also have figured therein as one of four prose poems, but we have no manuscript or other record indicating the exact constitution of this work.

connu") and a subsequent acceptance of the void as constituting the center or essence of self.[2]

The enterprise undertaken in *Igitur* is unquestionably the replacement of a long-standing metaphysical concept of being with its opposite. Though the story ends in his suicide, Igitur, the young, Hamlet-type hero explores not so much the question of whether to be or not to be as the question of what being and non-being are. As with the previous texts it will be useful to begin our analysis of *Igitur* by briefly examining the "plot."

In his quest for a metaphysical absolute, Igitur undertakes an exhaustive search of his inner self, which he paradoxically projects outward into the claustral universe of his castle in an attempt to fix it in time and space. This projection of the inner self into the material world surrounding it is itself inevitable and symptomatic of Igitur's duality, of the fact that his mind or consciousness is trapped in his body. At the end of the tale Igitur's corpse is associated with his now pure or uninhabited castle, "reste le château de la pureté" (443).[3] Yet the scene (or *décor*) in *Igitur*—the chamber, the staircase, and the tombs—is also clearly symbolic of the structure of Igitur's mind. The chamber with its ubiquitous reflections and echoes renders concrete the mirroring activity of consciousness. The spiral staircase renders tangible the apparent deepening and refinement of ideas (the remnants of consciousness that reflexively turn back on themselves yet seem to lead somewhere) as we proceed toward the unconscious, which lies underneath. And the tombs and ashes of the ancestors below the staircase symbolize a conceptual *Néant,* which the mind would (if it could) encounter at its core. Thus, what Igitur finds at the end of his quest is the necessity of his own death. After using his consciousness in a valiant but failed attempt to conceptualize Nothingness (failed because, as we shall see, consciousness inevitably prolongs itself), Igitur swallows the last drop of his "conscience de soi" (438), "la goutte de néant qui manque à la

2. This 1867 letter to Henri Cazalis perhaps best reveals Mallarmé's discovery of Nothingness and loss of his sense of self: "Je viens de passer une année effrayante: ma Pensée s'est pensée, et est arrivée à une conception pure. Tout ce que, par contrecoup, mon être a souffert, pendant cette longue agonie est inénarrable, mais, heureusement, je suis parfaitement mort, et la région la plus impure où mon Esprit puisse s'aventurer est l'Eternité, mon Esprit, ce solitaire habituel de sa propre Pureté, que n'obscurcit plus même le reflet du Temps. J'avoue du reste, mais à toi seul, que j'ai encore besoin, tant ont été grandes les avanies de mon triomphe, de me regarder dans cette glace pour penser et que si elle n'était devant la table où je t'écris cette lettre, je redeviendrais le Néant. C'est t'apprendre que je suis maintenant impersonnel et non plus Stéphane que tu as connu,—mais une aptitude qu'a l'Univers spirituel à se voir et à se développer, à travers ce qui fut moi" (Mallarmé 1959, 240).

3. All references to *Igitur* are to the *Œuvres complètes* edition (Mallarmé 1945, 421–51).

mer" (443). That drop is "la substance du Néant" (439) contained in a glass phial, which like the inkwell in "L'Action restreinte" symbolizes consciousness: "L'encrier, cristal comme une conscience, avec sa goutte, au fond, de ténèbres relative à ce que quelque chose soit" (370). In short, Igitur must consume the cup of consciousness to its last dregs in order to attain that zero degree of consciousness where Nothingness is. In this way he puts an end to his own duality and wholly reenters the world of pure material presence, which is also a world of metaphysical nothingness—that is, one where the opposition between presence and absence does not exist.

While Igitur ends in the evocation of this pure, material presence—"Le Néant parti, reste le château de la pureté"—it is the Idea, or a principle of Being founded on non-Being (or of presence founded on absence), that is explored within the tale. Being is defined as having the structure of consciousness itself. It is designated as a composite of dualities linked by a central nothingness, or void. This perception of Being explains the extraordinary choice of Igitur as the name of the hero and title of the work; for the tale recounts through a personification, the death, or annihilation, of the causal conjunction—*therefore*—that holds Being together or, rather, that allows Being to be (as, for instance in Descartes, "I think, therefore I am"). By virtue of the fact that this causal conjunction functions as a pivot fixing the various conceptual and material nonentities into Being, the word *Igitur* can be understood as the linguistic equivalent of the "substance of Nothingness" contained in the glass phial symbolizing the human mind.

Although the choice of the adverb *igitur* is not a direct reference to the famous Cartesian proof "Cogito ergo sum," hostile references to the logic of mathematicians within the tale ("vous, mathématiciens expirâtes—moi projeté absolu") cannot help but alert the reader to the fact that a negation of this classical ontological argument is at work in the text.[4] Furthermore, when this conjunction is read within its context—*Igitur ou la Folie d'Elbehnon*, the full title of the work—it is obvious that the text will undertake the subversion of reason itself and its lofty position in the Judeo-Christian perception of the universe. As many of *Igitur's* critics have pointed out, the implied unity and order of God's creation stated in Genesis, "Igitur perfecti sunt cœli et terra et omnis ornata eorum," are inverted in the text (negated by the discovery of "l'infini" and "le Hasard"). This inversion is clear from the outset, since the title designates

---

4. In "*Igitur* ou l'argument ontologique retourné" René Nelli analyzes this overturning of the Cartesian formula (1948, 147–53).

"madness" as the true mode of thinking of God (or his representatives, the sons of the angels), alluded to in the name "Elbehnon."[5]

As Kristeva points out in *La révolution du langage poétique* (1974), the death of logic symbolized by the self-consumption, or expenditure, of Igitur ("la dépense d'une conclusion logique") also implies a rupture in the traditional function of literary language, which was to represent something exterior to the text. By virtue of its circularity, *Igitur* (like *Hérodiade* and *L'après-midi d'un faune*) binds the reader to the practice of the text.[6] Here language shifts from an instrument of creation (its demiurgic function) to an instrument of self-negation and death, a reversal in the traditional system of metaphysics. In the Bible the Word is clearly set at the beginning of time—it creates. In *Igitur* we progress toward the death of "la parole" and its inevitable physical complement, gesture: "fin de parole et geste unis." This extinction occurs through Igitur's suicide, his blowing out of the "bougie de l'être" (434).[7]

In *Igitur* the dual self is projected as the model of the absolute. Its decomposition into mind and body and into their respective modes of expression—speech and gesture, or word and deed—is emphasized in numerous instances within the text. The importance of this dichotomy is clearly expressed by its repeated articulation within the plot summary, which the Pléiade editors have subtitled the "[Argument]":

> A peu près ce qui suit:
> Minuit sonne—le Minuit où doivent être jetés les dés. Igitur

5. André Rolland de Renéville was the first to argue that *Igitur* was inspired by the above-cited line from Genesis (2:1): "Thus the heavens and the earth were finished, and all the host of them." He was also the first to suggest that "Elbehnon" refers to the angels, the sons or messengers of "Elohim," a Hebrew name for God (1938, 99).

6. Kristeva presents *Igitur* as an important step toward a new type of literary language (more clearly exemplified in *Un coup de dés*) in which the activity of the "chora sémiotique" (defined as the subject's sensory-motor organization and site of creation) resurges at the surface of the text, pulverizing its logic—its syntax—and thereby revealing the dialectic between the symbolic aspect of language and the more basic psychic drives that both engender and transgress it (1974, 197–98).

7. The choice of a candle as the symbol of Igitur's life recalls the famous passage from *Macbeth* in which life is represented as a candle and player and, also, as a tale told by a madman "signifying nothing" (Shakespeare 1967, 132). Given the mind/body duality context, the candle might also recall Descartes's contemplation of "un morceau de cire" in his "Méditation seconde" (De la nature de l'esprit humain; et qu'il est plus aisé à connaître que le corps) (1979, 91). For Mallarmé (unlike Descartes), the essence of a "corps" cannot be wholly grasped by virtue of an introspection of the mind that perceives it. (*Igitur*, in fact, demonstrates that such an introspection is infinitely circular and therefore fruitless.) Rather, the being of a *corps* can be perceived only through the combination of a sensorial process ("une vision," "un attouchement") and its imaginative reflection.

descend les escaliers, de l'esprit humain, va au fond des choses: en "absolu" qu'il est. Tombeaux—cendres (pas sentiment, ni esprit) neutralité. Il récite la prédiction et fait le geste. Indifférence. Sifflements dans l'escalier. "Vous avez tort" nulle émotion. L'infini sort du hasard, que vous avez nié. Vous, mathématiciens expirâtes—moi projeté absolu. Devais finir en Infini. Simplement parole et geste. Quant à ce que je vous dis, pour expliquer ma vie. Rien ne restera de vous—L'infini enfin échappe à la famille, qui en a souffert,—vieil espace—pas de hasard. Elle a eu raison de le nier, —sa vie—pour qu'il ait été l'absolu. Ceci devait avoir lieu dans les combinaisons de l'Infini vis-à-vis de l'Absolu. Nécessaire—extrait l'Idée. Folie utile. Un des actes de l'univers vient d'être commis là. Plus rien, restait le souffle, fin de parole et geste unis—souffle la bougie de l'être, par quoi tout a été. Preuve.

(Creuser tout cela)

(434)

In this passage we find three instances in which speech and gesture are explicitly juxtaposed. In the first instance Igitur is playing out the game (or performing the verbal and gestural rite) that will result in his discovery of the absolute: "Il récite la prédiction et fait le geste." The prediction is "la parole humaine en le grimoire . . . annonçant cette négation du hasard" (442). That is, the statement passed down to Igitur from his ancestors affirming that one member of their race would capture the absolute and thereby conquer chance (a principle that the family, contrary to Igitur, had always denied). The gesture is the dice throw, the act by which Igitur will attempt to turn chance against itself or, as stated in the paragraph, extract a principle out of a necessity: "Nécessaire—extrait l'Idée." Should he succeed in his attempt to throw the perfect number 12 (a number that represents the union of temporal contraries, Midnight), he would paradoxically disprove the principle of chance, which by definition implies randomness, the opposite of causality: "*si je compte, comédien, jouer le tour—les 12—pas de hasard dans aucun sens*" (442). In fact this correspondence between the number of the hour and that of the dice is achieved (as is that between the configuration of the dice and that of the constellation in *Un coup de dés*): "Il jette les dés, le coup s'accomplit, douze, le temps (Minuit)—qui créa se retrouve la matière, les blocs, les dés" (451). Particularly emphasized, in both the plot summary and throughout the text, is the fact that Igitur goes through two parallel yet different processes, speaking and acting, in order to capture the absolute and that in so doing he accepts chance as the determining factor of both his speech and his acts.

The one-word sentence "Indifférence" that follows the reference to the prediction and the gesture is significant, for Igitur's mental and physical indifference toward what he is saying and doing ("pas sentiment, ni esprit") results from the fundamental lack of a *difference in value* between speaking and acting. The difference between these modes of expression is, like the division of the self (and all other dualities), merely the consequence of chance: "le hasard, cet antique ennemi qui me divisa en ténèbres et en temps créés" (438). The reader is thus alerted early on that both speech and gesture have been divested of any unique or "original" power to express a unified presence. The two modes of expression can neither say anything nor do anything beyond revealing their respective existences. There is no reference to a fundamental unity or causal link between the two aspects constituting the self; they merely coexist. Thus, in contrast to his predecessors (such as Baudelaire and Hugo), Mallarmé proposes a model of duality that is ultimately irresolvable.[8] It remains purely reflexive.

This infinite, irreducible duality of the self is articulated more clearly still in the second reference to speech and gesture in which Igitur designates the self as the model of the absolute: "Vous, mathématiciens expirâtes—moi projeté absolu. Devais finir en Infini. Simplement parole et geste." The adverb "simplement" underscores the irresolvable quality of the duality; there is no transcendent unified Being veiled behind the

---

8. In the works of Hugo and Baudelaire, duality is often reconciled in the birth of some form of transcendent being. Two examples of this are Baudelaire's "L'aube spirituelle" (1982):

> Quand chez les débauchés l'aube blanche et vermeille
> Entre en société de l'Idéal rongeur,
> Par l'opération d'un mystère vengeur
> Dans la brute assoupie un Ange se réveille.
>
> (229)

and Hugo's "Mors" (1967):

> Les peuples éperdus semblaient sous la faulx sombre
> Un troupeau frissonnant qui dans l'ombre s'enfuit:
> Tout était sous ses pieds deuil, épouvante et nuit.
> Derrière elle, le front baigné de douces flammes,
> Un ange souriant portait la gerbe d'âmes.
>
> (663)

For these poets, death does not generally constitute the end of the metaphysical quest, as it does in *Igitur* (cf. Baudelaire's "Voyage" and Hugo's "Ibo"), and all modalities of expression are considered to participate in a higher form of language, "la parole divine": "Il y a dans le mot, dans le *verbe,* quelque chose de sacré qui nous défend d'en faire un jeu de hasard" (Baudelaire in his "Préface à l'œuvre de Poe"); "Car le mot, c'est le Verbe, et le Verbe, c'est Dieu" (Hugo 1969, 29).

two aspects of the self. At the moment when the self's duality is brought to a close, in death, the subject from which it originates no longer exists. This explains the removal of the *je* in "Devais finir en Infini."

In the third reference to speech and gesture the point of conjunction between these two modes of expression is presented as "le souffle," which is neither the breath of God nor "le souffle poétique" but that of life itself. It is Igitur's breath that (although brought into existence by chance) will put an end to the battle between Igitur (logic) and *le hasard* because it blows itself out rather than leaving its extinction up to chance: "Plus rien, restait le souffle, fin de parole et de geste unis—souffle la bougie de l'être, par quoi tout a été." The conquest over *le hasard*, which this suicide represents, is underscored by the play on *souffle* as both subject and object of the annihilation. Like John the Baptist in *Hérodiade*, Igitur finds the long-desired end to his mind/body duality in death.

It is the fundamental, issueless, dichotomy of the self that determines both the inevitable concomitance of speech and gesture and the intervention of theatrical signs within the text. In a brief introductory passage entitled "Ancienne étude," there is a suggestive reference to Igitur's transposition of the absolute from the prediction inscribed in the language of the magic book ("le grimoire") into a natural, eternal, and exterior form, a moon that he will finally reveal as a mystery, perhaps theatrically: "Puis—comme il aura parlé selon l'absolu—qui nie l'immortalité, l'absolu existera en dehors—lune, au dessus du temps: et il soulèvera les rideaux, en face" (431).

There are signs of the theater within the plot summary: the inclusion of the sound effect "Sifflements dans l'escalier" and the inclusion of words apparently recited by Igitur to his ancestors, "Il récite la prédiction . . . 'Vous avez tort.' " But because these references to theater are not structurally isolated from a mass of what look like carelessly composed notes, they do not strike the reader as forcefully as do those within the actual text of the *conte* which seems otherwise finished and artfully composed. The references to theater are, for the most part, *isolated* from the body of the *conte*. Their differential structure implies that the language of the text is shifting into a different, nonassimilable mode. It appears that in its references to the theater (which often occur within the white space or margins) the text is adding a performative supplement to itself. The following analysis demonstrates that this dividing of the text into a performative mode and a nonperformative mode is overdetermined by the self's fundamental decomposition into "parole et geste."

The first reference to theater occurs in the epigraph: "Ce Conte s'adresse à l'Intelligence du lecteur qui met les choses en scène, elle-même" (433).

At first reading the epigraph appears to state nothing but a truism. It is self-evident that the *conte* as a literary genre activates the imagination. Its representations remain purely within the mind. The genre is not inherently theatrical, it is not (other than intellectually) *mis en scène.* There is irony apparent, however, not only in the statement of what goes without saying but also in the demonstrative adjective *ce,* which implies that what is stated in the epigraph applies particularly to this *conte* and not to the genre as a whole. And the irony increases as the reader comes to realize that, contrary to the conventions of the genre, this *conte* carries the mark of the theatrical text; it incorporates signs of the unnecessary *mise en scène.*

As in *Hérodiade* the division of *Igitur* into several sections that reflect various stages in the evolution of the "drama" evokes the conventional structuring of the theatrical text. Four of these sections are listed above the plot summary:

1. *Le Minuit*
2. *L'escalier*
3. *Le coup de dés*
4. *Le sommeil sur les cendres, après la bougie soufflée*

Like dramatic scenes, all of these subtitles seem to anchor the narration in isolated moments in terms of an action, time, or place. Within the text another section is added that does not fit this pattern because of its broader scope; at the center of the tale we find (the section) "VIE D'IGITUR," which like the central section in *Hérodiade,* functions as a flashback subverting the systematic progression of the narrative.

This semitheatrical structure might not, in itself, warn the reader that the text (contrary to the epigraph) is preparing a kind of theatrical staging. But we cannot help forming this impression as we become aware of marginal and parenthetical notes that, unlike the text of an ordinary *conte,* seem to support the narration with elements that are external to it. As in *Hérodiade* and the *Faune* some of these notes appear theatrical in genre, and others do not. Thus, the "ambiguïté entre l'écrit et le joué" (319) permeates every aspect of the text, even the marginal and parenthetical space to which the *mise en scène* is conventionally assigned.

In section I, "LE MINUIT" there are no references to theater isolated from the text. This is because the Midnight scene (more than any other) focuses on the *dream* of a pure presence, which is the corollary in consciousness of a conceptual absence, or "le Néant." In the narrative description of "le rêve pur d'un Minuit, en soi disparu" (435), we are almost unaware of any manifestation of a living presence that (like the heartbeat and sound effect in section II) mars the purity of Midnight's dream, endlessly prolonging itself in shadows and echoes within the chamber. There are, however, two moments in which Midnight *speaks*. It is significant that the representation of shadows and echoes within the chamber is transposed into a representation of speech, for the change in register (from indirect to direct discourse) emphasizes the resurgence of "la parole" in a context where it is inappropriate, the depiction of a scene supposedly devoid of any plausible speaking subject. Indeed, by virtue of the fact that it speaks, a personification of Midnight is achieved that functions to alert the reader that Midnight is merely an avatar of Igitur himself. Midnight is represented as a person dreaming of its pure self. The image of its presence reverberates in the chamber: "Et du Minuit demeure la présence en la vision d'une chambre du temps où le mystérieux ameublement arrête un vague frémissement de pensée" (435). And like Igitur who simply inhabits the Midnight-chamber, "l'hôte, dénué de toute signification que de présence" (435), Midnight is ever conscious of itself, its "*moi* pur longtemps rêvé" (435). It possesses the attributes of a subject ("parole" and "geste"), hence the impossibility of maintaining the image of its presence as a unity or pure dream. In one case the words uttered by Midnight are described as marring its purity, or "stérilité: "subsiste encore le silence d'une antique parole proférée par lui, en lequel, revenu, ce Minuit évoque son ombre finie et nulle par ses mots: J'étais l'heure qui doit me rendre pur" (435). As the words of Midnight explain, Midnight can never, in fact, be pure, for like Igitur, it presupposes a division. As a conjunction between the past and the future, Midnight exists only insofar as it unites two opposites, yesterday and tomorrow. The silence of the book symbolizing the purity of Midnight's dream is also inevitably divided, violated by both the memory and the anticipation of the utterance of the written words by Midnight (or Igitur).

One paragraph succinctly expresses this difficulty in achieving a state of pure presence, this difficulty in being one that results from the insurmountable duality of the cognitive subject:

> Depuis longtemps morte, une antique idée se mire telle à la clarté de la chimère en laquelle a agonisé son rêve, et se reconnaît à l'immémorial geste vacant avec lequel elle s'invite, pour terminer l'antagonisme de ce songe polaire, à se rendre, avec et la clarté chimérique et le texte refermé, au Chaos de l'ombre avorté et de la parole qui absolut Minuit. (436)

The impenetrable quality of this description of the idea (a variant of Midnight, and Igitur) results from its circularity, the endless "dédoublement" of its thought. The acrobatic turning-on-itself of the idea symbolizes the mirroring process of consciousness. The idea projects itself as both a dead and living presence, one that grasps itself by means both of an open, candle-lit text and an age-old yet meaningless gesture, the "immémorial geste vacant." The vacant gesture is here the extinction of the candle of life, which implies both the negation of its presence (symbolized as the light that illuminates the text) and its absence (the shadow of its presence) contained in the words of the closed text. The gesture terminates "l'antagonisme de ce songe polaire" by surrendering the image of the presence of light "la clarté chimérique," not merely to its shadow (which would testify to its presence-in-absence) but to the Chaos of "l'ombre avorté." It also ends this antagonism by surrendering the text (which had also manifested the presence-in-absence of speech), to a Chaos of "la parole" in which, no longer signifying anything, words could absolve Midnight (or the idea, or Igitur) of its duality, its impurities or faults.

In the last instance in which Midnight speaks, we find, however, that the acquisition of its purity (like that of its "Eternity") is destined to remain in the domain of a possible future, for it recreates itself by virtue of the fact that it is impure—it always splits itself into two: "l'heure se formule en cet écho . . . 'Adieu, nuit, que je fus, ton propre sépulcre, mais qui, l'ombre survivante, se métamorphosera en Eternité' " (436).

These instances of cited discourse within the narrative are unique to the Midnight section. Although they may not initially strike the reader as bizarre (since we are accustomed to the incorporation of direct discourse within narrative and also to the personification of time), the emphasis on the fact that Midnight speaks, and on a polarity between "la parole" and "le texte," is rather strange. We are thus subtly prepared for the more flagrant instances of an unconventional differentiation between types of language employed further on in the *conte:* the presence of signs evoking a theatrical genre, whose inappropriateness to the narrative is emphasized by their structural isolation from the body of the text. As earlier mentioned, these isolated fragments of discourse occupy the space of the *mise en scène;* some have a conventionally theatrical value, and others do not. We recognize that the text is communicating to us in two different modes, but we have difficulty in distinguishing one from the other. As in the texts previously examined, this seemingly unjustifiable ambiguity is an important aspect of the message of *Igitur.* By virtue of this ambiguity the text suggests that there is nothing meaningful behind such oppositions as the textual and the theatrical (these contraries, like the mind and the body, thinking and acting, and illusion and reality are virtually identical) and yet that there is an inevitable differentiation nonetheless.

The first example of such a theatrical use of language occurs in an isolated parenthetical note following the subheading of section II. The subheading itself appears more like a stage direction than a proper chapter title, indicating the movement and location of Midnight/Igitur:

IL QUITTE LA CHAMBRE
ET SE PERD DANS LES ESCALIERS
(au lieu de descendre à cheval sur la rampe)
(436)

We have difficulty reconciling the absurdity of the parenthetical note with the grave, metaphysical tone of the tale; it is very hard to conceive of Midnight behaving like a child at play. Moreover, although the note looks like a stage direction, it could not possibly function as such. In this respect it is similar to several of the stage directions in *Hérodiade* and in the early versions of the *Faune*. This *didascalie*, in fact, functions like several of the stage directions in Ionesco's "anti-pièce," *La cantatrice chauve*, in which alternative instructions such as "*Mme Smith, tombe à ses genoux, en sanglotant ou ne le fait pas*" underline the difficulty of translating options (easily expressed in literary language) into the concrete language of an actual *mise en scène*.[9] To borrow Mallarmé's formula (in "Le genre ou des Modernes"), this theatrical index is actually a sign of literariness, for it is relevant only to "*la scène à ne pas faire*" (319). An irony of genre is produced by the simultaneous association and disassociation of literary and theatrical modes.

The two other notes within this section are more conventionally theatrical in genre. As Igitur examines "cette inquiétante et belle symétrie de la construction de mon rêve" (that is, its symmetrical images in the stairwell), he is bothered by the beating of his own heart, "le cœur de cette race (que j'entends battre ici) seul reste d'ambiguïté." His heartbeat reminds him that he has not really reached a state of nirvana, or pure awareness. His vision of the *Néant* (his pure "conscience de soi") is marred by an insurmountable awareness of his own mind/body duality. His body is the

---

9. In *La cantatrice chauve* several stage directions are quite obviously impossible to translate into a *mise en scène:* of the alternative type, such as that cited above, e.g., "*Il embrasse ou n'embrasse pas Mme Smith*" (59; of a negative type, "*La pendule ne sonne aucune fois*" (16); and of an indifferent type, "*Le pendule sonne autant qu'elle veut*" (32). These ironic stage directions (ironic in that they cannot be used as such) serve as reminders that we are not reading an ordinary play but, rather, an "*anti-pièce*" (Ionesco 1954).

"travestissement" of his "Ombre incréée et antérieure." The heartbeat as a manifestation of his bodily presence, tangible in time and space and brought into existence by chance—"le hasard, cet antique ennemi qui me divisa en ténèbres et en temps créés" (438)—interferes with his conceptualization of absence. Igitur's narration of this problem resulting from his duality is interrupted by a note that cannot be interpreted otherwise than as a stage direction, a parenthetical "(chuchotement)."

It is not surprising that the noise of which the narrator speaks should be transposed into a theatrical reference, a sound effect, which breaks up the unity of the text. The "(chuchotement)" echoes various bothersome noises to which Igitur refers in the text as manifestations of his duality: a "scandement" (the beating of his heart) and a "frôlement" (the brushing of a bird's wings as, conscious of its own proximity to annihilation, it fearfully takes flight): "Ce scandement n'était-il pas le bruit du progrès de mon personnage qui maintenant le continue dans la spirale, et ce frôlement, le frôlement incertain de sa dualité" (438–39). What Igitur had thought at first to be a sound emitted by a bird—a conventional symbol for the spirit—was in fact the noise emanating from his own body, his heart beating in fear of his progress toward annihilation. This is a noise Igitur must shut out, one from which he must detach his spirit, in order to purely conceptualize his absence:

> Enfin ce n'est pas le ventre velu d'un hôte inférieur de moi, dont la lueur a heurté le doute, et qui s'est sauvé avec un volètement, mais le buste de velours d'une race supérieure que la lumière froisse, et qui respire dans un air étouffant, d'un personnage dont la pensée n'a pas conscience de lui-même, de ma dernière figure, séparée de son personnage par une fraise arachnéenne et qui ne se connaît pas: aussi, maintenant que sa dualité est à jamais séparée, et que je n'ouïs même plus à travers lui le bruit de son progrès, je vais m'oublier à travers lui, et me dissoudre en moi. (439)

Thus, the structural separation of the noise, the "(chuchotement)," from the body of the text presages the desired and imagined but in fact impossible separation of Igitur's mind from his body. It also reflects the impossibility of clearly disengaging the self's two modes of expression, "parole et geste," since the gesture, the whisper, although it may not say anything, implies a minimal form of speech.[10]

---

10. The bothersome "scandement" that the chuchotement echoes creates a similar ambiguity, since although it refers to a not-necessarily signifying noise (Igitur's heartbeat), it also suggests verse. Cohn also notes that "the chuchotement is like the earlier sifflements [in the

At the end of the section we find another stage direction in the margin informing us that all the progress made—the descent in the staircase toward the tomb and the implied separation of the mind from the body—was only on the level of conceptualization. In fact, Igitur has never left his chamber; the meanderings of his mind have revealed to him that he cannot attain the vision of the "Néant" as long as he remains conscious (present-to-himself) within the chamber. Since the perception of his person mars the purity of his consciousness (which the chamber symbolizes), he recognizes that he must now (bodily) leave the room:

> L'heure a sonné pour moi de partir, la pureté de la   *Il quitte la*
> glace s'établira, sans ce personnage, vision de moi—   *chambre.*
> mais il emportera la lumière!—la nuit!
> Sur les meubles vacants, le Rêve a agonisé en cette fiole
> de verre, pureté, qui renferme la substance du Néant.
>
> (439)

It is the marginal stage direction that emphasizes for the reader that up until this point no real progress has been made; all that has occurred happened only on the level of conceptualization. And the conceptualization of purity has failed; Igitur still hears the beating of his heart—"Son heurt redevient chancelant comme avant d'avoir la perception de soi" (439) and the mirroring walls like the glass phial still contain the presence of a body ("la substance du Néant"). It is only when Igitur leaves (and it is implied that he will take the candle of life with him—"il emportera la lumière!—la nuit!") that all oppositions formerly contained within the chamber will die or be reconciled into pure nothingness.

Because of its unexpectedness the stage direction serves as an emphatic marker. By abruptly recalling our attention to the *scène* and breaking up the circularity of the text, it enables us to grasp an important point—the action has not yet advanced. As long as Igitur is only *thinking* about his journey toward Nothingness, no progress in reaching it can be made.[11] As the tale proceeds, the isolated, italicized notes

---

"Argument"], a stirring of the ancestral ghostly public and hence of his sentimental fear" (1981, 113). But he does not comment on this note's isolation from the body of the narrative text—the formal aspect that, in fact, creates this theatrical effect.

11. Here is an example of a theatrical reference so troubling in its disruption of the text's logical and sequential coherence that critics have implied that it somehow got there by mistake. R. G. Cohn (1981) writes, for example, "In the next paragraph, the reference to 'Il quitte la chambre' (in the margin) and the mirror and other furniture all indicate that this paragraph belongs to an earlier episode, in the Midnight room; I do not know how it got to be in this spot" (118).

increase, and they become increasingly ambiguous. They take on an exegetical function as well as their theatrical one. As we come closer to the moment of the gesture or act, the notes begin to *explain* what is happening in the text. They interrupt the narrative not only to help us reconstitute its theatrical staging but also to comment on the narration, to explicate its literary representations. This double role further undermines our ability to distinguish the language and space of theater from the language and space of the *conte*.

In section III, "VIE D'IGITUR," Igitur speaks to a public before whom the action will take place and to whom this *conte* is implicitly addressed. In a note directly following the title, the reader/spectator is prepared for a kind of monologue in which Igitur sums up his life:

> *Écoutez, ma race, avant de souffler ma bougie—le compte que j'ai à vous rendre de ma vie—Ici: névrose, ennui (ou Absolu!)*
> (439)

The monologue is very short. It is followed by a third-person narrative recapitulating all that was said in the preceding sections. It narrates Igitur's presentiment of Nothingness, his ennui, which he wants to (but cannot) pursue to its core. It recounts his attempt to isolate himself in time and space, to detach himself from his self-consciousness (from his image in the mirror) and thereby create an "absence d'atmosphère," the appropriate context for the undertaking of his suicidal act. In a marginal note at the beginning of the monologue, Mallarmé sums up the quality of Igitur's life as though it could be evoked in a tangible scene. The *didascalie* designating this scene is ironic because it is itself so intangible. We are invited to visualize time—to see hours that are empty and negative. Yet the marginal note retains a theatrical value; it functions like the earlier *chuchotement* in that it looks like a stage direction and intrudes within a discourse in which Igitur *describes* how he always tried to render time material—to absorb it and thereby give it a greater degree of tangibility, or presence:

> J'ai toujours vécu mon âme fixée sur l'horloge. Certes, j'ai tout fait pour que le temps qu'elle sonna *restât* présent dans la chambre, et devînt pour moi la pâture et la vie
>
> *Heures vides, purement négatives.*
>
> (439)

The fourth section, "LE COUP DE DÉS," also begins with a stage direction, an indication as to the *décor:* "*(Au tombeau).*" Although this note is conventionally theatrical in genre, it is followed by another isolated and italicized note, an explicative passage with no bearing on the *mise en scène.* The note comments on the significance and nature of the Act that is finally about to take place. Its philosophical tone disorients us; owing to its isolation from the body of the text one expects to find a development of the reference to the *décor* rather than an exegetical gloss:[12]

IV

LE COUP DE DÉS

(Au tombeau)

(SCHÈME)

> *Bref dans un acte où le hasard est en jeu, c'est toujours le hasard qui accomplit sa propre Idée en s'affirmant ou se niant. Devant son existence la négation et l'affirmation viennent échouer. Il contient l'Absurde—l'implique, mais à l'état latent et l'empêche d'exister: ce qui permet à l'Infini d'être.*
>
> *Le Cornet est la Corne de licorne—d'unicorne.* (441)

The note explains how the dice throw cannot get the better of chance but can only serve to prove its principle. The chance Act, which pits itself against the chance Idea, inevitably establishes the principle of chance, because the dice are themselves but a metonym of chance ("le hasard," whose etymology is the Arabic word *al-zahr,* "jeu de dés"). This is also the final message of *Un coup de dés:* "Toute Pensée émet un Coup de Dés" (477). The act and the idea are virtually identical, yet their differentiation is important, for it allows them to serve each other as reciprocal proofs.

Thus, it is not surprising that the philosophical articulation of the paradox is followed by a more concrete-seeming demonstration in the last part of the note: "*Le Cornet est la Corne de licorne—d'unicorne.*" The text refers to an object to demonstrate how the dice horn (a symbol of Igitur's new metaphysics of Chance) and the unicorn's horn (a symbol

---

12. In "Une lecture d'Igitur," Pierre Rottenberg (1967, 84) comments upon this passage as a means of integration of Hegelian thought into the game of writing, a writing that, contrary to that of Hegel, draws no conclusions.

linked from the Middle Ages with the Christian metaphysical system)[13] are in fact one and the same thing, except that one turns the other upside down. The significance of this reversal in the context of *Igitur* can be summed up as follows: whereas duality and chance are traditionally considered merely to constitute appearances veiling an underlying principle of unity and order, for Igitur, behind the apparent unity and order of the world are the fundamental principles of duality and chance. Thus, in *Igitur,* every possible strategy and device is used to create paradox rather than to solve it.

Several exegetes, such as Cohn (1981, 28), have suggested that the allusion to the unicorn's horn is "a profound symbol of resolution, of

13. In the Middle Ages the unicorn was linked with Christ. Its symbolism is explained in the following extract from *Le bestiaire divin,* a thirteenth-century text:

> Iceste mervellose beste,
> Qui une corne a en la teste
> Senefie nostre Seignor
> Jhesu-Crist, nostre Sauveor.
> C'est l'unicorne esperitel,
> Qui en la Virge prist ostel,
> Qui est tant de dignité;
> En ceste prist humanité. . . .
> Icele beste veirement
> N'a qu'une corne seulement,
> Senefie sollenpnite.

> [This marvelous animal
> Who has one horn on his head
> Symbolizes Jesus-Christ our Savior
> Who found protection in the Virgin's womb,
> She so great in dignity,
> And took on Him human form. . . .
> This animal truly
> Has but one horn only
> It symbolizes truth.]

There is, in fact, a striking similarity between the "unicorn" line in *Igitur* and the following lines from this text:

> Et dex dist meisme uncors,
> Par Davi qui si crie et corne:
> "Si cum li corn de l'unicorne,
> Sera le mien cors essaucie"

> [And God said further,
> By David who cries and sounds the horn:
> "Even as the horn of the unicorn,
> So will my body be exalted."]
>
> (Guillaume, clerc de Normandie, 1970, 236–37)

overcoming the linear duality of Becoming in favor of a triumphant singularity, as in countless texts of our mystical heritage." This interpretation would be difficult to resist if the evocation of the dice horn and the animal horn were to result only in the word *unicorn*. Then we might well state that duality had been overcome. But the fact that the latter symbol represents something that is nothing (nonexistent) and that, by chance, it can be expressed in two words, *licorne* and *unicorne* only reaffirms (as in the preceding philosophical statement) there is no real solution to the paradox. The *cornet* and the *corne,* the *licorne* and the *unicorne* may be one and the same thing, but ultimately (like Idea and Act) they cannot be fused: duality remains unshaken. This fact is asserted within the body of the text, where the Idea (of chance) and the (chance) Act are presented as the necessary and distinct proofs of each other and as reciprocal proofs of the self.

> Mais l'Acte s'accomplit.
> Alors son moi se manifeste par ceci qu'il reprend la Folie: admet l'acte, et, volontairement, reprend l'Idée, en tant qu'Idée: et l'Acte (quelle que soit la puissance qui l'ait guidé) ayant nié le hasard, il en conclut que l'Idée a été nécessaire. (441)

The negation of chance resulting from the Act is not yet, however, the negation of Chance as an absolute or metaphysical principle; it is only the negation of the meaninglessness, or absurdity, of Chance. Indeed, what actually occurs here is a radical inflation of the value of Chance. When Igitur discovers the all-encompassing power of Chance, he feels that he has captured the Infinite and transformed it into an Absolute for himself:

> Tout ce qu'il en est, c'est que sa race a été pure: qu'elle a enlevé à l'Absolu sa pureté, pour l'être, et n'en laisser qu'une Idée elle-même aboutissant à la Nécessité: et que quant à l'Acte, il est parfaitement absurde sauf que mouvement (personnel) rendu à l'Infini: mais que l'Infini est enfin *fixé*. (442)

This elevation of chance to an Absolute paradoxically causes a devaluation of the two elements that served as its instruments: *la parole,* which predicted the negation of chance (in the affirmation that the absolute would be discovered), and *l'acte,* the dice throw that sought to "abolir le hasard," to negate chance by turning it against itself (in the successful attainment of the desired number through a lucky *coup de dés*). Both the conceptualization of the absolute in thought (and its reflection in both written and spoken language) and the deliberate gesture, or act, are rendered useless in light of the discovery of the *infinite* quality of chance. Igitur's search for the absolute through "parole et geste" is *vain* because his word and deed already contain that absolute (Chance) within themselves. Thus, while Igitur goes through the motions of predicting the end of chance and acting against it, he is fully aware of the inanity of his speech and the uselessness of his gesture. The uselessness of the act is clearly expressed within the body of the text: "Le personnage . . . trouve l'acte inutile, car il y a et n'y a pas de hasard—il réduit le hasard à l'*Infini*—qui, dit-il doit exister quelque part" (442). The inanity of the prediction, or speech act, is articulated at the end of a marginal theatrical note juxtaposed to the narrative description of Igitur's vain gesture:

SCÈNE DE THÉÂTRE,
ANCIEN IGITUR
Un coup de dés qui accomplit
une prédiction, d'où a dépendu
la vie d'une race. «*Ne sifflez pas*»
aux vents, aux ombres—si je
compte, comédien, jouer le
tour—les 12—pas de hasard
dans aucun sens.

———

Il profère la prédiction, dont il
se moque au fond. Il y a eu folie.

Igitur secoue simplement les dés—mouvement, avant d'aller rejoindre les cendres, atomes de ses ancêtres: le mouvement qui est en lui est absous. On comprend ce que signifie son ambiguïté.

Il ferme le livre—souffle la bougie,—de son souffle qui contenait le hasard: et, croisant les bras, se couche sur les cendres de ses ancêtres.

Croisant les bras—l'Absolu a disparu, en pureté de sa race (car il le faut bien puisque le bruit cesse).

(442)

When the reader recalls the axiom of the argument, "moi projeté absolu," it is clear that within the narrative the designated disappearance of the Absolute is the consequence of the death of the self, which follows Igitur's last words and gesture, the crossing of his arms over his body (the assumption of the position of death). The cessation of the heartbeat signals the end of his duality. And with the mortal heartbeat go all the pure Ideas that were the goal of Igitur's quest: the Absolute, the Infinite, and even the principle of Chance. The theatrical note in the margin underscores the fact that if Igitur were to play his game of chance out to the end, the Chance principle itself would be denied. It would be denied not only because his successful arrival at the perfect number ("les 12,") would belie the possibility of any randomness to his act, but also because, were he only playing, the confirmation of Chance would not count. It would lose its authenticity in the game.

In the fifth and last section of the tale, the Chance principle is indeed conquered, but in a more definitive way. The victory results from the fact that the game of Chance is over for Igitur is dead. Igitur has swallowed his self-consciousness and, with it, the concept of *le Néant,* that "drop of nothingness that the sea lacks." Thus, Nothingness itself departs, as does *le hasard,* so that a long-sought-after purity is finally found, not in any concept, or Idea, but in the images of various empty shells, the remains of the stars and the family, Igitur's corpse, and the empty phial:

IL SE COUCHE AU TOMBEAU

Sur les cendres des astres, celles indivises de la
famille, était le pauvre personnage, couché,
après avoir bu la goutte de néant qui manque à   *ou les dés—*
la mer. (La fiole vide, folie, tout ce qui reste du   *hasard absorbé.*
château?) Le Néant parti, reste le château de la
pureté.

(443)

The victory over chance is expressed in a final ironical theatrical instruction: the *didascalie* evoking the image of a pair of pure white dice that have finally absolved themselves of any significance; the dice have absorbed their signifiers, the numbers that symbolize chance.

Although the theatrical signs of *Igitur* do not at first appear to have a homogeneous function (some fulfilling the traditional role of *didascalies,* others presenting themselves as a kind of meta-commentary on what is happening in the text), we have seen that they all function to undermine the self-sufficiency of a *conte* whose desired but impossible autonomy is emphasized from the epigraph. The shifting back and forth (in the marginal notes) from a theatrical to an exegetical function serves to underscore for the reader an insurmountable yet ineffectual *differentiation* between the types of language or modes of expression occurring within the text. This formal differentiation reflects the thematic exploration of an identity-in-difference relating both components of the self (the mind and the body) and their respective media of expression, "parole et geste." In maintaining signs of this paradoxical identity-in-difference (which results from Chance) at the level of the structure of the text, Mallarmé achieves a form that corresponds as closely as possible to his message.

Part *pièce de théâtre,* part *conte, Igitur* provides, even through its generic ambiguity, an image of the inevitable duality governing human life. Although, in death, duality may be overcome, in life, duality and Chance prevail over all our dreams for an Ideal of ultimate unity and order—even, paradoxically, within the domain of reason, whose purpose seems to be to overcome Chance. This, of course, is also the message of what Claudel (1965, 510) called "le geste suprême d'Igitur," the poem *Un coup de dés*. In that text we shall see how Mallarmé's perception of the identity-in-difference of contraries (a principle tested in *Igitur*) motivates a unique combination of literature and music that curiously announces simultaneously the birth of concrete poetry and performance art.

CHAPTER TEN

Un coup de dés

In *Hérodiade, L'après-midi d'un faune,* and *Igitur,* as we have seen, Mallarmé uses a performing-arts code to create an ambiguity of genre; the signs of performance framing these texts simultaneously underscore the difference between literature and the performing arts and their sameness. In *Un coup de dés* literature and performing arts are also combined, but the model of combination is quite different. Instead of being confined primarily to the text's perimeters, the performing-arts reference is superimposed on the body of the text. It no longer subtly, intermittently interferes with the unity, or closure, of the text but, rather, completely and dramatically explodes it.

Mallarmé says in his "Préface" (which, like the epigraph in *Igitur,* ironically presents itself as an unnecessary key, or "mode d'emploi") that the text's highly unconventional structuring supplements the verbal signifying process with both a visual and a musical aspect. The two aspects are designated as pertaining to a *performance* of the text. He describes the poem's arrangement as kinetic rather than static, that is, as being the textual representation of a mental "mise en scène." The poem is thus a concrete pattern, or "dessin," of its own signified, but it is one that must be animated, or mobilized, by the work of a reader/spectator. And this pattern, which allows a visual staging, also offers the necessary indications for a "mise en musique," an auditory supplement. That is, the disposition of the poem provides the reader/viewer with a musical score, which he or she is also invited to interpret or perform.

Though the model of this literature/performing-arts combination is different from that in the texts previously discussed, we shall see that its effect is very much the same. The reader is disoriented by the mimesis of the nonliterary, of performance, in the structuring of the poem and (in spite of the direct references to performance in the "Préface") seeks either to ignore it or reason it away with a more or less conventional literary explanation. Although *Un coup de dés* has been (of necessity) universally accepted as a concrete poem, its presentation of itself as a performance piece has been almost equally widely rejected.

Although unfortunate, this rejection is not altogether surprising, coming as it has from generations of critics who have shared (despite their many philosophical differences) a far more narrow and conventional concept of what may compose a literary text than Mallarmé's.[1] Without pretending to equal the many brilliant poetic analyses of *Un coup de dés*, I shall simply try to underscore that this 1897 poem, Mallarmé's last finished "masterwork," makes the same point about the role of performance in literature as do his earlier and unfinished "theatrical" texts. It strives to represent the combination of literature and performative modes in a relationship of simultaneous similarity and difference, autonomy and interdependence, and thereby to aesthetically exteriorize, or express, the insurmountable duality of all Being perceived by the human self.

Before I examine the references to performance in the "Préface" and in the structure of the poem, it will be useful to introduce the work's principal themes, which are, of course, intimately related to its revolutionary form. The title and seminal sentence of the poem, "Un coup de dés jamais n'abolira le hasard," itself constitutes the clearest expression of its central idea. The phrase is an effective verbal demonstration of the identity-in-difference of contraries: the dice throw seems at first to fulfill the function of a unique and deliberate act pitted against an eternal and fortuitous condition in order to modify it. But the dialectic between the act and the condition produces circularity rather than synthesis because these contraries are not simply opposite; they are also identical. As in *Igitur*, in this text the supreme, voluntary act and its corollary are none other than the verbal-nonverbal gesture (the signifier) and its reflection, the idea (or signified) of chance.

This strangely circular dialectic (which Robert Greer Cohn [1951, 1981] has called "tetrapolarity" and has thoroughly described) is concretely and dramatically symbolized in the poem through a succession of pre-negated births that result from the annulled syntheses of identical

1. For very different comprehensive analyses of *Un coup de dés*, see Robert Greer Cohn's *L'Œuvre de Mallarmé: Un coup de dés* (1951); Gardner Davies's *Vers une explication rationelle du "Coup de dés"* (1953); and Claude Roulet's *Elucidation du poème de Stéphane Mallarmé: Un coup de dés jamais n'abolira le hasard.* (1943). Other important, more recent analyses concentrating on various aspects of the poem are Julia Kristeva's discussion of its syntax in *La révolution du langage poétique* (1974); Malcolm Bowie's treatment of its obscurity in *Mallarmé and the Art of Being Difficult* (1978), and Virginia A. La Charité's reading of its use of space in *The Dynamics of Space: Mallarmé's Un coup de dés jamais n'abolira le hasard* (1987).

contraries, or from marriages that, paradoxically, never take place. In this respect *Un coup de dés* is very similar to *Hérodiade* and *L'après-midi d'un faune* and to the last two sonnets of the previously mentioned "Triptyque."

As in yet another sonnet, "A la nue accablante tu . . . ," the main event of *Un coup de dés* is the supreme shipwreck, a "naufrage" of cosmic proportions, which is itself presented as uncertain. The hypothetical quality of this disaster is emphasized by the element of doubt in the boldfaced, subjunctive "SOIT" that introduces its description and later by the similarly accentuated phrase that concludes it: "RIEN N'AURA EU LIEU QUE LE LIEU" (474–75).[2]

All related images and details of the event are similarly phantasmagoric: all that appears disappears by virtue of a verbal strategy of syntactical imprecision and self-dissolution (or disintegration), which the text itself aptly describes as the dispersing of an "acte vide / . . . dans ces parages / du vague / en quoi toute réalité se dissout" (475). How is this perpetual self-dissolution maintained? The semic content of one syntagmatic unit produces others that constitute at once its context and its metaphorical (or more precisely metonymic) substitution.

This process, through which the birth of an all-encompassing, univocal symbol is alternately offered and denied, begins on double-page 3 with the conflict between the sea and sky-wings of the cosmos, "l'Abîme." And it continues until the emergence of the very last image—the constellation, which is presented as though its value might "perhaps" transcend the duration of the game, that is, the signifying process of the text.

The stormy wings of the cosmos (on double-page 3) engender the image of a sinking, oscillating ship that in turn, gives rise (on double-page 4) to the image of its captain, "LE MAÎTRE," also oscillating—hesitating over whether to throw the dice and reveal "l'unique Nombre qui ne peut pas être un autre." This flesh-and-blood hero is then himself transposed (on double-page 5) into a paradoxically anachronistic specter: "l'ultérieur démon immémorial," "son ombre puérile." This image is said to be drawn from that of the drowning Master and ship, born of the conflict between the old man and the sea: "soustraite / aux durs os perdus entre les ais / né / d'un ébat / la mer par l'aïeul tentant ou l'aïeul contre la mer / une chance oiseuse." The birth of this paradoxically younger and older avatar of the Master (further on periphrastically

---

2. All references to *Un coup de dés* are to the *Œuvres complètes* edition. I have also assigned numbers to each double page (there are eleven of these) in order to help the reader follow the progression of the text.

evoked as Hamlet, "prince amer de l'écueil") is also anachronistic; he is born from a not yet accomplished union ("Fiançailles") between the Master and the sea. And their engagement engenders an equally phantasmal gesture, "le fantôme d'un geste," a simulacrum of the dice throw. This gesture against *le hasard* is not a real one, because it is inane, invalid as an *act*. It is neither deliberate (the hand wavers with its secret and then lets go, "chancellera / s'affalera") nor significant; because this dropping of the dice is accidental, it is without consequence, resulting in an absurdity, "folie" (464).

The absurdity of the Master's gesture is developed in a series of related parenthetical images. The highly abstract image of a mystery's "insinuation" into a "tourbillon d'hilarité et d'horreur" (on page 6)—implicitly the mystery, or "vierge indice" of the dice—gives way first to an evocation of Hamlet's vain metaphysical hesitations (page 7) and then to the equally vain yet more tangible contortions of a *sirène* (page 8).[3] Each of these parenthetical images is introduced by a conditional marker "COMME SI . . . COMME SI . . . que SI," revealing that the series functions as a set of hypothetical analogies.

The poem's "secondary motif" (marked typographically by the second-largest size of type) is then clearly resumed (on page 9) with the completion of the conditional "rire que SI" that introduced the series of parenthetical analogies in "SI . . . C'ÉTAIT LE NOMBRE . . . CE SERAIT LE HASARD" (472–73). And this important motif is itself modified by a number of subordinated phrases expressing doubt with regard to the very existence of the "NOMBRE": "EXISTÂT-IL / COMMENÇÂT-IL ET CESSÂT-IL / SE CHIFFRÂT-IL / ILLUMINÂT-IL." (It should be noted that the Number, "l'unique Nombre qui ne peut pas être un autre," is itself symbolically the product of a *divided* number, the added sum of the two faces of the dice.)

---

3. The horror and hilariousness of the whirlpool (symbolic of metaphysical Nothingness) recall the union of similarly contrary sentiments at the theater where the "lustre" (also a symbol of Nothingness) was described as the horrifying echo of the poet's yawn (1945, 293). The parenthetical description of the feather/hero's oscillation is very similar both in its implications and its imagery to Mallarmé's description of Hamlet (*"le seigneur latent qui ne peut devenir"*): "Son solitaire drame! et qui, parfois, tant ce promeneur d'un labyrinthe de trouble et de griefs en prolonge les circuits avec le suspens d'un acte inachevé, semble le spectacle même pourquoi existent la rampe ainsi que l'espace doré quasi moral qu'elle défend, car il n'est point d'autre sujet, sachez bien: l'antagonisme de rêve chez l'homme avec les fatalités à son existence départies par le malheur" (300). In "The Dancer and the Becoming of Language" (1977), Carol Barko draws an interesting parallel between the movement of this siren and that of Loïe Fuller, "[qui] darde sa statuette, stricte debout—morte de l'effort à condenser hors d'une libération presque d'elle des sursautements attardés décoratifs de cieux, de mer, de soirs, de parfum et d'écume" (309).

As the feather, the last vestige, or sign, of a human presence—that is, of the Master's taut, outstretched hand, which had previously turned into the feather of Hamlet's cap—dissolves back into the abyss, the lack of difference between the contrary aspects of the "Abîme," the sea and sky, is again underscored: "Choit / la plume / . . . flétrie / par la neutralité identique du gouffre" (473). And the inanity of the Master's *coup* and of all previously suggested images and events is further emphasized by the boldfaced phrase on the following page, "RIEN N'AURA EU LIEU QUE LE LIEU." Here (on page 10), it is clearly stated that the whole catastrophe described, the human gesture of rebellion against chance, will finally result in nothingness.

Does this gesture's nothingness itself have meaning? Yes, at least insofar as it manages to represent itself, or to find its own reflection/negation on an ideal plane. This game whereby nothingness becomes the absolute (and the playing of which *is,* we recall, alternatively, "la musique et les lettres") is precisely what takes place on the last page of the poem. The dice throw, the fortuitous gesture, is miraculously transformed and projected onto a lofty site: "UNE CONSTELLATION / froide d'oubli et de désuétude / pas tant / qu'elle n'énumère / sur quelque surface vacante et supérieure / le heurt successif / sidéralement / d'un compte total en formation / veillant / doutant / roulant / brillant et méditant / avant de s'arrêter / à quelque point dernier qui le sacre" (477). Here, the correspondence implied between the movement and configuration of the stars (the hesitating movements of "un compte total en formation" before arriving at a "final consecrating point") and the staggering trajectory of the dice before arriving at the "unique Nombre" ("chancellera/s'affalera" [464]) strongly suggests that contrary to the poem's title, the once merely arbitrary gesture will at last acquire an elevated, enduring, and profound significance, one that transcends the game of signifiers in the text.

Yet, the seemingly unique, transcendent value of even this new signified—of the correspondence between the Idea and chance, the Number of the constellation and that of the dice—is undermined by the poem's concluding phrase, which brings the text full circle to the words with which it began: "Toute Pensée émet un Coup de Dés" (477). This axiomatic phrase functions like the moral of the text, summarily exposing the identity-in-difference of various contraries whose negated dialectic had, paradoxically, persistently aborted meaning from the text. These identical contraries are uniqueness and multiplicity (the many = the one), thinking and acting (the thought = the gesture or deed), and determinism and chance. In short, the final phrase effectively convenes the text's various contrary signifieds under the banner of *le hasard* and implicitly includes its own signifying process as being simultaneously unique (owing to the capital letters) and as nothing special, that is, just another *thought* and *throw* of the dice.

Just as the text preserves yet neutralizes its oppositions on the level of signification, so is it structurally arranged to preserve yet neutralize the difference between literature and other aesthetic forms. By virtue of its extraordinary typographical disposition, the text functions not only as a poem, a verbal signifying body, but also as a score for a visual *mise en scène* of its idea, as well as a *mise en musique*.

Of what does the poem's novel typographical disposition consist?[4] The work's most striking structural feature is its spacing. The white spaces that surround the ordinary poem are here not confined to the perimeters of the text but, rather, assimilated within it, producing varying expanses of emptiness between the fragments of verse.[5] Another arresting feature, which is related to the poem's assimilation of its white spaces, is the "éclatement," or explosion, of any horizontal or vertical margins that ordinarily confine a text. The words are disseminated alone or in groups over the eleven folded or double pages of the text, at various levels, toward the top, middle, or bottom of the page. A third surprising feature is the use of several different sizes of italics and roman type.

The most obvious effect of this novel typography is that it draws the reader's attention to the material aspect of the text, an aspect conventionally considered to be secondary. In our search for the meaning behind this unusual exploitation of the text's concreteness, for the correspondence between its figurative value and its signification, the obvious place to turn to is Mallarmé's "Préface," which, as mentioned earlier, ironically presents itself as an unnecessary explication of the form of the text.

Indeed, all of the novel features of the poem's typography are explained in the "Préface." It is the extraordinary spacing of the poem that constitutes the greatest surprise for the reader, and it is to this aspect that Mallarmé devotes the majority of his comments. He begins by asserting

4. My textual description pertains specifically to the 1914 *Nouvelle Revue Française* version (reproduced in the *Œuvres complètes*), whose principal variation from the first (that of the *Cosmopolis*) is that the material is tipped in broadside, i.e., a single page is spread over the breadth of two, according to Mallarmé's instructions in his final manuscript.

5. We have seen that Mallarmé considers the value of this whiteness to be authenticated by the blackness of written characters on the page. In this regard the reader should recall the passage cited earlier in which writing is presented as the identical opposite of its absence. Reading is the act of transposing signifiers into a conceptual nothingness that is equal to the material nothingness or blankness of the page. Thus, the text itself is a tangible manifestation of the dual aspects (material and immaterial) of the Idea, creating a "Virginité qui solitairement, devant une transparence du regard adéquat, elle-même s'est comme divisée en ses fragments de candeur, l'un et l'autre, preuves nuptiales de l'Idée" (387).

that the text's form is not nearly so unconventional as it appears, the only novel feature being its spacing: "le tout sans nouveauté qu'un espacement de la lecture." He justifies his use of space as deriving from a necessity that has always been recognized in a conventional literary genre, lyric poetry:

> Les "blancs" en effet, assument l'importance, frappent d'abord; la versification en exigea, comme silence alentour, ordinairement, au point qu'un morceau, lyrique ou de peu de pieds, occupe, au milieu, le tiers environ du feuillet: je ne transgresse cette mesure, seulement la disperse. (455)

Beyond this avowal of semi-adherence to the rules inherent in that genre, Mallarmé offers visual and musical justifications for his use and particularly, for his dispersal of blank space.

He maintains that the typography functions to guide us in our reconstitution of the visual, or figurative, aspect of the Idea, which the poem verbally signifies. What the poem makes happen in the mind is presented as having its corollary in space. The poem's pattern becomes a concrete, plastic model of the signifying process, or the *process* of thinking itself, by exteriorizing not what simply *is* but, rather, what *is happening* in the reader's mind.

> Le papier intervient chaque fois qu'une image, d'elle-même, cesse ou rentre, acceptant la succession d'autres et, comme il ne s'agit pas, ainsi que toujours, de traits sonores réguliers ou vers— plutôt, de subdivisions prismatiques de l'Idée, l'instant de paraître et que dure leur concours, dans quelque *mise en scène spirituelle exacte,* c'est à des places variables, près ou loin du fil conducteur latent, en raison de la vraisemblance, que s'impose le texte. (emphasis mine, 455)

It is essential to note the extent to which Mallarmé emphasizes the mobile, or kinetic, quality of this process. The white space functions as a scanning mechanism, an exteriorized marking, which announces the rhythm, dynamics, or movement that lies latent (waiting for a reader) in the text:

> L'avantage, si j'ai droit à le dire, littéraire, de cette distance copiée qui mentalement sépare des groupes de mots ou les mots entre eux, semble d'accélérer tantôt et de ralentir le mouvement, le scandant, l'intimant même selon une vision simultanée de la

> Page: celle-ci prise pour unité comme l'est autre part le Vers ou
> ligne parfaite. La fiction affleurera et se dissipera, vite, d'après la
> mobilité de l'écrit, autour des arrêts fragmentaires d'une phrase
> capitale dès le titre introduite et continuée. (455)

Thus, although the pattern of the text undoubtedly functions here and
there to provide the reader with plastic images, or icons, of various
elements that it signifies (i.e., a listing ship on page 3; a whirlpool on
page 6; a constellation, the Big Dipper, on page 11), its unifying feature
as a signifying pattern is that of an ideogram of the process it evokes, or
summons: its reading-in-performance.[6]

Since Mallarmé presents the typographical position of his poem as a
pattern that must be realized kinetically, or set into motion, its function
is analogous to that of a choreographic score; that is, the pattern is not
an embodiment but, rather, a record and set of instructions for perfor-
mance. Indeed, his description of the visual performance that the poem's
arrangement announces and evokes is very similar to his description of
the function and aesthetic principle of dance (and ideally of all theatrical
arts). It is essential to recall that what Mallarmé is attempting to achieve
in his arrangement of *Un coup de dés* is (according to his own theoretical
writings) achieved by dance: a reciprocal, and therefore mutually conse-
crating, reflection between the ever-evolving mental, or imaginative,
world of the reader/spectator and the material figure that exteriorizes
and supports it:

> la représentation figurative des accessoires terrestres par la Danse
> contient une expérience relative à leur degré esthétique, un sacre
> s'y effectue en tant que la preuve de nos trésors. A déduire le
> point philosophique auquel est située l'impersonnalité de la
> danseuse, entre sa féminine apparence et un objet mimé, pour
> quel hymen: elle le pique d'une sûre pointe, le pose; puis déroule
> notre conviction en le chiffre de pirouettes prolongé vers un autre
> motif, attendu que tout, dans l'évolution par où elle illustre le

---

6. The pictorial value of the text has been extensively explored and diversely interpreted. In
Les dessins trans-consciens de Stéphane Mallarmé (1960), Ernst Fraenkel claims to expose the
underlying significance of the text in his drawings of its abstract patterns. In *Stéphane Mal-
larmé le presque contradictoire* (1975), Simonne Verdin presents another set of graphics (more
angular than Fraenkel's). In *Mallarmé, Manet, and Redon* (1986), Penny Florence analyzes the
poem's relationship to its illustrations by Redon. In his general analysis of the text, Cohn
identifies various isolated icons as well as more abstract structures, which are representative of
Mallarmé's epistemology: cycles, spirals, and the all-pervasive undulation, or "crête à creux" of
a wave.

sens de nos extases et triomphes entonnés à l'orchestre, est, comme le veut l'art même, au théâtre, *fictif ou momentané.*

Seul principe! et ainsi que resplendit le lustre, c'est-à-dire lui-même, l'exhibition prompte, sous toutes les facettes, de quoi que ce soit et notre vue adamantine, une œuvre dramatique montre la succession des extériorités de l'acte sans qu'aucun moment garde de réalité et qu'il se passe, enfin de compte, rien. (296)

In *Un coup de dés,* this sole aesthetic principle—the point that every thought, chance-determined and ultimately insignificant though it may be, expresses (in the original sense) its corollary concrete gesture—is also "exteriorized" in a visual *coup de dés* that serves as a concrete demonstration of the poem's dénouement. "Toute pensée émet un Coup de Dés." And given the admission of *le hasard* into this all-pervasive play of *correspondences,* any search to pin down more precisely the signified of the text's visual, or concrete, aspect must be recognized from the outset as ultimately vain.

The correspondences between the text's verbal and musical aspects are, of course, equally arbitrary, equally indeterminant. The musical analogies suggested by the poem's structure have inspired almost as much analytical commentary as the text's pictorial aspect. And in their efforts to remain coherent, critics are naturally forced to choose which aspect, the musical or the pictorial, is the more important—which one *really* determines the structuring of the text. Critics for the most part have validated the text's pictorial aspect but have dismissed its musical aspect (since within the general context of literature this poem's musical, performative aspect is by far the more revolutionary and unsettling). They have justified this dismissal by appealing to our common sense, to our knowledge that music and poetry are not one and the same thing.

Yet Mallarmé clearly invites the reader to use his text as a musical score:

Ajouter que de cet emploi à nu de la pensée avec retraits, pro-longements, fuites, ou son dessin même, résulte, pour qui veut lire à haute voix, une partition. La différence des caractères d'impri-merie entre le motif prépondérant, un secondaire et d'adjacents, dicte son importance à l'émission orale et la portée, moyenne, en haut, en bas de page, notera que monte ou descend l'intonation. (455)

Unable to conceive of such a performance, many critics (who other-wise take Mallarmé very seriously) dismiss this set of guidelines as an error or joke. For instance, Gardner Davies (1953, 73) writes that "le poète ne pouvait guère croire sérieusement à cet aspect de son œuvre." Suzanne Bernard (1959), in particular, emphasizes the ridiculousness of various attempts to sing or otherwise musically interpret Mallarmé's score, and she attributes an especially naïve attitude to Mallarmé for even suggesting that it might be done:

> Il est vrai que lui-même ne manque pas de naïveté lorsqu'il envisage une "lecture à haute voix" de cette partition. . . . Ici on a beau jeu de railler Mallarmé: une telle lecture est inimaginable, et contredit au principes mêmes de la lecture. . . . Mallarmé semble avoir oublié que la langue française possède des accents d'intensité plutôt que de hauteur. . . . En réalité, il n'est pas question d'"exécuter" le *Coup de dés* comme un morceau de musique, et sa "partition" est purement intellectuelle: c'est une partition d'idées. (126–27)[7]

In fact, it is irrelevant to an understanding of both this poem and Mallarmé's general aesthetic theory whether such a performance could be successfully realized or to ponder, as other critics have, exactly what kind of music the score would produce.[8] What is important is that the auditory supplement (like the visual) is offered to the reader in the "Préface" and suggested by the mimesis of musical notation in the typographical disposition of the text itself.

7. Bernard (1959) is forced to explain away this portion of Mallarmé's "Préface" in order to safeguard the coherency of her own thesis (implied in the quotation above), that Mallarmé's text offers a synthesis of the arts whose value is purely literary, since (she claims), his approach to other arts is purely intellectual: "L'originalité de Mallarmé est d'avoir posé en principe que le Livre ne devait pas seulement supplanter les autres arts, mais se les annexer. Il deviendra ainsi à lui seul un véritable 'système de beaux arts' . . . théâtre mental, chorégraphie de signes, et, surtout, concert intérieur—puisque pour Mallarmé, la vraie musique, c'est la poésie, nous l'avons vu" (150). As I have already stressed at many points, this conclusion, while inviting, does not account for the fact that it is precisely the nonintellectual and tangible aspects of other arts that interest Mallarmé. As we have seen, it is specifically these aspects that he perceives as missing from literature, and (as *Un coup de dés* well demonstrates) it is these aspects that, successfully or not, he is trying to "annex" to the literary text.
8. Claude Roulet (1943), for example, is very specific about how the poem should be musically interpreted: "La modulation majuscule CE SERAIT forme la note prolongée, et le stiche scalaire [I assume, the line in the form of a descending scale] qui lui succède forme à son tour une suite d'accords, un *decrescendo* ponctué de *pizzicati* qu'on entendra jouer par des violons ou des violoncelles." In "The Musical Analogies in Mallarmé's 'Un coup de dés,' " Calvin S. Brown (1971, 67–79) cites this passage along with many other examples showing how diversely critics have dealt with the musical aspect of the text. For a deconstructive reading of the interrelations of poetry and music in the poem see Christie McDonald's "Unsettling the Score: Poetry and Music" (1986, 254–63).

Can we conclude (along with many critics, as different from one another as Bernard and Cohn) that *Un coup de dés* offers the reader a literary synthesis of all the arts? We cannot, because though the text may serve as the basis or *score* for its own performed audiovisual representations, these representations are clearly not contained within the text; rather, paradoxically, they become the various signifying processes of the text, insofar as the receiver chooses to visually or musically *interpret* the text, rather than to read it.

Synthesis implies a meshing, or mixture, of various elements. Yet *Un coup de dés*, despite its concrete aspect, is integrally poetry, self-sufficient in its literariness; surely we do not need to reconstitute the kinetic, or performative, representations that the text also records in order to understand the poem. Though this point is more difficult to verify and accept (since, in fact, we generally read *Un coup de dés*), it follows that the performed audiovisual representations, which the text-as-score might be used to call forth, would be equally self-sufficient, not in relation to the material text but in relation to its verbal, literary representations. The text might thus be perceived as signifying *simultaneously* yet integrally in literary, pictorial, or musical terms. In fact, the poem itself invites us to accept the autonomy of the text's representations since it tells us that all systems signify equally and that there is only an arbitrary correspondence between the signifier and the signified, between meaning, or concepts, and forms.

Thus, while the typographical disposition of the text presents itself as a point of conjuncture between literature and other aesthetic modes, each mode retains its independence, so that their concurrence would be more properly described as structural syllepsis than as synthesis.[9] Indeed, syllepsis rather than synthesis accurately describes the ideal combination of music and letters as Mallarmé presents it in the passage earlier cited from the essay of that name:

Je pose, à mes risques esthétiquement, cette conclusion . . . : que la Musique et les Lettres sont la face alternative ici élargie vers l'obscur; scintillante là, avec certitude, d'un phénomène, le seul, je l'appelai, l'Idée.

L'un des modes incline à l'autre et y disparaissant, ressort avec emprunts: deux fois, se parachève, oscillant, un genre entier.

9. Michael Riffaterre (1978) describes syllepses as forms representing the "equivalence of two signifying systems," as forms "equally pertinent to two codes or texts" (81). And it should be noted that the syllepsis of poetry and music's writing, or notation, in Mallarmé's "score" seems, paradoxically, the ideal textual concretization of these two art forms' ideal *alternative* interrelations, which (as we saw in Chapter 2) Boulez attempted and described.

> Théâtralement pour la foule qui assiste, sans conscience, à
> l'audition de sa grandeur: ou, l'individu requiert la lucidité, du
> livre explicatif et familier. (649)

Given the autonomy of literature so consistently implied both in the
structuring of Mallarmé's poetry and in his own theoretical statements—
i.e., his insistence that literature does not require any theatrical comple-
ment—the reader cannot but wonder why *Un coup de dés* so persistently
refers to its own performance. Why, in this his last, most complete, most
perfect published text is Mallarmé still representing the combination of
textual and performative aesthetic modes and representing them in the
same supplementary relation suggested in his earlier, imperfect, unfin-
ished "theatrical texts"? As I have tried to demonstrate throughout this
study, the answer to these questions lies in his perception of literature and
the performing arts as contrary, superlative forms of corporeal-spiritual
Language; of Language itself as a reflection of the metaphysical "Idea"
(*le Verbe*); and of all of these elements as projections of the unity-in-
duality of mind and body that is the human Self.

But, one might object, in *Un coup de dés*, in contrast to the other texts
examined here, representations of the Self are, or at least become, con-
spicuously absent. Indeed, this poem is, as has often been pointed out,
the drama of the Self's disappearance and also, implicitly, of the Poet's
withdrawal from the poem. It must be remembered, however, that, for
Mallarmé, it is only and precisely through such a self-sacrifice that the
poetic act can finally be projected into the heavens, or the poem trans-
posed onto an ideal, metaphysical plane. What we ultimately find in
place of the traditional poetic Self, or lyric subject, in *Un coup de dés* is
the carefully structured yet highly flexible empty space of the Ideal,
metaphysical Self that every human subject must be allowed, paradoxi-
cally, to enter and fill. We saw that Mallarmé describes the theatrico-
religious structuring of this space in "Offices," and he describes its tex-
tual structuring in a famous passage from "Crise de vers":

> L'œuvre pure implique la disparition élocutoire du poëte, qui
> cède l'initiative aux mots, par le heurt de leur inégalité mobilisés:
> ils s'allument de reflets réciproques comme une virtuelle traînée
> de feux sur des pierreries, remplaçant la respiration perceptible en
> l'ancien souffle lyrique ou la direction personnelle enthousiaste
> de la phrase.
>
> Une ordonnance du livre de vers poind innée ou partout,
> élimine le hasard; encore la faut-il, pour omettre l'auteur: or, un
> sujet, fatal, implique, parmi les morceaux ensemble, tel accord

quant à la place, dans le volume, qui correspond. (Mallarmé 1945, 366)

The literary depersonification of the world that occurs through the drowning of the Self in *Un coup de dés* is itself, in fact, the identical contrary, the authenticating reflection, of the far more common idealizing gesture that Mallarmé describes in his exceedingly liberal translation of George Cox's textbook of mythology, *Les dieux antiques.* Here, in a number of passages added to Cox's introduction, Mallarmé once again and perhaps more clearly than anywhere else states that all *Mythologie* (or poetic fiction), be it religious or secular, primitive or modern, is ultimately a *personification* of the infinite, irresolvable conflict of contraries that both creates and destroys the natural world:

> Tel est, avec le changement des Saisons, la naissance de la Nature au printemps, sa plénitude estivale de vie et sa mort en automne, enfin sa disparition totale pendant l'hiver (phases qui correspondent au lever, à midi, au coucher, à la nuit), le grand et perpétuel sujet de la Mythologie: la double évolution solaire, quotidienne et annuelle. Rapprochés par leur ressemblance et souvent confondus pour la plupart dans un seul des traits principaux qui retracent la lutte de la lumière et de l'ombre, les dieux et les héros deviennent tous, pour la science, les acteurs de ce grand et pur spectacle, dans la grandeur et la pureté duquel ils s'évanouissent bientôt à nos yeux, lequel est: LA TRAGÉDIE DE LA NATURE. (Mallarmé 1945, 1169)

But the final disappearance of the poet-self represented in *Un coup de dés,* the withdrawal that finally permits the poem's transposition onto an ideal plane, cannot actually take place, in Mallarmé's aesthetic system, unless or until the poetic text finds its own reflection (its own identical contrary) in a theatrical performance. In short, just as the ancient personifying myths necessarily authenticated themselves through ritual gestures, so must this modern, abstract, depersonalized myth find its own ideal consecration in a modern, abstract, depersonalized performance.

Although it may only strike the reader as subtly disconcerting, the search for and representation of a reciprocally reflecting, mutually consecrating text-performance relationship is, I hope to have shown, one of the most significant, revolutionary aspects of all of Mallarmé's most ambitious critical and poetic texts. We shall now see that the effort to realize such a relationship is by far the most important and furthest developed aspect of *Le Livre,* his manuscript consisting of plans for a sacred and metaphysical text to be presented in a series of ritual performances.

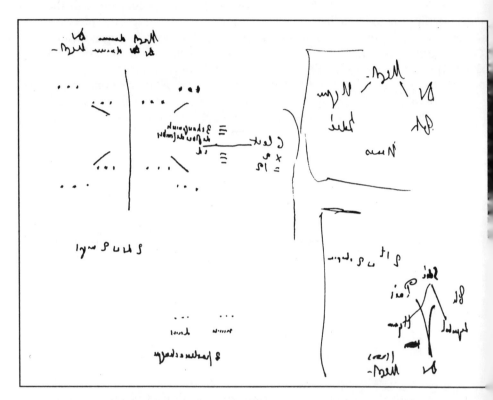

Fig. 4.   Le "*Livre*," folio 15. By permission of the Houghton Library, Harvard University.

CHAPTER ELEVEN

Le Livre

As we saw in the previous chapters, the performing-arts code in Mallarmé's poetic texts is supplementary. The reference to absent, or extratextual, performances appears paradoxically superfluous yet necessary to the completion of these works of art. That is, although the performances referred to are always felt to be missing, they seem extraneous in relation to the texts' literary closure; without the theatrical references these texts would surely appear to be more complete, self-sufficient, literary monuments. Like the ideal "scène à ne pas faire" (Mallarmé 1945, 319), that Mallarmé either recognizes or reads into Shakespeare's *Macbeth,* and like Loïe Fuller's illuminated veils, the representations of performance in Mallarmé's most ambitious poetic texts fulfill the function of a "prolongement transparent," suspending the reader's "crainte contradictoire ou souhait de voir trop ou pas assez" (Mallarmé 1945, 311). As the performing arts play such a striking and equivocal role with respect to the completion of these poetic texts, it is not surprising that they figure prominently in Mallarmé's conception of the ultimate Book—the all-encompassing text for which the world exists.

Such a Book is referred to in one of Mallarmé's most celebrated statements: "tout, au monde, existe pour aboutir à un livre" (378). Like the poetic texts previously examined, the Book presents itself as more than a text. It is the product of a literature that provides us a Theater, a Work whose purpose would be both to ritually celebrate and explicate human nature:

> Je crois que la Littérature, reprise à sa source qui est l'Art et la
> Science, nous fournira un Théâtre, dont les représentations seront

le vrai culte moderne; un Livre, explication de l'homme, suffi-
sante à nos plus beaux rêves. (875–76)[1]

   In this chapter I undertake an analysis of Mallarmé's references to the
Book in *Le Livre,* for therein we find the most striking and problematic
examples of the text/performance duality that we have been examining.
The performing arts play their most prominent role in Mallarmé's texts in
relation to his project for the Book. Whereas references to performance in
his poetic texts have been largely ignored, no one has failed to recognize
the preeminent and problematic character of these references in *Le Livre.*
But despite this widespread recognition, few critics have even addressed
the difficult question of why Mallarmé—for whom literature existed
"seule, à l'exception de tout" (1945, 646)—demanded as the integral
corollary of the ideal text, a ceremonial, theatrical performance.[2]
   It is essential to emphasize from the outset that Mallarmé's Book does
not exist (and has never existed) as such. Though Jacques Scherer's 1957
publication, *Le "Livre" de Mallarmé: Premières recherches sur des docu-
ments inédits,* consists of a manuscript filled with notes pertaining to
such a Work, the manuscript itself is not the Book but, rather, an incom-
plete and generally incoherent compilation of plans for it.[3] Nevertheless,

   1. In this context "Art" and "Science" are variants of the aesthetic (concerning beauty) and
the metaphysical (concerning truth). This becomes clear further in the passage as the Theater is
said to provide a manifestation of truth, "a true cult," and the Book, an "explication" adequate
to beauty, or to "our most beautiful dreams."
   2. Many critics, such as Bernard, Richard, Scherer, and Paula Gilbert Lewis, have correctly
explained that the Book would have been performed in order to attain for it the kind of
communion and communication with the public that occurs in the performing arts. But their
explanations have not, in my view, sufficiently accounted for *how* this communion was to be
achieved in the Book, for *why* it was deemed necessary, or for which qualities particular to the
performing arts it was to depend on. I shall take up this point further on, in relation to Scherer's
discussion of the theatricality of the Book.
   3. In 1977 Scherer issued a new edition of this publication, *Le "Livre" de Mallarmé.* All
references to *Le Livre* in this chapter are to the 1977 edition, which includes a new preface by
Scherer and Mallarmé's play, *Quelque chose ou rien* (composed entirely of fragments of the
manuscript), but no significant alterations of the manuscript or of Scherer's analysis introduc-
ing it. The manuscript should not be equated with the text of Mallarmé's Book, not because
Mallarmé did not intend it to be published but because it does not present itself either as a
literary text in the ordinary sense or as the text of the literary/theatrical work that it describes.
For those who still regard some measure of intentionality as relevant in determining the status
of a work, it should be noted that there is no apparent order to the collection of sheets of notes
that constitute *Le Livre.* (This is not necessarily significant, as we cannot determine whether or
how they were meant to be ordered, though Scherer is careful to insist that he has scrupulously
respected the order in which they came to him from Henri Mondor, to whom they were passed
on from Mallarmé's son-in-law, Edmond Bonniot.) Moreover, there is no reason to think that

a literary-theatrical Book functions as a model toward which *Le Livre* and many other of Mallarmé's texts point, and we are able to learn much about its nature through an examination of the many references to it, both within the posthumously published manuscript and in its critical prose. To realize that an understanding of this project is highly relevant to understanding his texts on the whole, we need only consider the impact of Scherer's publication on Mallarmé studies. Whatever literary status critics have chosen to attribute to it, *Le Livre* has come to figure as a fundamental text in Mallarmé's corpus, referred to in most of the recent criticism of his work.[4]

Unlike other posthumously published manuscripts of Mallarmé (e.g., *Les noces* and *Igitur*), *Le Livre* does not read like a literary text, but like a set of preparatory notes.[5] It also lacks the unity, order, and coherence necessary for precise literary explication. The manuscript does not, however, resist explanation altogether. I shall attempt to elucidate the meaning of several notes pertaining both to its structure and thematic content, to reveal the similarities between the manuscript and the poetic and critical texts examined previously, and finally, to demonstrate the critical role that performance plays in consecrating Mallarmé's art and in providing it with a ritual function.

The manuscript consists of 202 pages of notes. These notes can be broadly classified into three groups. The majority constitute a category referring to the material aspects of the Book—that is, the text and the "séances" in which it would be performed. This category includes (a) notes indicating the number of the Book's volumes and pages, its geometrical dimensions, the quantity of editions, the manner and price of publication; (b) notes indicating the number of performances, the number and nature of spectators, the price of tickets, the seating arrangement, and the staging of the spectacle from the perspective of the performer (who is most often called the "opérateur"); and (c) notes revealing the correlations, or

---

this manuscript includes *all* of the notes pertaining to the Book, since many of Mallarmé's notes were burned as he had requested. The reader will find a different theoretical analysis of the literary status of *Le Livre* in Blanchot's *Le livre à venir* (1959, 271–97).

4. The most useful and comprehensive analysis of the manuscript to date remains Scherer's 1957 introduction. The reader will also find interesting discussions of it in Blanchot (1959), Derrida (1972), Eco (1984), Kristeva (1974), and Richard (1961a). Scherer gives a more complete list of criticism pertaining to *Le Livre* in his 1977 preface (1977, x).

5. In this and many other respects *Le Livre* is very similar to *Pour un tombeau d'Anatole* (1961b), Jean-Pierre Richard's previously mentioned publication of a collection of Mallarmé's notes describing a work that would have commemorated the death of his son (Mallarmé 1961). Although a discussion of this ritualistic work would be highly relevant to this study, I have chosen not to include one for personal reasons.

"identity" between the various aspects of the text and its performance, correspondences between the number of volumes and performances, the number of pages and spectators, and the price of the performance and the text. The second category of notes contains diagrams illustrating the relationship between various textual and performative genres employed in the Book. And the third category consists of schematic references to the Book's thematic content of poems, or myths (as Scherer appropriately calls them, since they present themselves as the content of a rite and sacred text). We shall see that these myths are primarily significant in their symbolization of the nature of the Book as a composite of text and theatrical presentation.[6]

The sole unifying feature in all of these notes is their exposition of the principle of unity-in-duality. All entities are irreducibly dual, divided into contraries, but all contraries are presented as reversible and therefore identical. It is important to recall how consistently we have encountered expressions of this principle throughout this study.

As Scherer points out in his introduction to the manuscript, the various correspondences set up by the notes appear to function as reciprocal proofs. When one aspect of the Book shows itself as identical to another, each aspect is thought to become valid, and the ensemble of the Book, to convey its objective truth:

> Dans l'ordre littéraire, il est indispensable que le Livre montre sa réalité interne par une "preuve." La notion de preuve est une conséquence immédiate de l'idée de confrontation ou de comparaison. A défaut de la comparaison externe qu'est la ressemblance, le Livre devra trouver en lui-même deux aspects qui se rejoignent; s'ils se rejoignent, c'est qu'il y a quelque chose de réel dans ce jeu; l'existence d'un point de jonction montrera l'objectivité de ce qui est en question. (Scherer 1977, 91–92)

Indeed, comparison and inversion are two procedures ubiquitously employed in Mallarmé's plans for the Book. He begins by comparing one thing to another in order to demonstrate their "identity" and then inverts, or reverses, the equation as if to confirm that they are indeed equal. The use of this double procedure is most explicitly articulated on the fifth page of the manuscript, where we find its abstract formulation in an "equation" that is immediately used to establish the identity and

---

6. The manuscript also includes several notes, or "brouillons," pertaining to previously published letters and articles, for example, a letter to Charles Morice and an article entitled "La littérature: Doctrine" (published in the *Oeuvres complètes*, 872 and 850, respectively).

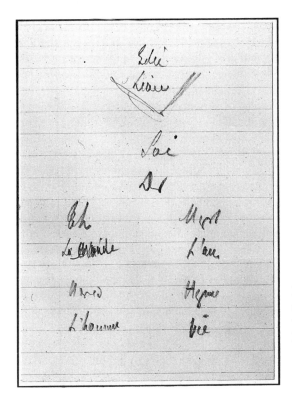

Fig. 5. *Le "Livre,"* folio 111. By permission of the Houghton Library, Harvard University.

reversibility of the theater and the hero and of the various aesthetic genres involved in the Book (I shall, of course, focus on these particular issues further on):

le Dr est en le mystère
de l'équation suivante   faite d'une double
                                    identité
                           équation ou idée
                        si ceci est cela
                         cela est ceci
                              (5 [A])

In *Le Livre* no element is presented as existing wholly in and of itself. The wholeness of every element is achieved or attained through its juxtaposition with another element that is found to be identical to it, hence, the constant confrontation and comparison of the various aspects of the

Book. This point is important enough to repeat, but for the sake of variety I can put it (as the notes themselves often do) in an opposite yet equivalent way. Whatever the entity in question, the manuscript presents it as split into two halves. These halves, in turn, often find their corollaries in another entity that is also divided into two.

Let us examine some examples of this obsessive search for symmetry and for proof of the Book's identity via internal correspondences. The intellectual exercise that these notes require of the reader is exhausting, and we naturally resist going through an analytical process that the schematic presentation of the notes discourages as much as invites. In the context of this study an examination of these notes is, however, essential, for through their circularity, and despite their global incoherence, we find a persistent demonstration of the principle of identity-in-difference tied to the mutually consecrating function of text and performance.

I shall begin with notes pertaining to the material constitution of the Book. The number of projected volumes in the Book is four, and the ensemble of these parts is thought to create a fifth, representing their sum. This summation is achieved by a juxtaposition of the four "half-parts" to themselves five times (that is, 5 × 4 halves + 4 halves). This results in the designation of either twenty or twenty-four as the total number of fragments of the book: twenty fragments perceived as grouped into ten double fragments. This strange numerical symmetry is expressed as follows in the manuscript:

Les quatre volumes sont un | | Livre, | / | le même,
présenté deux fois en tant que ses deux moitiés,
première de l'un et dernière de l'autre juxtaposées à
dernière et première de l'un et de l'autre : et peu à
peu l'unité s'en révèle, à l'aide de ce travail de comparaison
en deux sens différents, | montrant que cela fait un tout / en tant qu'une cinquième
partie, formée de l'ensemble de ces quatre fragments,
apparents ou deux répétés :
ceci aura donc lieu 5 fois
ou 20 fragments groupés
en 2 par 10, trouvés identiques

(173 [A])

The projected number of pages to be contained in each volume is also based on multiples of four and five. In several calculations it looks as if a volume would consist of either twenty or twenty-four "feuillets." Folded in half, one *feuillet* would produce four pages, and the ensemble of *feuillets* either eighty or ninety-six pages. This number of pages multiplies itself either by four or by five; giving the options of 320 (80 × 4), 384 (96 × 4) or 480 (96 × 5) as the total number of pages in each volume, and 1,600 (320 × 5), 1,920 (384 × 5), or 2,400 (480 × 5) as the total number of pages in the Book.[7]

The number of copies of the Book and the financial gain accrued from its publication also correspond. Mallarmé envisages 480,000 as the appropriate number of copies to be printed, from which he would gain an equal financial benefit, 480,000 francs. This amount is projected as half the cost of the Book's publication.

We find the same search for symmetry in Mallarmé's design for the realization of the *séances*. All projected numbers convey an inner correspondence as well as a correspondence to the numbers involved in the text. In its theatrical aspect the Book is conceived of as a "quadruple Pièce juxtaposée en cinq actes" [175 (A)]; corresponding to the twenty fragments of the text (also called "volumes"), there are twenty *séances* [176 (A)]. The number of spectators for one double reading (or "double séance") of the text, is projected as twenty-four (the number of *feuilles* in one volume) and the total number of spectators invited is, like the total number of *feuilles*, 480: "480 places, 480 feuilles" [176 (A)]. These spectators would not actually pay but would guarantee the value of the performance at 1,000 francs per seat, thereby allowing Mallarmé to publish a cheap, one-franc edition for the crowd of 480,000 people who will buy the Book, never having witnessed the *séances*:[8]

> Ainsi, en convoquant ces 480 personnes, à qui
> je donne lecture (par 8 et 3 fois = 24) de vingt volumes,
> ce qui vaudrait * de la part de chacune 1000 francs,
> pour rien; j'acquiers le droit de rentrer dans cette
> somme (de 480 mille francs,) en publiant
> le tout, soit en 480 mille volumes à I f :
> ou autant de mille exemplaires que de places; . . .
> (114 [A])

---

7. The reader will find these figures and others dispersed throughout several pages of the manuscript; many of them appear together on page 201 (A). Scherer examines these and other numerical correspondences in the portion of his analysis entitled "Grandeur et servitude de l'analyse combinatoire" (1977, 85–90).

8. These figures concerning the Book's financing are unrealistically high given the value of money in Mallarmé's time. As Scherer points out, they suggest that Mallarmé aspired to acquire a readership comparable to the Bible's.

This correspondence between the price of the performance and that of the text is said to provide a "reciprocal proof" of the value of the Book, in the unequal yet proportionally fair investment on the part of those who will benefit from it—the rich and elite group of spectators and the crowd who will purchase the text: "*établir que cela vaut 1000 francs (le fait: que / la foule achètera) / preuve réciproque" [114 (A)].

The geometrical dimensions of the Book and its manner of presentation in the *séances* must be similarly symmetrical. In its textual form the Book is conceived of as a rectangular "bloc" whose dimensions—length, width, and thickness—must all correspond. Mallarmé examines various possible shapes and appears to decide on a parallelepiped consisting of two cubes: "sa largeur quand, en bloc / devient son épaisseur . . . l'on obtiendrait des / en quelque sens, couché ou debout / deux blocs un rectangle présentant sa / hauteur même que sa largeur ou 2 largeurs de vol. / ou épaisseur / ici." The purpose of the *séances,* or "lectures," is to reveal the mathematical foundation of the Book, to show through its all-encompassing symmetry that it is not a product of "le hasard": "il n'est pas chu / au hasard, / sacre à un seul- / on l'en sort-. . . . Les Lectures n'ayant d'autre but / que de montrer ces rapports scientifiques— / dans découverte du livre" [40–41 (A)].

The *opérateur* accomplishes this by performing various permutations of the text, before an audience of twenty-four "assistants" who are themselves symmetrically arranged in either eight "triple places" or six "double places" on either side of an auditorium. He changes the order of the distribution of the *feuillets* in a "meuble de laque" containing six open vertical slots and reads the fragments in two different ways as if to demonstrate their perfect congruity and that of the text as a whole: "La séance, implique la confrontation d'un / fragment de livre avec lui-même" [112 (A)]. "Ce n'est que grâce à deux textes / répétés que l'on peut jouir de / toute une partie / ou grâce / au retournement / du même texte / —d'une seconde façon / de relire / qui permet d'avoir le tout / successivement" [179 (A)]. Every fragment of the work is read twice [89 (A)]. Every text is presented through two different readings in a double *séance* [36 (A)]. Each double *séance* lasts two hours, consisting of a preliminary 15-minute waiting period, a 15-minute intermission, and two 45-minute reading periods, in which the *opérateur* directs his attention toward either half of the audience. Two double *séances* are given in one day.

Analogous to this search for symmetry in the material constitution of the Book is the search for correspondences between its various genres and states. These genres are referred to in a number of diagrams that seem to express the nature of their interrelations. The diagrams constitute perhaps the most impenetrable aspect of the manuscript, for their forms and the terms they set up are constantly changing. No sooner does one devise a theory about the expression of relationships in one particular diagram than one finds another structure, either within the same diagram or in another, in which the previously discovered set of relationships is significantly changed.

The many permutations in these diagrams suggest that neither their terms nor their interrelations can be fixed. Although the structures convey symmetry, they also appear unstable and fortuitous, subject to almost any alteration. Thus, the overall effect of the diagrams is to express the impossibility of establishing a definitive order or of ridding order of its inherent disorder. The diagrams appear to illustrate Mallarmé's belief that absolute order and disorder are, finally, one and the same thing. Indeed, his often-stated conviction that *all* things are interrelated and that order is all-pervasive quite logically leads to the contrary conviction that there is no particular, or absolute, order of relationships—in short, to the principles of chaos and chance. This point may well be the key to the significance of the ensemble of the diagrams, since it was also made emphatically in *Igitur* and *Un coup de dés*.

The reader may wonder, then, whether anything further can be said about the diagrams and the terms that they arrange. We can, in fact, acquire a better understanding of them by responding to their invitation to analytically order their elements—that is, by attempting to classify their terms into categories and by examining the relationships expressed in their arrangement.

For the most part, the terms in the diagrams can be classified under the following binary categories: (a) they pertain either to texts or performances; (b) they suggest either what is sacred (hidden and contained within a religious space) or what is profane (visible, exterior, "hors du temple," "profanum"); and (c) they represent either poetic (emblematic) or prosaic (direct) modes of human expression. I shall reproduce and analyze a number of diagrams in order to illustrate this point.

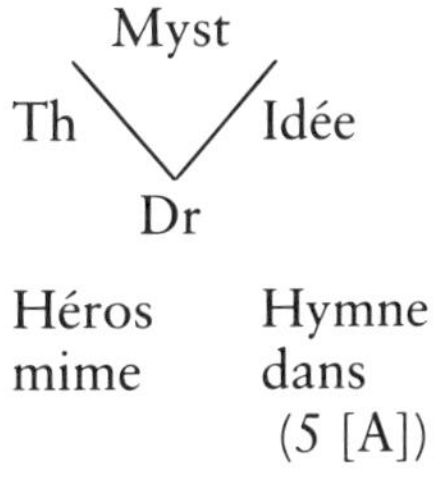

Diagram 1.

At the center of Diagram 1 we find (abbreviated) "Drame" and "Mystère." These terms are similar in that they both refer to theatrical genres. These genres, however, are also different; the former is profane, and the latter is sacred. Drama does not concern the divine but is the theatrical exposition of an incident in the life of a person. By contrast, a mystery necessarily concerns whatever surpasses human understanding. The medieval *mystère*, for example, portrayed miracles in the life of Jesus, Testament figures, or the saints. A similar contrast is apparent between the other terms that are juxtaposed: "Theater" connotes a world of appearances, while the "Idea" is considered to transcend appearances; a "Héros" is a human character whom we see, while an "Hymne" is expressive of that which transcends humanity, either God, or whatever is elevated in the hero, his greatness or his glory.[9] Similarly, "mime" (whether it refers to the artist or the art form) strives to imitate or represent things as they appear, while "dans" (referring either to the dancer or dance) is emblematic, signifying at a higher level of abstraction.[10] We sense "Drama," "Theater," "Hero," and "mime" to be more prosaic (that is, direct) and profane than their counterparts, "Mystery," "Idea," "Hymn," and "dance" (or "dancer").

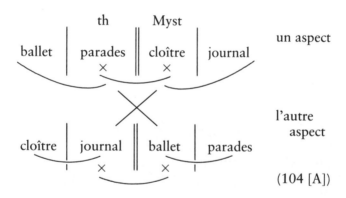

Diagram 2.

9. In other notes the "Hymne" is described as both the mother and child of the "Héros": e.g., "—le Héros / dégage—l'Hymne maternel qui le crée" (4 [A]). I shall return to the relationship between the hero and the hymn further on.

10. Recall that Mallarmé emphasizes such a distinction between mime and dance in "Ballets": "Un art tient la scène, historique avec le Drame; avec le Ballet, autre, emblématique. Allier, mais ne confondre; ce n'est point d'emblée et par traitement commun qu'il faut joindre deux attitudes jalouses de leur silence respectif, la mimique et la danse, tout à coup hostiles si l'on en force le rapprochement" (Mallarmé 1945, 306).

In Diagram 2 the juxtaposition of "theater," "Mystery," and the terms they subsume also suggests an opposition between the profane and the sacred and between prosaic (open and easily accessible) and poetic (hermetic) forms of expression. The subsuming of "ballet" and "parades" under "theater" (in "un aspect") implies that theatrical expression has its poetic and prosaic genres. "Parades" can be understood as the equivalent of "mime" (in Diagram 1), for a parade is an open and direct exhibition, while ballet (its counterpart) is more hermetic and enigmatic. It is more difficult to account for the subsuming of "cloître" and "journal" under "Mystère." This structure can be explained, however, if we recall that in Mallarmé's critical writing mystery is often equated with the literary text. (This association constitutes the central theme of such articles as "Hérésies artistiques: L'art pour tous" and "Le mystère dans les lettres.")

"Cloître" (subsumed under "Mystère") is very similar in its connotations of encasement and protection to words such as "coffret" and "tombeau," which Mallarmé employs in his critical prose to designate the Book.[11] "Cloître" then relates to its counterpart, "journal," similarly to the way "parades" relates to "ballet." Thus, we can understand "Mystère" in this context as a metaphor for the textual and "cloître" as referring to the "clôture," or closed quality, of the Book and (given the religious connotations of "cloître") to the idea that the Book constitutes a sacred space. The inversion of the subsumed pairs in "l'autre aspect" conveys the sense that while one pair seemed to belong (as metonyms) to theater and the other to Mystery (metaphorically, literature), these pairs are actually equivalent.

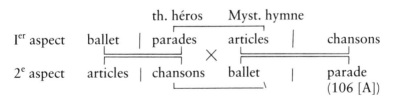

Diagram 3.

---

11. Mallarmé uses the term *tombeau* in reference to the Book in "Le livre, instrument spirituel": "Le pliage est, vis-à-vis de la feuille imprimée grande, un indice, quasi religieux: qui ne frappe pas autant que son tassement, en épaisseur, offrant le minuscule tombeau, certes, de l'âme" (Mallarmé 1945, 379). The Book is compared to a *coffret* in "Le genre ou des modernes": "Oui, le Livre ou cette monographie qu'il devient d'un type (superposition des pages comme un coffret, défendant contre le brutal espace une délicatesse reployée infinie et intime de l'être en soi-même) suffit avec maints procédés si neufs analogues en raréfaction à ce qu'a de subtil la vie" (Mallarmé 1945, 318).

In Diagram 3 we again find the juxtaposition of "théâtre" and "Mystère," now coupled (as they were in Diagram 1) with "héros" and "hymne," respectively. In the pattern described as the "Ier aspect" we find subsumed under the couple "th. Héros," the terms "ballet" and "parades" (whose relationship was explained above), and under "Myst. hymne," two potentially textual genres, "articles" and "chansons." Although as a generic term "chansons" generally refers to popular, playful verse forms, in this context it appears to refer to poems in general as it is juxtaposed to "articles," which suggests prose. The diagram suggests that the relationship between "articles" and "chansons" is analogous to that between "ballet" and "parades" and to the relationship previously expressed (in Diagram 2) between "cloître" (referring to the closed and arcane text) and its contrary "journal." "Articles" can clearly be understood as the content of "journal," while "chansons" (as a metaphor for poems) can be understood as the content of the arcane "cloître" (book).

The relationship between the terms in the primary couples of Diagram 3, "th. héros" and "Myst. hymne," expresses a parallelism. More precisely, the arrangement of the terms constitutes an analogy (a : b, c : d): "theater" is to "hero" as "mystery" is to "hymn." The juxtaposition of these two pairs conveys an opposition and identity between the profane and the sacred and also between the performative and the textual, insofar as we continue to read "Mystery" and "hymn" as metaphors for the text and for poetry. Such a reading is justified by the textual/performative opposition suggested in the terms these primary couples subsume. Theater can be understood as containing the hero, as well as ballets and parades, while mystery (as a metaphor for the text) can be seen as containing a hymn, as well as articles and poems (or "chansons"). A passage in "Le Livre, instrument spirituel" supports this metaphorical interpretation describing the Book as consisting of: "l'Hymne, harmonie et joie, . . . des relations entre tout" (378).

We can discern the same set of relationships (of container to contained) if we consider the terms of the primary couples as arranged in a chiasmus (a : d; b : c). The small cross at the center of the diagram suggests this option, as does the crossing of the secondary couples in the "2e aspect." Theater can be understood as containing a hymn just as it can be understood as containing a mystery ("La scène . . . est la majestueuse ouverture sur le Mystère dont on est au monde pour envisager la grandeur" [1945, 314]). The corresponding relationship between "héros" and "Mystère" (in a chiasmus) appears more problematic. How can a hero contain a mystery in the same way that the theater can contain a hymn? This does not seem plausible, but elsewhere in the manuscript just such a relationship is expressed. A hymn is described, paradoxically, as buried both within the hero and in a mystery that lies beyond his reach. Thus, the mystery containing the hymn is both within and outside of the hero:

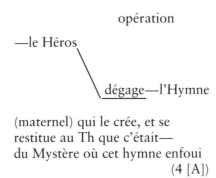

opération

—le Héros

dégage—l'Hymne

(maternel) qui le crée, et se
restitue au Th que c'était—
du Mystère où cet hymne enfoui
(4 [A])

This paradoxical location of the hymn (in a mystery that lies both within and outside of the hero) corresponds to the intermediary position of the anagram of "hymne," "hymen."[12] However, a more contextual meaning for its location in relation to the hero can be found if we look to Mallarmé's discussion (in "Offices") of the hymn as the "not understood" song that comes out of each participant in the Mass, allowing him access to, or communion with, the "héros" of that "Mystère." The hero of the "divine Drama" appears to transcend each individual, but, in fact, is each individual who takes part in the hymnal chant:

> quiconque y peut de la source la plus humble d'un gosier jeter aux voûtes le répons en latin incompris, mais exultant, participe entre tous et lui-même de la sublimité se reployant vers le chœur: car voici le miracle de chanter, on se projette, haut comme va le cri. Dites si artifice, préparé mieux et à beaucoup, égalitaire, que cette communion, d'abord esthétique, en le héros du Drame divin. (396)

Thus, Diagram 3 can be understood as expressive of either of two contrary rhetorical figures, the analogy or the chiasmus. The chiasmus, or cross, is explicit in the pattern of several of the diagrams. Diagram 4, whose terms are nearly identical to those of the primary couples in Diagram 3, is one example.

---

12. Cf. Derrida's discussion of the "hymen" as signifying the identity-in-difference of the inside and the outside (1972, 237–45).

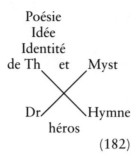

(182)

Diagram 4.

The terms in the cross are "Théâtre," "Mystère," "Drame," and "Hymne." The symmetry of the form and the word "Identité" written over it lead the reader to seek parallelism, or identity, between all of these terms. "Idée" and "Poésie" look like variants, or possible substitutions, for "Identité." We note initially that all of the terms in the cross are similar in the sense that they are generic, potentially either texts or performances, and indicative either of the sacred or the profane. We may then seek to discover the particular relational parallels of the six possible pairs: Theater/Mystery; Drama/Hymn; Theater/Drama; Mystery/Hymn; Drama/Mystery; Theater/Hymn.

Along with suggesting an identity between metonyms (in several of the pairs, between elements containing and elements contained), Diagram 4 suggests (as does Diagram 3) an identity between the inner and the outer and between the sacred and the profane. For example, the parallelism implied in the crossing of Mystery and Drama suggests that the former is the hermetic, interior equivalent of the latter. This equivalence is borne out by other notes in the manuscript:

> ⌊ne sont que même chose retournées [sic]
> Myst et Dr., Dr. et myst.et ⌉ présentant
> l'un en dehors ce que
> l'autre cache en dedans.
>
> Dr. les personnages en dehors et Myst. en dedans
> (89 [A])

Though less obvious, a similar equivalence can be posited between the other crossed terms, "Théâtre" and "Hymne." "Théâtre" can express the same exteriority in relation to "Hymne" as does "Drame" in relation to "Mystère."

In this diagram, as in the others, one is led to interpret "Mystère" and "Hymne" as metaphors for the book and poetry, since the book and poetry are the more hermetic counterparts of "Théâtre" and "Drame." Indeed, in another group of four terms on the same page (182) we find "Livre" substituted for "Mystère" and "vers" substituted for "Hymne." Whether or not we interpret these last terms metaphorically, however, the terms in Diagram 4 can be read as signifying various symmetrical relations—that is, interpreted in such a way as to conform to the all-pervasive "Identité" expressed in their arrangement. The symmetry of the diagram is so complete that it prevents us from establishing any definitive order of relationships between the terms.

On another page of the manuscript the reader again finds the pattern of Diagram 4 with the same terms. But Mallarmé complicates the diagram one step further by dividing the four terms into half-terms and then juxtaposing (or adding) the half-terms to themselves, so that the figure consists in a double half-cross (Diagram 5).

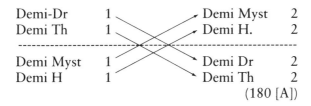

Diagram 5.

In notes beneath this diagram the pattern is described as revealing the four halves of two "states," or conditions, of the Work that complete each other, yet each state is designated as paradoxically self-sufficient, that is, as containing one complete text of the Œuvre:

> Ainsi 2 états d'Œ. qui se complètent,
>   chacun des deux n'étant qu'une moitié
>   fait de 4 moitiés dont les 4 autres
> moitiés sont en l'autre
>   mais chacun contenant 1 texte
>   complet de l'Œ. répété 2 fois par le fait
> qu'une partie

What are the "deux états de l'Oeuvre," and how do these four terms relate to them? An answer is implicit in my reading of "Mystère" and "Hymne" as metaphorical for the Book and Poetry. The diagram would in this case suggest that one "état de l'Oeuvre" pertains to the Work in its textual aspect, the Book ("Mystère") and its Poetry ("Hymne"), while the other pertains to its performed state (the "Théâtre" and its "Drame"). This interpretation is strongly supported by the fact that everything in the manuscript points to two principal conditions, or modes of being, of the Work: the Work would be published in a text and would be presented in a performance.

The double status of *l'Oeuvre* as both text and performance is, moreover, explicitly referred to on another page of the manuscript, and here, this duality is linked to the performer. The enigma of the Work is "reduced to" the symbol of the "operator's" identity, his hat:

Pièce
|ou
cette représentation avec concert
dialogue poème et symphonie
pour scène et orch
—occupe le fond de l'Œ—

vers

et comme publiée en livre
journal et vers
s'adapte—à un journal régulier
une fois pour toutes, et,
toutes les questions traitées,
par quelqu'un qui les réduit à son
chapeau⌋   façon de tout rendre
vierge—ce qui est exté-
rieur au poème⌋
(171 [A])

One face of the Oeuvre is a multigeneric performance, while the other is a multigeneric text. These two faces are presented as inhabiting one another, and the function of the *opérateur* is to demonstrate the sameness and reversibility of these seemingly contrary states. His hat appears to hold the answers to all questions raised by the Work; he shows that everything is reducible to it. What is the nature and function of this hat? We find clues to its identity in Mallarmé's prose. In "Réponses à des enquêtes" he refers to the top hat as something dark and supernatural, as a "mystère" that he has dedicated himself to solving in a lengthy, obscure book:

> Ce mystère, vous prenez la belle audace de l'épuiser, peut-être, dans la colonne d'un quotidien: moi, il fournit, presque seul, voici des temps, ma méditation, et je n'estime à moins que plusieurs tomes d'un ouvrage compact, nombreux, abstrus, la science pour le résoudre et passer outre. (881)

In this brief article, as in the manuscript, the meaning of the hat remains mysterious. In several hyperboles Mallarmé merely stresses the grave implications of this fashion accessory, which for him paradoxically constitutes the eternal, the immutable: "Le monde finirait, pas le chapeau: probablement même il exista de tous temps."[13] The object is finally described as the possible (because undecipherable) Sign of man's superiority:

> Apparu, l'objet convient à l'homme, évident autant qu'inexpliqué, ni laid ni beau, échappant aux jugements: Signe, qui sait? solennel d'une supériorité et, pour ce motif, institution stable. (882)

All we really learn about Mallarmé's concept of the hat is that (contrary to most hats) it is inseparable from the one who wears it. The hat is not an accessory; rather, it constitutes the identity of a person and thus cannot be taken off: "Qui a mis rien de pareil ne peut l'ôter. . . . je le considère, chez autrui, avec qui il me semble faire un—et, me salue-t-on, je ne le sépare, en esprit, de l'individu; je l'y vois, encore, pendant cette politesse. Immuablement" (882).

Since, for Mallarmé, the hat makes the man, the performer's hat must in some way incorporate his identity as "opérateur" of the Work. His function, we have seen, is to demonstrate the all-pervasive symmetry of the Book by rendering its various contrary aspects identical. Now the primary two contrary aspects of the Book are its conditions as "livre"

---

13. The tone of this article is ironical. Mallarmé appears to be joking about the high significance of the top hat, but the resurgence of a hat in the manuscript leads the reader to wonder whether he was *only* kidding. While *Le Livre* is absurd, even farcical at times, like *Igitur* it does not strike the reader, overall, as a playful, parodic text. I explore the symbolism of the top hat further in "Mallarmé, Pre-postmodern, Proto-dada" (Shaw 1992a).

and "représentation." The *opérateur* reveals that these are, in fact, identical by demonstrating that the latter occupies the former as its "fond" (center, or matrix). By performing the Book, he mediates the difference between the text as publication and spectacle. Through performance he neutralizes, or erases, the otherness of that totality that, constituting the *représentation,* is exterior to the text: "façon de tout rendre vierge—ce qui est extérieur au poème" [171 (A)].

Finally, in the context of this note implying an abolition of the difference between the container and the contained (the text and its theatrical representation) one must recall the position and purpose of the hat. As "couvre-chef" the hat is a container and extension of the head. The head is a paradigmatic symbol of the mind it contains, but as container, it is also a metonym of the body. In this light the note can be understood as suggesting (albeit circuitously) that the secret of all identities can be reduced to the hat as symbol of the identity-in-difference of the operator's mind and body. The impersonal operator is simply every man.

The diagrams referring to the generic constitution of the Book can thus be understood as expressing various oppositions. But the expression of particular oppositions is clearly not their central point. More important is the principle of reversibility of terms and relationships expressed both within each diagram and in the shifting of elements and patterns in the diagrams as a whole. Far more than an inventory of binary oppositions and distinct relationships, what the reader finally retains from the dizzying experience of analyzing these diagrams is an awareness that entities that appear different are also the same. It is important to stress that this identity is not recognizable from the start. Rather, it consistently *results,* or proceeds, from a discovery procedure involving juxtaposition, comparison, and reversal. Thus, it is not surprising that Mallarmé submits the two primary states of the Work (book and theatrical representation) to this treatment in order that its total "identity" might be established as a text equal to and reversible with a performance.

The poems, or myths, sketched out in *Le Livre* articulate this principle of reversibility as persistently and emphatically as the diagrams do, but in a manner less abstract. Scherer writes that in Mallarmé's conception of the Book, form and structure take precedence over content—that is, dictate the nature of its images and themes. But this assertion cannot be demonstrated, and the constant underscoring of the principle of reversibility suggests that such conclusions regarding the order of the Book are irrelevant; here, all relationships can be inverted. Although unsettling, this state of affairs does not preclude a unifying analysis of the myths. Along with presenting themselves as concrete, symbolic representations of the concepts of reversibility and identity-in-difference informing the ensemble of the manuscript, these fragments of the Book's poetic content are consistently dramatic in their themes and structures and explicitly refer to theater and performance.

The first myth, "le mythe de l'appel," is a dramatic representation of the relationship between "la parole" and "le geste," the principal modes of expression employed in theater and in the performance of the Book. A character responds to his verbal summons by means of a contrary yet identical gesture. He hears his name called, but rather than simply obeying (going in the direction from which he hears himself called), he hesitates. In his hesitation he is represented as responding to an ambivalence inherent in his name, "ce mot d'une langue humaine et qui désigne quelqu'un" [12 (A)]. The "nom propre," more than most words, appears to be what it says (to be one with its referent); yet as name or sign it also necessarily implies a distance, a difference, between itself and the referent it symbolizes:

> Toujours est-il que ce mot d'une langue
> humaine et qui désigne quelqu'un
>
> s'il fut proféré
> ⌈à demi
> non semble⌉dire celui qu'il eût
> lui
> appelé, prêtant l'oreille
> tête penchée visage souriant
> d'un côté, un peu haut*, comme qui
> ⌈ écouter afin d'obéir, ce qui suit
> va⌉obéir—
>
> <u>Rien</u>
> (<u>12</u> [A])[14]

14. This recognition of the inadequacy of the name runs contrary to the onomastic ideal described, for example, by Barthes in *Le degré zéro de l'écriture:* "Il est une classe d'unités verbales qui possède au plus haut point ce pouvoir constitutif, c'est celle des noms propres. Le Nom propre dispose des trois propriétés que le narrateur reconnaît à la réminiscence: le pouvoir d'essentialisation (puisqu'il ne désigne qu'un référent), le pouvoir de citation (puisqu'on peut appeler à discrétion toute l'essence enfermée dans le nom, en le proférant), le pouvoir d'exploration" (1953, 124). Indeed, the proper name is usually held to be particularly full of meaning and to retain a strong, motivated relation to its referent. Mallarmé often alludes to this, e.g., in the earlier quoted passage on the name Hérodiade, and in the sonnet dedicated to the memory of Ettie Yapp, "Sur les bois oubliés quand passe l'hiver sombre . . ." (1945, 69): "Ame au si clair foyer tremblante de m'asseoir, / Pour revivre il suffit qu'à tes lèvres j'emprunte / Le souffle de mon nom murmuré tout un soir."

The character appears at first to be contradicting the order of the call.
He does not move or act to join his corporeal self (the referent) to his
name but, rather, appears to do nothing, "*Rien.*" But in his resistance to
being called he is presented as *acting* nonetheless, as responding to a
more profound order hidden or implicit in the calling of his name. He
assumes an attitude of departure but does not really leave, just as his
name symbolically implies his presence yet does not embody him. His
gestural *posturing* functions as a corporeal symbolization of the resis-
tance of referents to signs or of the discrepancy (the lack of absolute
proximity) between words and things. By merely miming his departure,
the character shows his recognition that the "proper" name, which incor-
porates him, which *is* him, "qui est lui là," has, in fact, yet to be called:

> Le mot n'est donc pas pour lui proféré
> à ce moment où il l'entend, s'il le
> fut jamais (non—semble-t-il dire à
> ce doute, ne connut sa tête libre—il
> non pas non à l'ordre, qui neutre l'appelle et le laisse
> libre*
> ne le fut pas)
> proféré, ce mot qui est lui là et + , et tout en restant.
> il se plait   ⌈l'attitude qui est celle d'un départ—
> comme pour
> le montrer   penché en avant, un pied en avant
> à reprendre⌋
> ⌈et même cesse, avant—par attitude—
> diagonale⌋
> mais
> sans cependant quitter de l'autre pied—sans
> partir, obtempérant à l'ordre caché en la
> neutralité ferme et bienveillante de ce mot
> exagère peut-être le défi secret de son
> acte parti quand même
> défi
> que quelqu'un—ce
> ne sera pas lui
> une fois sommé
> par ce mot et sachant qui
> il est.
> (puissance
> d'un mot bien dit
> (14–15 [A])

The defiance of this character, and of his act, consists, then, of his resistance to being identified with his name, "sommé par ce mot" ("sommé" functions here as a syllepsis meaning "summed up by" as well as "summoned by"), in his refusal to be called, "appelé ainsi enfermé en le cercle d'un mot" [13 (A)]. It also consists of his denial of the power of human speech, "ce mot d'une langue humaine," which (unlike its divine, omnipotent model, the "Verbe") can neither eradicate the distance between the sign and its referent nor cleanly separate the idea (or concept) from material form—that is, constitute a pure language of the signified. Had the word never been uttered or otherwise tangibly expressed, the character's presence might have been summoned as a pure concept, or Idea, for divine language implies either the perfect union of form and concept or their complete separation. But the character rejects the possibility that man has any access to such a language; he recognizes that the calling of his name has no bearing on its referent, his corporeal being, and yet it calls him, or constitutes his identity nonetheless. The concept of his identity signified in his proper name is at the same time not his corporeal self and yet bound to it. Freedom to separate the former from his body would imply that his mind had a life of its own "non—semble-t-il dire à ce doute, ne connut sa tête libre" [14 (A)]. He doubts that a word could ever fully represent him either as a being in flesh or spirit (here, symbolically, a bodiless head), because the signifying word is neither its referent nor its signified. This is not to say, however, that there is no correlation between the character's sign (his name) and its referent (his being as a composite of concept and form). There *is* a correlation, and even "identity," between them in their mutual inadequacy to constitute a unified presence. It is this inadequacy that the character demonstrates in his gestural posturing of the ambivalent act of "l'appel."

Thus, "le mythe de l'appel," like several of the manuscript's diagrams, points to the identity-in-difference of two apparent contraries, verbal language (or words) and gestures, and also points to the reversible quality of their relationship. Like the dual aspects of the self, the mind and the body, these two modes of expression are presented as equal in their incapacity to function independently and equal in their incapacity to incorporate fully the quality of the other.

This first myth exposes the fundamental sameness and difference of verbal and gestural language in a manner we have already encountered both in Mallarmé's critical prose and in his poetic texts: the gestural mimesis of the nature and limits of verbal language. For example, the mime mimes the self-effacing libretto in "Mimique," and like the mimetic gestural response to the self-canceling act of naming in the myth, the ballet included in the "Finale" of *Les noces* is represented as the mirror image of the circular and self-negating poem. In "le mythe de l'appel" the paradoxical relationship between language and gesture is further underscored by an ambivalent reference to its own dramatic genre. The reader does not know whether the representation sketched out in the notes is itself verbal or gestural. Is "le mythe de l'appel" conceived of as a poem or as a pantomime, or as both, "ici rien dit de / poème mimique" [13 (A)]?

The second myth, "le mythe des deux femmes," recalls *L'après-midi d'un faune*. Here, the central character, or hero, finds himself confronted by two women who (like Iane and Ianthé) symbolize the two aspects of the world in which he lives, the earth and its imaginative reflection in the dream. These two women constitute at once the hero's home or country, "une belle patrie," and his feminine counterpart, his "other half" with whom he is not yet united, his fiancée:

> ↑ ma seule fiancée!   la terre
> ou fiancée
> et ce rêve revenu
> (16 [A])

The character considers the relationship between these two women, who are not yet united and who consequently cannot be united to him, with contradictory feelings: "gloire et amertume" or "déception et gloire." His reaction toward his fiancée is ambivalent; it is his distance from these women (his fiancée is divided into two) and their distance from each other that permit them (this double woman) to be his "other half," to correspond to what is dual in him.

These two distances are symbolized in a *mise en scène* in which the two women are set on a beach, stretching their arms toward each other, mirroring each other, and, through this mirroring process, engendering a multiple reflection, a kind of *mise en abîme* of their image.

> tendant les bras, sur la grève
> ....
> et comme des deux côtés revenues, par
> un habile mélange ici et là de celles
> que l'on a vu [*sic*] d'un côté puis de l'autre, la
> double troupe, est là cette [fois]
> _____
> y apparaissant alors comme moitié
> deux moitiés d'une troupe
> (17 [A])

The "habile mélange" (or, in a variant, "habile entrelacement") that brings these two women together is, at the same time, an operation of the mind pulling them apart, a perception that sees them distinctly and separately enough so that they can be considered to reflect each other as contraries. In order to achieve this perspective, the character/hero considers the two halves of "la double troupe" "sur la grève" as though each half were placed on two separate beaches ("sur deux grèves"), thus increasing the distance between them. Then, through an ideal operation of "l'esprit," each woman can be joined to her distant counterpart or reflection, "son absence":

> ... la
> double troupe, est là cette
>
> fois tendant en effet les bras d'une
> part et d'autre, ainsi que sur deux
> grèves très lointaines,
> mais entre lesquelles, à travers l'esprit sans
> doute (à travers lui)
>   et idéal
> il s'opère un mystérieux rapproche-
> ment, chacune
> tendant d'où elle est,
> y soit allée ou
> les bras à son absence
>
>   (17–18 [A])

The primary recurring image in this portion of the myth is that of a *demi-femme* (one who is missing her other half, yet paradoxically complete). Two similar images (images of "wholes" that are halves or vice versa) are evoked below the above-cited notes: that of a one-eyed monster who looks upon them, "hémisphère—et œil du monstre qui les regarde" and that of Amazon-like women who are portrayed as crossing their arms over their absent breasts: "bras croisés sur seins absents." This gesture is described further as a half-crossing of arms in the manner of the dancer: "un bras bas, un autre levé, attitude de danseuse" [19 (A)]. (This attitude recalls the fourth-position *port de bras* in ballet.)

The women (or, more precisely, dual-woman) are represented as having a split personality as well as a split physique. They are portrayed as desiring both a real marriage, with its worldly acquisitions (a diamond, a marriage bed, a fortune) and, along with the hero, a more ideal marriage (symbolized as a bird, apparition of the spirit of the diamond, "l'oiseau de diamant vraiment apparu"). But the latter, we have seen, depends on preserving the distance between the two halves of the woman as well as between the double-woman and the man:

> Et il entend leurs rires—tu me rapporteras—
> ceci, cela—diamant—diamant—il n'enten-
> dait que cela (lui, gloire, elles couche, fortune, etc.)
> elles cessant leur rire en l'oiseau de diamant
> vraiment apparu—là et qu'elles voudraient toutes avoir
>   car ce
>   rêve
>   est fait
>   de leur
>   pureté
>   gardée
>   à
>   toutes
>   (19 [A])

The myth is interrupted approximately midway through by several pages of notes containing an explicit discussion of various dualities inherent in theater. This long parenthesis in the development of "le mythe des deux femmes" begins with an exploration of the nature and function of the intermission, which divides the spectacle from itself.

The "entracte" is at first described as an "ouverture sur un milieu (solitaire en soi)." This milieu is the space of theater. It comprises an "avant mystérieux" (the proscenium, which is in front of the curtain), a "fond" (stage rear), and the "salle" (space of the audience), which is designated as equal to the *fond*, "fond = salle" [20 (A)]. The intermission reveals the identity between these contrary spaces. During the *entracte* the curtain closes, coming *between* the *avant mystérieux* and the *fond* and thus causing a "confusion des deux / avec interruption du fond ouvert" [20 (A)]. Similarly, the *entracte* serves as a temporal bridge for the audience; it both prepares them for, and reminds them of, the primary spectacle in which the *entracte* is inscribed: "préparation à la fête . . . (rappel de la fête (regrets, etc.)" [20 (A)]. The *entracte* also provides the audience with a sense of unity in action, for it is itself a spectacle framed by the rising and falling of the curtain: "l'action dans le fond—reprenant [le spectacle] où on le quitte" [20 (A)]. This intermediary performance functions as a mirror image of the spectacle it interrupts; it reveals the identity between itself, the activity of the spectators in the *salle,* and that of the primary spectacle (the mythic representation) remaining in the background, the *fond:*

> et   lever du rideau—chûte [*sic*]   salle
>   et fond
>   Correspond à <u>fond</u>   l'au dela
>   et <u>avant</u> mystérieux—correspond à
>   ce qui cache le <u>fond</u> (toile, etc.) en fait le
>   mystère—
>   (20 [A])

Not surprisingly, the performance occurring during the *entracte* appears to be a dance.[15] Although dancers are not explicitly mentioned at this point in the manuscript, their presence was just evoked in a parenthesis toward the end of the first part of the myth ("un bras bas, un / autre levé, attitude de / danseuse"). Their presence in the *entracte* is, moreover, further suggested by the term "arabesque" and the series "déchirure sacrée du voile," which link the functional value of dance (as described in Mallarmé's prose) to that of the previously described *entracte.*

>   l'arabesque électrique
>   s'allume derrière—et les deux
>   voiles
>   —sorte de déchirure sacrée du
>   voile, écrite là—ou déchire—
>   et deux êtres à la fois oiseau
>   et parfum—semblable aux deux d'en
>   chaire
>   haut (balcon) com
>   ———————————————————————
>   l'œuf   église
>   (21 [A])

Dance functions similarly to the intermission, for Mallarmé, because it creates an opening within the spectacle in two senses. It permits the penetration of the spectacle's mystery, and it provides a pause—an opportunity for rest and regeneration. Recall that in the closing phrases of "Ballets," for example, the dancer is presented as transporting the spectator across a veil, a metonym of mystery symbolizing the identity-indifference between the dance-step signifiers and their signifieds:

---

15. Up until Mallarmé's time ballets were, of course, most often presented as *entractes.*

> par un commerce dont paraît son sourire verser le secret, sans
> tarder elle te livre à travers le voile dernier qui toujours reste, la
> nudité de tes concepts et silencieusement écrira ta vision à la
> façon d'un Signe, qu'elle est. (307)

In the essay "Parenthèse," dance assumes the function of a pause.[16] Like
Symbolist poetry (in essays such as "L'Action restreinte"), dance is pre-
sented as the misunderstood art of an "interrègne," and the dancer, still
waiting in the wings to reappear, as the supreme force in the purification
and preparation of the Theater of the future: "Cependant non loin, le
lavage à grande eau musical du Temple ... ne l'entendez vous pas? dont
la Danseuse restaurée mais encore invisible à des préparatoires cérémo-
nies, semble la mouvante écume suprême" (322).

This representation of an *entracte* in "le mythe des deux femmes"
gives way (not yet to the second act but) to other notes describing, in a
more mythical language, the site where the action takes place. There are
references to the disclosure of a mystery, "les clefs du sans borne" in a
"Vision magnifique et triste" [22 (A)]. The Vision is that of a grand
theater described as "Les restes d'un grand palais, —grand comme une
ville—ou d'une ville unie comme un seul palais," also as a "nef, ville
flottante ... ville du poète futur" [22 (A)]. This "nef" is a syllepsis
referring both to the ship as vehicle of the venturing poet (who leads the
people) and to the nave of the church. Underneath the note representing
the *entracte* (beginning "l'arabesque électrique ...") the terms "l'œuf"
and "église" also refer to this site of revelation [21 (A)]. In the essays
entitled "Offices" and, in passing, in other critical essays (such as the one
quoted above from "Parenthèse") Mallarmé refers to the Theater of the
future as a church, or "temple"; he also refers to it as an "œuf." In the
essay "Crayonné au théâtre," contemporary theater is labeled a "sim-
ulacrum" of the "célébration des poëmes étouffés dans l'œuf de quelque
future coupole" (298). The current theater is a mere simulacrum of the
œuf-église, because while the ignorant spectators go to see themselves
represented there, they do not perceive the Vision they seek, that of the
mystery or divinity the crowd holds within. Their reflection in the
theater does not constitute for them a "divinity" but, rather, its "*image-
rie* brute" (emphasis mine, 298).

In the manuscript notes the "Vision magnifique" is presented as inac-
cessible (this is why the vision is also "sad"), as beyond the reach of a
"peuple maudit" who come to sit before their image and yet sleep,

---

16. The title is a syllepsis alluding to this function as well as to the fact that for two years no
ballets had been shown at the Eden Theater where Mallarmé had enjoyed seeing them.

refusing to see themselves. "Tout ce qu'on sait, c'est qu'elle / gît en le passé ténébreux— / . . . à moins qu'elle ne gise en / l'avenir—fermé aux / yeux humains, là / au fond / Devant—double fontaine, ou son / rêve / peuple maudit—qui dort—, ne / vient plus se mirer* / * dans le regard de son orgueil immense" [22–23 (A)].

It seems that the poet, who is a seer, cannot reveal to the people the secret of his Vision (that is, the mystery of the spectacle) or explain to them the meaning of their "modern" apathy toward it, although they beseech him to do so: "Moderne est ce calme—homme dompteur—dis-nous le secret" [24 (A)]. At this point in the notes our attention is abruptly returned to the resumption of the spectacle, "le mythe des deux femmes," which the *entracte* had equally abruptly interrupted. The ballet interlude gives way to a more prosaic and tangible demonstration of the same principle of reversibility and identity-in-difference exposed in the first part of the myth:

—Pendant ce temps-là—rideau
dioramique s'est aprofondi [*sic*]—ombre
de plus en plus forte, comme creusé
par elle—par le mystère—

(24 [A])

A protective curtain, which functioned as a "store" (awning or blind), inverts, or "annuls," itself into a dioramic scene deepened by its own mystery. Now we see clearly wild animals, previously "entrevues" "sur le fond de store," owing to the opening of the *voile* in the *entracte:*

Le store s'est annulé—avec—
les acquêts que ne pouvait rendre la
musique et qui sont là, éléphants, etc.

(24 [A])

Les bêtes sauvages ont été vues en
effet sur le fond de store, dans
ce repos (et n'ont point oser [*sic*] y
feu
entrer—

(25 [A])

The second act of the spectacle now crystallizes as a circus in stage rear. There, wild beasts who were frightened to come forward during the *entracte* demonstrate their ability to jump through and across dangerous barriers, symbolized by hoops of fire and snakes. In doing so they mime, in a more concrete fashion, the interaction between the two women in the first part of the myth. In spite of their ignorance and fear, they cross through an empty barrier in order to join one another and to grasp thereby their reward, a "parcelle" (perhaps an invisible piece of meat, bestial equivalent of the two women's diamond), which they feel rightfully belongs to them: "elles ont comme aperçues [*sic*] une parcelle à elles, mais invisibles, et ont sauté—par deux fois—comme l'une contre l'autre . . . sauté à travers les anneaux / mobiles des / du serpent, pour montrer que pas de glace là" [25 (A)]. Once the animals have crossed one another, jumping from one side to the other of the barrier, and have thus proved the hollowness of its center, they appear to be pacified and tamed. They come forward from the background (*le fond*) carrying "ces deux femmes idéales," whom, we recall, the hero's mind had formerly subjected to a similar, though more "ideal," or intangible, "entrelacement" through an equally empty center [26 (A)].

On the last pages of this sequence the "bêtes sauvages" are associated with both the heroines of the myth, "ces deux femmes," and the theatrical public. Like the two women and the spectators, they constitute the center of the spectacle yet are ignorant of the role they play there: "les bêtes ignorantes mais au milieu" [25 (A)]. And, like the bear in *La bête et le génie* (a performance at "le petit théâtre de prodigalités" described in Mallarmé's prose poem "Un spectacle interrompu"), these beasts mime the attitude both of the puppet-hero (or, in this case, heroines) and the real hero, the crowd of spectators, "bêtes sur deux pattes, exprimant le désir de voir" [26 (A)].[17]

The unifying feature in the very disparate parts, or stages, of "le mythe des deux femmes" is their repeated presentation of the identity and reversibility of the various elements that make up theater. We have seen, for example, the identity and interchangeability of the characters (the two women and the hero); of the primary spectacle and the *entracte;* of

17. In the prose poem, the spectacle is interrupted when a dancing bear rises on its hind legs in an attempt to discover the meaning of the "génie['s]" gesture: "Au geste du pantin, une paume crispée dans l'air ouvrant les cinq doigts, je compris, qu'il avait, l'ingénieux! capté les sympathies par la mine d'attraper au vol quelque chose, figure (et c'est tout) de la facilité dont est par chacun prise une idée: et qu'ému au léger vent, l'ours rythmiquement et doucement levé interrogeait cet exploit, une griffe posée sur les rubans de l'épaule humaine. Personne qui ne haletât, tant cette situation portait de conséquences graves pour l'honneur de la race: qu'allait-il arriver? L'autre patte s'abattit, souple, contre un bras longeant le maillot; et l'on vit, couple uni dans un secret rapprochement, comme un homme inférieur, trapu, bon, debout sur l'écartement de deux jambes de poil, étreindre pour y apprendre les pratiques du génie, et son crâne au noir museau ne l'atteignant qu'à la moitié, le buste de son frère brillant et surnaturel" (Mallarmé 1945, 277).

the stage and the hall, or house; and of the roles played by the actors and spectators.

This last form of identity and reversibility, the exchange between the performer and the public, constitutes the central theme in the third and fourth myths, which are similar in imagery and structure. Both fragments describe a sacrifice in a theater. The hero exchanges himself (and his attributes) for the public (and their attributes) in view of their mutual redemption.

In the third myth, which concerns "le truc de la mort de faim," an old man is portrayed as suffering from various forms of torture and deprivation; these are most often referred to in terms of carnal desire—"hunger"—and spiritual desire—"thirst." This basic opposition arises at several points: "faim et amour de cieux" and "faim de ta chair soif de tes yeux." The old man hesitates over which of these needs he should attend to and questions whether both can be satisfied in the theater:

> tandis que meurt de
> faim
> ou +
>
> doute, tout est là
>   n'a qu'un louis!
>   hésite (dîner)
> les deux   ou
>   en Th?,   boit
>   (27 [A])

He opts to go into "le truc de la mort de faim," which I read as a metaphor for the Book, as theater/text. Theater feeds the public's hunger, as Mallarmé remarks twice in the essay "Crayonné au théâtre." Recall that toward the beginning of the article he refers to the theater as "le trou magnifique ou l'attente qui, comme une faim, se creuse chaque soir" (294). And he returns to this hunger imagery toward the end: "il a fallu formidablement, pour l'infatuation contemporaine, ériger, entre le gouffre de vaine faim et les générations, un simulacre [du Théâtre] approprié au besoin immédiat" (298). While there are no further direct references to theater in the fragment, we find several references to its various elements and functions as Mallarmé describes them in relation to the Book.

The old man's burial in a "tomb" appears, at first, to be his sole means of access to fulfillment, but this tomb is not really a permanent grave but, rather, a "truc": a (closed) tomb/Book that is simultaneously open, like a Theater. (In "Le livre, instrument spirituel," we saw that the volume was referred to as a *tombeau*.)

> aller—«dans le truc de la mort de
> faim»
>
> si—etc|foule|supplice ignoré
>   ici
> jusqu'à la tombe inclu-
> sivement
>   elle est—et pas
>   elle est fictivement, condi-
>   tionnelle   (littérairement)
>   il s'y met pour montrer
> ce qui adviendrait si . . .
>   (28 [A])

The old man feels that he must physically cloister himself, that the tomb must be covered (or closed) so that he can achieve a spiritual renaissance:

>   mais elle doit se
>   (selon lui, car|
> couvrir { |mort de faim lui donne droit
>   (à recommencer . . .
>   (28 [A])

Thus, he physically shuts himself off, "c.-à-d. s'être fait comme prêtre privé de tout" [29 (A)], and deprives himself of carnal knowledge—that is, of women and of the experience of procreation: "prêtre doit ignorer, pour gloire humaine, le mystère de la femme—d'où (enfant dans les jambes) tout se résoudra par cela" [29 (A)]. This corporeal confinement is conceived of as only partial, "sorte de claustration 1/2," for it does not restrict his mind; on the contrary it is in the *tombe*/Book that he gains access to the spiritual mystery, "libre pensée en soi" [29 (A)].

As we recall, however, the old man had two different needs to fulfill, and this corporeal confinement meets only the first. He cannot fully penetrate the mystery without fulfilling his bodily needs as well, his desire for food and women. In order to do this he must bring another into the tomb, another who has the carnal knowledge he now lacks and who will exchange it for the spiritual knowledge of the old man/priest:

mais le truc (d'où : à nous deux, etc.)
est que pas trouvé le mystère cherché (si pas aidé, foule?)
et que ce n'est que là en tombe qu'il peut le trouver
(30 [A])

This other who comes to his rescue is a younger avatar of himself, and an "ouvrier," ambassador of the (spiritually) ignorant "foule."[18] He, too, desires access to the tomb ("le truc de la mort de faim") and dreams of setting it in motion, "pour savoir le mystère":

d'où———
          d'autre part il faut que jeune *
          en lui se livrant au rêve de mettre en branle
                    la grande machine, un ouvrier
     * homme—   mais qui
     n'est que vieux—   vienne
     en tombe   (y ensevelissant fiancée
prêtre—claustration
     inconnue)   pour savoir
     mystère, avant de se marier
     —que dire à enfanter
(30 [A])

Among other things, this myth can be understood as an allegory of the relationship between the text and theater in the Book. We have seen elsewhere in the manuscript that terms like *tombe* (e.g., *cloître* and *bloc*) refer to the text as Book. And we know that Mallarmé often refers to the literary text as a tomb.[19] It is likely that "la grande machine" here refers to theater, that "machine crue" that Mallarmé (in *Crayonné au théâtre*) describes as a mechanism causing insatiable hunger (298) and as "la majestueuse ouverture sur le mystère" (314). Moreover, there is a clear correlation between theater as public outlet for the claustral Book and the *vieillard/prêtre*'s escape from his *tombe,* thanks to the presence of the *foule/ouvrier.* Thus, the latter might be understood as playing the role of the public in the Work, and the former as playing that of the *opérateur.* In the *séances*, the Book is brought to life, "mis en branle," by virtue of an exchange between the "operator" and his public, serving their mutual benefit.

18. In "Conflit" Mallarmé describes the similarities and differences between the worker and the writer/intellectual. They work together to build a better future, to create something "qui puisse servir, parmi l'échange général," but the labor of the intellectual is "transféré[e] des bras à la tête" (Mallarmé 1945, 358).
19. Cf. note 11 above, the many *tombeaux* poems, and *Pour un tombeau d'Anatole.*

Indeed, the remaining notes in this mythic sequence describe the dual hero's effort to assemble and fulfill the contrary desires of the opposite faces of himself, "unissons nos deux besoins." This is achieved through the exchange of the two parts of the Mystery known to the *ouvrier/foule* and the *vieillard/prêtre*. It is important to note that these desires are never fulfilled except through an exchange of the one for the other. There is a constant reversal of roles between the *vieillard/prêtre* and the *ouvrier/enfant*. They deliver each other from the tomb in a cycle that appears to have no term:

———source—vieillard
lutte—et là le tout joué
          ouvrier laissé
     vieux échappé—

(30 [A])

jusqu'à ce qu'enfant qu'il avait en lui
(ouvrier) * au lieu de prêtre—qui
souffre indument de cette claustration—
          de
a faim et soif (colère) se plaint au nom
de justice, d'être ainsi cloîtré en le
prêtre—prêtre (chaste et mort de faim) chaste
enfant en lui—mort de faim, vieux.

     * revienne l'en tirer. . . .
de mystère qu'on ne peut savoir
qu'en l'accomplissant—amour—
preuve—enfant

(33 [A])

Significantly, the child who will ultimately unite (or synthesize) these two characters and who holds the solution to the Mystery is not yet born.

The fourth myth, "le mythe de l'Invitation," presents a similar scenario. Two characters come together and consume each other—they are represented as literally eating each other—in a theater. This narrative fragment is far briefer than those preceding (the notes describing it occupy only one double page), but it summarizes well the elements in the other three myths.

In this myth the hero once again finds himself in a "Cité/Théâtre" in which he would have performed what is variously referred to as a marriage ceremony, "fête—(noces)," a "Dr," an "Opération," and a "crime."

He was invited there by a lady who unknowingly inspired him to come and perform his act. Respecting the naïveté and candor of his hostess, the hero accordingly does not perform the act:

Il se trouve dans un endroit-Cité-où | dont il eût fait la
                                                                              fête—(noces)

                                              Th | Dr

L'exploit qui devait lui rapporter de la gloire | est un crime : il s'arrête à

temps en cette Opération; dont c'est un miracle que l'Invitation si bien comprise par lui, || ait suffi à la dame qui la lui fit à son insu peut-être.   lueur
⌈ de celle qui la lui inspirait ⌉ génie. farce   —

                                                                                       (169 [A])

If we look to Mallarmé's critical essays, we find several clues to the identity of this lady. In "Crayonné au théâtre" the poet invites a lady to the theater. She is a personification of his soul: "ô mon âme . . . une si exquise dame" (293). In "Le mystère dans les lettres" the lady, who reacts impetuously to the obscurity of the text, personifies the public, "la Foule (où inclus le Génie) . . . notre Dame et Patronne" (383). Thus, the lady in question here might be perceived as a personification of the soul of the poet, of the crowd, or both. This last interpretation equates the poet with the crowd. It seems the most plausible, as Mallarmé considers the poet and crowd identical in that they are guardians of Mystery (the former guards the mystery expressed in literature by writing obscure verse, and the latter guards that expressed in music by using its own "riche mutisme" to protect music's secrecy or refusal to signify); "La foule qui commence à tant nous surprendre comme élément vierge, ou nous-mêmes, remplit envers les sons, sa fonction par excellence de gardienne du mystère" (390).

Given the innocent character of the lady's invitation (she does not know what she is inviting him to do), the hero wonders how he ought to respond:

                                    mais laisser l'Invitation sans y répondre
                                             ordre

et que la dame ait eu peur de ce   fut-ce Non.
qu'elle venait lui faire. A son insu   on ne peut—   alors qu'elle s'est à ce
peut-être. S'accorde. chapeau   point livrée à lui est
                il la couvre   un vol. que cela pris
                  en soi⌋

                                              opération | qui n'est
                                              (169 [A])

Respecting the woman's fear of her own gesture, the ambivalence of "l'Invitation," the hero responds in a manner similar to that of the character in "le mythe de l'appel." He performs an act, or operation, that is not one: "une opération / qui n'est," "Opération * / crime serment? / * qui n'est ni. ni." [169 (A)]. His decision is to withhold the aspect of the mystery that is under his jurisdiction. Indeed, he shows the same "pudeur" as the woman and does not expose to her his "esprit"; rather, he covers his head with his hat: "on n'a / jamais pu savoir que- / + chapeau éclate soleil," "S'accorde. chapeau / il la couvre / en soi" [169 (A)]. Thus, he performs his "opération" in a manner congruent with the limited terms of the lady's invitation: "Invitation à fête / à tout excepté au repas d'où sa faim" [169 (A)].

In this myth, as in the preceding one, two characters attempt an exchange of either aspect of a Mystery uniting the spiritual and the physical, the sacred and profane. Here, the lady offers but withholds her food, and the hero does the same with the brilliant mind ("le soleil") he holds under his hat. In this they are presented as safeguarding the Mystery and as abiding by its "loi," which dictates an insatiable hunger. In this fragment (as in the preceding one) the Mystery is described as a "truc de la mort de faim." Mystery hides and consumes itself, even as it reveals and feeds itself: "La loi se tait / S'il est une / loi c'est celle-là / mange- puisqu'on mourrait sans manger / n'ose se montrer telle elle se voile" [169 (A)]. He who would know an end to mystery or hunger is forced to consume the object of his desire. Thus, while it is preposterous, it is not altogether illogical that the hero finally consumes the lady ("la foule") who withheld from him her food. The hero eats the lady, a meal for which he pays the price of 20 francs: "manger la dame / 20 f. pour elle" [169 (A)]. Since the lady personifies the public, the resurgence of diagrams (within these notes) assembling terms referring to public places, activities, and ceremonies makes sense. The terms listed might each represent a portion of what the hero will have consumed in eating his hostess:

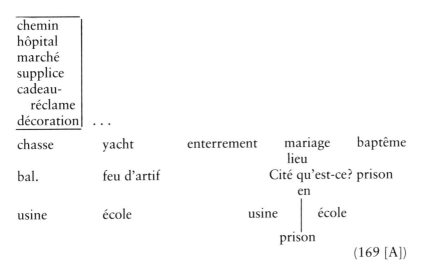

(169 [A])

If this myth is to reveal, like the others, a certain reciprocity, we must find what the lady (crowd) will consume in exchange for her sacrifice. Logically, this food would be the hero or would consist of that portion of the mystery lying under his jurisdiction (symbolically his hat)—that is, the knowledge resulting from his *opération*. On the next page of the manuscript, the notes pertaining to this mythic sequence give way to notes referring to the formal or material aspects of the *séances*, the public reading of the Book. These notes are definitely related to "le mythe de l'Invitation"; but in them the roles of the performer and *la foule* are reversed. It is the operator who extends a restricted Invitation to the public; they would pay 20 francs (the price of the lady, the performer's meal in the myth) for the right to be read the Book. The price of this Invitation is given in the context of a discussion of the number and placement of spectators at the "Lect. / séance" [170 (A)]. The public does not understand what it has paid for, but it gets the operator (or the Book's performer) along with its seats:

12 places doubles
comme si Personne—
et le lecteur   y est le même ici et là,
(ce qui suffit)   non 13ᵉ, 25ᵉ.
ou tenant |

ou I part, | l'ensemble ici,
Personne   lequel n'a de rap-   [soit 20 feuilles
n'entend   port direct avec   à l f
rien   leur nombre   * * * 20 fr × 12 =
                  présent ou pas,   240 f* *
                  mais avec le prix
                  fictif
                  de l'Invitation
                  mais repose
                  sur le prix
                  d'invitation * * *

                                              (170 [A])

    This striking interpenetration of notes developing the poetic content of the Book and notes describing its theatrical presentation points clearly to the inseparability of its literary and theatrical states. So significant and all-pervasive are the references to performance in Mallarmé's projected Masterwork that a basic understanding of these references provides considerable insight into both the general thrust and detail of its seemingly impenetrable poetic content. Thus, it is especially unfortunate that the references to theater in Le Livre have been largely neglected, as they have in the ensemble of Mallarmé's corpus.

    Even Scherer, who as an eminent scholar of French classical theater is particularly interested in Mallarmé's concept of theater, concludes that Mallarmé's Book is a purely textual phenomenon with little relation to actual theater. Although he thoughtfully discusses Mallarmé's theatrical criticism in his introduction to Le Livre and correctly states that "théâtre et livre ne sont que des traductions équivalentes de l'Œuvre" (Scherer 1957, 35), he finally strives to eradicate all that is specifically theatrical from Mallarmé's ideal theater and also from his ideal Work.

    Le Théâtre parfait selon Mallarmé se refuse à l'efficacité de l'auteur, à l'activité des personnages, à l'intérêt de l'action, à la réalité du temps, à l'utilité de la représentation: une fois qu'il est ainsi dépouillé, il est aisé de l'identifier au Livre. (42–43)

Like Suzanne Bernard (1959), who divests Mallarmé's concept of music from all that is properly musical (in order to preserve his image as a literary purist), Scherer constantly empties Mallarmé's theater of its theatricality in order to flatten, or neutralize, the difference between his conceptions of literature and theatrical performance, "un théâtre vidé de sa réalité concrète et qui n'est plus qu'allusion à la totalité du monde rejoint le Livre parfait" (27).

Scherer (like Bernard and others) readily concedes that theater has, for Mallarmé, one important advantage over literature in that it allows live communication and "communion" with the public:

> Et pourtant, il faut bien qu'il y ait dans le théâtre quelque vertu qui ne se trouve point dans le livre, sans quoi Mallarmé n'aurait pas consacré tant de pages à en élaborer la notion. Il n'aurait pas proclamé comme il l'a fait, péremptoire: "Le Théâtre est d'essence supérieure."
>
> Cette vertu est de communion, et sa nature est quasi religieuse. Le livre est solitaire. Le théâtre ne serait au fond qu'un livre mais il est social; et sur les hommes assemblés peut passer un souffle de grandeur, qui les exalte et les édifie. (43)

Indeed, taking part in the communion that all theatrical experiences provide was undoubtedly one of Mallarmé's primary aims. But reference to this general objective sheds little light on the peculiar nature of his theatrical project. It does not explain his unprecedented combination of text and performance as reciprocal proofs of the Book, nor does it explain the extraordinarily literal "communion" (or partaking in each other) of these two modes of expression in every aspect of the manuscript. Moreover, to concede with Scherer that the Book would have acquired for itself some kind of performance and through its performance, a communion with the public is to concede (contrary to Scherer's conclusion) that the Book would not have been devoid of theater in its "concrete reality." If, as Scherer suggests, the Book was to have been so divested of everything properly theatrical, we must ask ourselves how its communion with the public would have come about. Would it not have depended on precisely those elements that define theater and distinguish it from literature: the presence of an interpreting persona ("l'activité des personnages"), the unfolding of an action in time and space ("l'intérêt de l'action, la réalité du temps, l'utilité de la représentation")? The public's communion in the Book would, of course, have depended on all these things. Scherer (1977) must have realized this also, for although he divests the Book of all theatricality at one point, at another he clearly states that the Book employs, in order to communicate and establish its cult, not literary but theatrical devices: "Ce culte, il reviendra au Livre de l'organiser, en utilisant *tout ce qu'il peut y avoir d'efficacité affective dans l'action dramatique*" (emphasis mine, 45).

There is an underlying paradox in the Book's presentation that causes this kind of contradiction. It generally presents itself as a theatrical representation and a text, as (integrally) half the former and half the latter, not as the finished product of their synthesis. This unfinished totality of the Book cannot be explained away; it can only be recognized as such. The Book may well be difficult to imagine in either literary or theatrical terms, but its ubiquitous articulations of the principles of unity-in-duality and identity-in-difference help to explain, at least, Mallarmé's persistent references to the Work's dual nature, his constant presentation of the Book (in the manuscript and elsewhere) as partaking of two different states, or modes of being, one textual and the other performative.

The Book retains its status as literature. It would have been published and distributed like any other text, and in its bound form ("le bloc," "coffret," "tombeau"), it would indeed have been devoid of any theatrical element. We saw that, for Mallarmé, the bareness, or material simplicity, of black on white is a *necessary* condition of literature if it is to preserve its self-sufficient representational character, its singular autonomy in relation to the tangible world: "la littérature existe et, si l'on veut, seule, à l'exception de tout" (647). For Mallarmé, "Un livre ne remplace tout que faute de tout" (cited in Delfel 1951, 123). Because the text *replaces* things, it neither tolerates nor requires any complement: "Je suis pour—aucune illustration, tout ce qu'évoque un livre devant se passer dans l'esprit du lecteur" (878).

But the text does not substitute itself for the world merely by naming things. It accomplishes this substitution by affectively evoking, or calling forth, the referents replaced.

> *Nommer* un objet, c'est supprimer les trois-quarts de la jouissance du poëme qui est faite de deviner peu à peu: le *suggérer*, voilà le rêve. . . . Il doit y avoir toujours énigme en poésie, et c'est le but de la littérature, —il n'y en a pas d'autres—d'*évoquer* les objets. (869)

As we have seen throughout this study, Mallarmé's theory of poetic evocation is itself highly enigmatic, for his texts relate to referents that they simultaneously deny and suggest. His poetic texts curiously demonstrate their mimetic ability, their representational efficacity, by re-creating for the reader that which is not present within them, by supplying referents that the poems themselves are not. *Le Livre*, along with the poems and essays earlier examined, confirms that it is the tangible, sense-oriented aspect of "reality" that Mallarmé's texts attempt to supply in their evocation of the performing arts.

What is the difference between *Le Livre* and Mallarmé's other texts containing references to music, dance, and theater? *Le Livre* not only refers to supplementary theatrical performances but concretely projects them. In his plan for a Text that would show itself adequate to expressing totality, we see an important evolution in his aesthetic ambition: he shifts from the plane of representing performances to the beginning stages of producing them.

The various diagrams in the manuscript show that Mallarmé indeed dreamed of employing for the Book's performance "tout ce qu'il peut y avoir d'efficacité dans l'action dramatique" (Scherer 1977, 45). The bare, published text is said to be founded upon a "Pièce / ou / cette représentation avec concert / dialogue poème et symphonie pour scène et orch—" [171 (A)]. More significant than the alternative existence of these two seemingly contrary aspects of the Book is the fact that each aspect (text and performance) is presented as always *already* occupying the space of the other, as containing its contrary aspect within itself.

The theatrical "représentation" contains, indeed revolves around, a literary aspect, the reading of the unbound text (it is a "pièce," "dialogue poème"), and the signifying process of the (literal) text appears to be similarly dependent on an element of performance: "Rien ne sort que des séances" [130 (A)]. The reading *séances* of the Book, of course, constitute performances in and of themselves. As such, they are considered to compose a third genre, "livre suprême," i.e., a kind of absolute genre (like "le Verbe") *resulting* from the juxtaposition of the textual and theatrical aspects of the Book: "les Lectures seraient à proprement / parler le 3ᵉ genre qu'on tire de ce qui reste (ou / ballets-parades. articles-chansons) issu par / deux fois de cette juxtaposition (d'où 2 séries de Lectures)" [106 (A)].

These reading performances are not as stripped of theatricality as Scherer's understated presentation of them suggests: "Dans ce décor, Mallarmé ne peut se retenir d'imaginer, avec beaucoup de discrétion, des gestes d'acteur, et un minimum de mise en scène" (72). The staging of the *séances* is carefully plotted out, including indications as to lighting ("le lustre" or "la lampe électrique unique"—the fact that these are interchangeable is, of course, symbolic of the principle that unity and plurality are identical), props ("le meuble de laque"), sound effects ("timbre"), and the gestures of the *opérateur,* for example:

Il montre ceci, changeant
le feuillet intérieur de l'une à
l'autre feuille   soit les premières
deux, les deux secondes et troisièmes
posées momentanément à part, lit.

⌐à moins que ne se retournant par trois fois
vers la gauche. (sourire–patientez) à qui apparaît
mieux cet acte successif—un peu voilé pour la droite
   il ne prenne successivement les feuilles.⌐

                     ⌐jusqu'au moment
   ou le tout rejoint, l'opérateur, s'élance
droit devant lui, d'où il vient, emportant
   s'y identifiant
(vers la voix qui lut) ce fascicule comme
        pour chacun.
à lui

                              (193–94 [A])

These *séances* have three major purposes. One is to animate the text: "le volume malgré, l'impression fixe, devient par ce jeu, mobile—de mort il devient vie" [191 (A)]. A second is to demonstrate the absolute principle of identity-in-difference by juxtaposing and equating every aspect of the text to itself. Finally, the *séances* authenticate, or validate, the truth of this demonstration through the presence of witnesses: "on ne prouve que quant aux autres" [189 (A)].

Thus, while the Book is a literary monument, a text, it does not reject those paratextual elements that complete the theatrical work. On the contrary, what is exceptional about the Book is that it actually annexes these elements in the process of its being read. The Book is tied to space, not textual space (as in Derrida's "espacement de l'écriture") but theatrical space, since it takes place there as the operator performs the various permutations of its pages on stage. The Book incorporates a temporal factor by presenting itself during a specified period of time in the double *séances* that were to occur at various dates spread through five calendar years ("5 ans. le lustre") [50 (B)]. The Book presents itself as dependent on gestures or the operations of its interpreter, who employs mime as well as language to communicate its meaning. Finally and most important, the Book binds itself to a performer, the operator, who (because he is impersonal) is identifiable with every member of the crowd. Because of this appropriation of the fundamental elements of theatrical performance, the Book is capable not only of suggesting the total theater that it represents but also of *reproducing* it. By juxtaposing and identifying itself to its performative counterpart, the text validates its own representational efficacity. In short, it *proves* the authenticity of its literary representations by becoming a performance.

The need for a literature that proves itself is a consequence of the dual nature of the self. In the essay "L'Action restreinte," which presents itself as an intimate dialogue with a young friend, Mallarmé affirms that the writer must cross the space that appears to separate his mental and physical life. Being human, the writer needs to exercise his body as well as his mind. He has to have a physical outlet, to perform an exteriorized act testifying to his corporeal existence and corresponding to the transcription of his thoughts on paper. In other words, if the writer is to find in the world full testimony to his own existence, he cannot only write, he must also dance:

> Plusieurs fois vint un Camarade, le même, cet autre, me confier le besoin d'agir: que visait-il. . . .
>
> Se détendre les poings, en rupture de songe sédentaire, pour un trépignant vis-à-vis avec l'idée, ainsi qu'une envie prend ou bouger: mais la génération semble peu agitée, outre le désintéressement politique, du souci d'extravaguer du corps. . . .
>
> Agir . . . signifia, visiteur, je te comprends, philosophiquement, produire sur beaucoup un mouvement qui te donne en retour l'émoi que tu en fus le principe, donc existes: dont aucun ne se croit, au préalable, sûr. (369)

The only physical mode of action available to the poet is theatrical, since, as artist and metaphysician, he has chosen to sacrifice himself (and his worldly ambitions) to live in a world of absolutes, to contemplate and experience "les phénomènes ou l'univers" (294). In the theater the poet must subject himself to the same depersonalization, the same total commitment of self, to which he submits himself in the text: "L'écrivain, de ses maux, dragons qu'il a choyés, ou d'une allégresse, doit s'instituer au texte, le spirituel histrion" (370).

Through theatrical action and through writing, the artist transforms himself into an Other. His art is a scene of self-sacrifice in which he is resurrected, either as a "spirituel histrion" (the fragile, intangible, image of self transcribed on paper) or as an acting body transposed, a corporeal presence "en l'ordre réel" (here, the real refers to the theater as tangible, sense-perceived world):

Plancher, lustre, obnubilation des tissus et liquéfaction de miroirs gazée en l'ordre réel, jusqu'aux bonds excessifs de notre forme autour d'un arrêt, sur pied, de la virile stature, un Lieu se présente, scène, majoration devant tous du spectacle de Soi; là, en raison des intermédiaires de la lumière, de la chair et des rires le sacrifice qu'y fait, relativement à sa personnalité, l'inspirateur, aboutit complet ou c'est, dans une résurrection étrangère, fini de celui-ci: de qui le verbe répercuté et vain désormais s'exhale par la chimère orchestrale.

Une salle, il se célèbre, anonyme, dans le héros.

Tout, comme fonctionnement de fêtes: un peuple témoigne de sa transfiguration en vérité. (370–71)[20]

Significantly, Mallarmé deems this bodily resurrection of the hero to be self-sufficient, or complete. In performance the verbal expression of the writer is "vain," because his text is echoed in music, a nonverbal form: "le verbe répercuté et vain désormais s'exhale par la chimère orchestrale." It is the possible transformation (or translation) of text into performance, and vice versa, that affirms the self-sufficiency of each expressive mode.

Once the identity of literature and the performing arts has been proved through such an exchange, there is no longer any need for verbal expression in the performing arts or for the performing art in literature. The transposition has confirmed that they constitute different yet equal signifying systems. Mallarmé conserves a difference between the mind and the body and between their respective media of expression— literature and the performing arts—because this difference has, for him, an important functional value. It provides the *décalage* necessary for the discovery of a Mystery never resolved, the identity of the human Self. He presents mind and body, literature and the performing arts, and indeed all contraries as different yet identical, separate yet inseparable, as two faces of one and the same reality, one reality that can only be *perceived* as two.

Thus, it is not surprising that in "L'Action restreinte" he combines theater and literature in accordance with the text/performance model

20. This description of the sacrificial transfiguration of the hero closely resembles Mallarmé's description of Loïe Fuller's veil dance earlier discussed: "Ainsi ce dégagement multiple autour d'une nudité, grand des contradictoires vols où celle-ci l'ordonne, orageux, planant l'y magnifie jusqu'à la dissoudre: centrale, car tout obéit à une impulsion fugace en tourbillons, elle résume, par le vouloir aux extrémités éperdu de chaque aile et darde sa statuette, stricte, debout—morte de l'effort à condenser hors d'une libération presque d'elle des sursautements attardés décoratifs de cieux, de mer, de soirs, de parfum et d'écume" (1945, 309).

described earlier in "La musique et les lettres." Theater is not presented here as the complement of the text but, rather, as its "point d'aboutissement," its culmination and vanishing point: "Ainsi l'Action, en le mode convenu, littéraire, ne transgresse pas le Théâtre; s'y limite, à la représentation—*immédiat évanouissement de l'écrit*" (emphasis mine, 370).

In the preceding chapter, we saw the application of this same model of text/performance combination in reverse; that is, Mallarmé's poetic texts presented themselves as the vanishing points of theater.

Mallarmé's "musical" and "theatrical" poetic texts and *Le Livre* seem to test the value and viability of the self-restriction (or self-limitation) of various artistic modes in an aesthetic that aims, paradoxically, to express totality. In the case of *Le Livre* this testing is clearly a metaphysical enterprise. The reciprocal transposition of text and performance is undertaken in view of an "explication de l'homme" (875), an "explication orphique de la Terre" (663). It is only by mediating, or working through, the difference separating mental and physical life that Mallarmé perceives the artist as fully resurrecting himself in the world and providing proof of his own and the world's existence. In *Le Livre* this proof is attempted.

The mediation of difference between mind and body, thinking and living, word and deed, was also the functional operation of ritual as defined in the first chapter of this study. As in the case of Mallarmé's Book, the purpose of ritual in general, we recall, is not only (like that of myth) to symbolize the world as the human mind perceives it but also to tangibly *re-create* it. The Book is a striking example of how ritual (as the performance or enactment of myth) seeks to cross the barrier between mental structures and physical forms, between thoughts and gestures, between text and performance. It is also a paradigm of ritual in its ambition to constitute the line between fiction and reality, to represent itself as true.

Like every statement in *Le Livre,* Mallarmé's notorious proposition that "tout, au monde, existe pour aboutir à un livre" proves itself true in reverse; the obvious function of the Book's performance is to show that *un livre existe pour aboutir à tout au monde.* It is clear that once linked to the totality of man's world through its performance in the Theater, the Book transgresses the boundaries of ordinary literature and assumes the character of ritual: it symbolizes, constitutes, and consecrates the human experience of Truth.

Le Livre should thus be understood as representing a major breaking point in two related ideologies that Mallarmé has long been considered to embody: literary purism and "art for art's sake." This manuscript represents a radically new experiment. It is a literature fundamentally impure and an art that embraces the totality of human life. Although it cries out the death of God and the disintegration of culture, *Le Livre* is the unfinished Work of a *religio,* a rebinding of the "relations entre tout" (378). As Mallarmé wrote about the symphony, "il ne s'agit d'esthétique, mais de religiosité" (388).

CHAPTER TWELVE

Avant-Garde Performance

The increasingly radical application of Mallarmé's poetic principles leads, we have seen, to the unbinding of his ideal Book and to its performance in conjunction with other aesthetic modes. Although the aesthetic theory and texts we have been examining may be unique to Mallarmé within the context of late nineteenth-century literature, they are far from marginal in importance today. Along with anticipating the various discrete developments in literature and other arts already discussed, they prefigure the emergence in the twentieth century of a new multimedia art form, performance.

An oft-cited example of this art form and one that marked a midpoint in the course of its evolution was *The Untitled Event,* organized by John Cage in 1952 at Black Mountain College. Cage brought together several members of the Black Mountain community for a free exchange that would allow the arts to interpenetrate without undermining their autonomy. Although preparations for the performance were minimal, it was not absolutely unstructured. The performers determined individually what they would contribute, but they were given a precisely timed score indicating when they were to perform. The performance took place in a dining hall where seats, upon which white cups had been placed, were symmetrically arranged in four triangles pointing toward an empty center. Like the members of the audience, most of the participating artists had relatively fixed stations for the performance. Only Merce Cunningham and other dancers were allowed to move about freely.

Reminiscing on the event with Daniel Charles, Cage described it in *For the Birds* (1981):

> Free spaces were arranged everywhere. And the action wasn't supposed to occur in the center, but everywhere around the audience. That is, in the four corners, in the gaps, and also from above. There were ladders, which you could climb to read poems

or to recite texts. I climbed up there myself and delivered a lecture. There were also poems by M. C. Richards and Charles Olson, piano by David Tudor, films projected on the ceiling and on the walls of the room. Finally, there were Rauschenberg's white canvases, while he himself played old records on an antique phonograph and Merce Cunningham improvised amidst and around all that. The whole thing lasted forty-five minutes. (165)

As remote as this multimedia happening may seem from the rigorously structured literary-theatrical work sketched out in *Le Livre,* the two works have much in common. Like the Book and like countless other performed multimedia artworks, from the early twentieth century to the present, *The Untitled Event* implies (1) the equation of the artwork with the process of its creation, (2) a structure of wholeness-in-fragmentation, (3) an order that embraces disorder, (4) the reproduction (rather than the representation) of reality in art, and (5) the interpenetration of art and all other dimensions of human life. These five overlapping aesthetic principles form the theoretical basis of performance art.

The status of performance as a distinct new art form is evident not only from the proliferation of mixed-media theatrical presentations appearing from opera houses and cabarets to television screens. It is also attested to by the publication, beginning in the late 1970s, of works documenting its history and forging its theory. Even within the relatively conservative framework of academic institutions, performance art has of late been recognized as a phenomenon requiring critical examination.

But despite this heightened pitch of interest, there is little or no consensus on what performance art is. RoseLee Goldberg's first history of this art form (initially published in 1979 and reissued in 1988) is fascinating reading, but far from providing a clear sense of the confines of its topic, it states from the outset that performance art inherently negates the possibility of strict definition "since each performer makes his or her own definition in the very process and manner of execution" (9). And it proceeds to string together an extraordinarily large body of twentieth-century artworks whose sole unifying features are that they contain a performed element and are markedly avant-garde. Richard Schechner's ground-breaking *Essays on Performance Theory* (1977), although rigorously analytical throughout, are similarly eclectic. They do, however, consistently derive the fundamental principles of performance by exploring the ways in which contemporary avant-garde performance works resemble those occurring within the context of ritual and differ from those of traditional Western theater.

It is my hope that a close examination of the links between *Le Livre* (which projects a multimedia work at once explicitly ritualistic and markedly avant-garde) and a wide range of the performed multimedia works of the twentieth century will provide some further insight into the poetics of performance art. I shall therefore begin by showing how the Book, *The Untitled Event*, and other avant-garde performance works illustrate the five aesthetic principles listed above and by suggesting the reasons for the genesis of these principles. When this has been accomplished, I hope to justify the validity of my isolation of these five principles as key to the development of performance art by showing how consistently avant-garde artists have put them into practice from the time of Mallarmé to that of Cage.

Live Art: The Equation of the Work with the Process of Its Creation

Goldberg (1988, 9) asserts that "performance defies precise or easy definition beyond the simple declaration that it is live art by artists." And yet we saw that many of the components of *The Untitled Event*, which she herself cites as an exemplary performance work, were not inherently "live." Moreover, no hierarchy was suggested within the event's overall design that would lead one to conclude that its nonlive components—the films and slides projected on the walls and ceilings, Rauschenberg's white canvases, or the phonograph records that he played—had any less intrinsic value in the presentation than those components that were live—David Tudor's playing of the piano, the delivery of Cage's lecture, or the dancing of Cunningham.

Similarly Mallarmé's Book was designed to have its live dimensions, and at least one of these was to be performed by its "artist," Mallarmé, who during the *séances* was to fulfill the function of the reader/operator of the Book. But the Book, like *The Untitled Event*, was also to have incorporated a nonlive dimension, the unbound text, which in its bound, published state (or outside the context of the *séances*) would have preserved literature's traditional character as an autonomous art product—that is, one deliverable to the hands of other readers/operators.

As Goldberg's and others' studies of performance, e.g., Michael Kirby's *Happenings* (1965) or Richard Kostelanetz's *Theater of Mixed Means* (1968), reveal, one of this art form's most paradoxical and interesting aspects is that, far from implying the fusion of music, dance, and theater that one finds in opera or in musical comedy, it often consists predominantly of traditionally unperformed elements and almost always implies a combined yet defused presentation of performed and unperformed aesthetic modes.

Despite this mixture, performance works are essentially "live." This is true because, like *The Untitled Event* and the Book, they generally depend on a theatrical context not only to bring to life the various artistic gestures, products, and messages that they contain, but also to render present the dialectical process of art making and interpretation itself. That Cage attributed as much importance to this dialectical process in designing *The Untitled Event* as Mallarmé had in his plans for the Book is evident by the fact that he, like Mallarmé, placed as much emphasis on the various conditions under which the audience would receive the performance as on the design of the performance itself.

The staging of the audience that occurs in *The Untitled Event* and the Book (whose *séances,* we recall, provided for a restricted number of guests to be seated so as to correspond both numerically and geometrically with all other aspects of the work) is only one of the many means that performance artists have used to draw the audience into the center of their works. Like Mallarmé, who conceived of the Book's public not as spectators but as "assistants," contemporary performance artists have consistently structured their works to include various forms of audience participation. The audience's role has been conceived of as either active or passive. The audience has been sometimes left largely uncontrolled, as in many of Cage's performances after 1952. At other times, it has been carefully orchestrated, as in Allan Kaprow's *18 Happenings in 6 parts,* in which a restricted number of guests were invited to participate in an artwork in the making at the Reuben Gallery in New York and were given detailed instructions about what to do. But whatever strategies performance artists have chosen to transform their spectators into accomplices, their works have consistently suggested, as does Mallarmé's Book, that the ideal artwork is not the finished product of its "creator" but, rather, a vehicle for exchange and communion between the artist-performers and the interpreting public being addressed. Performance is essentially live because only by coming directly into contact with their audiences can artists render present the dialectical process through which their works are made and thus ensure the completion of the aesthetic "operation," which Mallarmé calls "[la] poésie, par excellence, et le théâtre" (1945, 296).

Absolute Unity, or Wholeness-in-Fragmentation

We have seen that *The Untitled Event* consisted of a wide variety of disconnected elements occurring in various locations in and around the spectators. Cunningham and others danced through the aisles chased by a dog. Olson's poetry was read in bits by various people seated in the audience. And Cage's imposition of moments of silence or inactivity on the performers ensured that within the context of the whole performance these disparate elements would appear, paradoxically, as interdependent yet autonomous fragments. Perhaps more important still, within the context of the total event, the scored performance itself seems to have taken on the character of a fragment. Although Cage contends that "the whole thing lasted forty-five minutes" (the time it took him to deliver his lecture), various spectators report that they did not perceive the performance to be thus circumscribed. Francine Duplessix-Gray wrote in her diary on the evening of the event that the "recital" lasted from 8:30 to 10:30, after which "Cage grinned while Olson talked to him again about Zen Buddhism, Stefen Wolpe bitched, two boys in white waltzed together. Tudor played the piano, and the professors' wives licked popsicles" (Duberman 1972, 352). Another witness, the sculptor and potter David Weinrib, contradicts both Cage's and Duplessix-Gray's descriptions of the temporal boundaries of the event, stating that the performance "was a long thing. Long" (Duberman 1972, 355).

The various conflicting accounts of what happened when and where in this "happening" (recounted with great humor in Martin Duberman's *Black Mountain: An Exploration in Community*) indicate that the fragmentation of the performance destabilized both the spectators' and performers' sense of its totality, or spatiotemporal boundaries. Like Mallarmé's Book, which constantly blurred the boundaries between the text, the *séances,* their various components, and factors pertaining to their planning and their reception, *The Untitled Event* clearly incorporated what Schechner has referred to as the preparatory and cooldown procedures of performance (1977, 1). An example is the spectators' initial questions about what they were supposed to do with the white cups on their seats and the ceremonial filling of these with refreshment, which for some occurred during the performance and for others after it.

Presenting themselves as uncircumscribed ensembles of compartmentalized fragments, both Cage's *Untitled Event* and Mallarmé's Book partially transgress the classical aesthetic principle of unity-as-closure, thus forcing us to question the notion that art, the arts, and artworks are well-defined totalities constituted through a hierarchical unification of their various incomplete aspects, or parts.

The classical ideal of unity-as-closure has in large part been responsible for the West's traditional subdivision of art into a number of discrete arts—literature, music, the visual and performing arts—as well as for the further subdivision of these art forms into genres, subgenres, and so forth. The very existence of all of these subdivisions has required that artists manipulate their rudimentary materials (e.g., sounds, words, or colors) within the organizational boundaries suggested by these relatively closed aesthetic systems in order to create particular works of art.

In most avant-garde performance works as in the Book and *The Untitled Event,* these subdivisions and organizational boundaries have rarely been left intact. On the contrary, the internally dehiscent, or compartmentalized, structure typical of performance works has consistently involved the dislocation of conventional parts from conventional wholes, the assertion of their aesthetic autonomy as fragments, and their combination with others in such a way as to discourage the impression that totality itself implies synthesis and closure.

The rejection of the principle of unity-as-closure that occurs in the overall structure of most avant-garde performances is also characteristic of the avant-garde music, dance, drama, visual art, and poetry that make up its parts. In avant-garde literature, for example, the rejection of closure is generally manifest (as it is in Mallarmé's texts) in the freeing of individual works from the unifying constraints imposed by genres and in the freeing of verses, phrases, and even individual words from the organizing principles of syntax and versification. In the most radical forms of avant-garde literature, such as concrete poetry, the thrust toward fragmentation and the attribution of aesthetic autonomy to fragments are so extreme that we often find individual syllables, sounds, and letters freed from (or signifying independently of) words.

When severely fragmented literature is combined in performance works with other similarly deconstructed art forms, its identity-in-difference with these and also with nonart becomes strikingly clear. By this I mean that although the compartmentalized structure of most avant-garde performances gives the impression that they consist of autonomous poetic, musical, and visual art elements, the fragmentary character of these elements impedes our ability, in turn, to identify them as music, poetry, and visual art and to clearly distinguish among them. Thus, the structural wholeness-in-fragmentation of multimedia performances points less, paradoxically, to an aesthetic of disunity than to one, like Mallarmé's, founded on the principle of unity-in-duality—that is, on a principle of absolute unity that knows no inner or outer bounds.

Absolute Order, or Order That Embraces Disorder

Cage is rightly regarded as revolutionary for having challenged with his music the classical premise that art must reflect both in its making and its finished state the existence of a fixed, or well-defined, order. He has vastly expanded our sense of what constitutes aesthetic order by consistently incorporating into the order of his compositions and performances such inherently disorderly factors as simultaneity, indeterminacy, and chance. It was around the time of *The Untitled Event* that he began to use these factors as the primary ordering principles of his work, and his employment of all three is to some degree manifest in *The Untitled Event* itself. The timing of various elements was, for example, derived by chance operations, and the elements were ordered so as to sometimes occur simultaneously and other times overlap. Faced with an event that was not only fragmentary in its structure but also anarchical in its order, both spectators and performers, not surprisingly, came away from it with considerably different views of what had transpired.

Owing to the syntactic complexity of his texts, Mallarmé has long been presented as a poet epitomizing the artist's desire to impose order on the world. Indeed, it has often been argued that the ultimate aim of his poetry was to abolish chance. And yet, we have seen that in their attempt to conquer chance, his most syntactically complex and obsessively ordered texts do not, paradoxically, banish chance but rather readily admit it into their play. The logical and sequential coherence of all of his most ambitious poetic texts is severely disrupted by their incorporation of contingent, indeterminant, and simultaneous elements.

In *Le Livre* an unequivocal break with the classical concept of order is achieved by Mallarmé's constant ordering and reordering of seemingly disconnected elements and also, conversely, by his constant disordering of either conventionally or intrinsically established patterns of order. Recall that nearly all aspects of the Book were presented as correlated and reversible with others, even aspects that in ordinary artworks are not perceived to be remotely related (e.g., the correspondence of the number of volumes and *séances,* of pages and seats; of the price of admission to the *séances* and of the cost of the Book's publication, etc.). In the diagrams, as we saw, the constant reordering and general reversibility of the terms interfere with our ability to determine fixed relationships among them and, therefore, to arrive at definitive conclusions about their meaning or sense. While certain terms such as *theater, idea, drama, mystery, ballets,* and *parades* reappear throughout these diagrams in a fairly consistent and logical way, their places are also occasionally usurped by other terms that either have never appeared before or that are placed in a new way that is inconsistent with the logic and order suggested by the diagrams in general. As I suggested, what is at work in these diagrams is an extreme application on Mallarmé's part of the principle of universal analogy, one paradoxically resulting in the demonstration that insofar as analogies are perceived *everywhere*, the principle of analogy no longer functions as a (restrictive) ordering principle at all.

While Cage's *Untitled Event* was expressly designed to avoid the establishment of causal links, or logical relationships, between its elements, many other contemporary performance works have undermined the classical concept of order, in a manner more similar to that of Mallarmé's Book. On the one hand, they have imposed a seemingly excessive degree of order on their various aspects through the establishment of multiple analogical relationships. On the other, they have destroyed our sense of the stability of these relationships either by introducing new elements into them or by simply changing the order of elements.

These two order-subverting processes figured prominently, for example, in Kaprow's previously mentioned *18 Happenings in 6 parts,* a 1959 series of performances described and analyzed in Kirby's *Happenings* (1965). For the most part, the ordering of this work reflected as obsessive a search for symmetry and internal (numerical and other) correspondences as Mallarmé's Book. The eighteen happenings occurred, for example, on six different evenings in a performance space that was divided into three rooms. Upon arrival at the Reuben Gallery, spectators were given three small cards stapled together and a program sheet with a list of participants, including the name of the six principals—three men and three women—on the left and instructions for the guests on the right. These instructions read "The performance is divided into 6 parts. . . . Each part contains three happenings that occur at once. The beginning and the end of each part will be signaled by a bell. At the end of the performance two strokes of a bell will be heard." They also explained that there would be two-minute intervals between parts and two fifteen-minute intervals when the spectators would change rooms. The cards stapled to the program gave precise directions on how the spectators were to be seated, reading "Part 1 and 2—take a seat in room 2," "Part 3 and 4—take a seat in room 3," "Part 5 and 6—take a seat in room 1"—instructions that the programs warned the audience to follow to the letter (Kirby 1965, 71). However, these instructions could not be followed. As there were an unequal number of seats in these rooms, some spectators were able to go to only two rooms rather than all three.

That this particular destabilization of the happenings' rigorously planned order was not accidental is suggested by the fact that there were parallel subversions of order in other aspects of the performance. For example, at one point during these events, "a series of slides was being projected rapidly on the window-shade screen," and according to Kirby, "all groups of slides had a set order of presentation." However, "the projector operator could," he adds, "rather than follow the sequence, show them in reverse order or merely reverse the order of the second half" and had, in addition, "the option of making his own arrangement" (74). The disruptions, or destabilizations, that one finds in the intricately planned order of Mallarmé's and Kaprow's works (as well as in the works of such mainstream contemporary artists as the composer Pierre Boulez) may constitute an even more effective attack on conventional concepts of order than Cage's virtual rejection of all conventional ordering principles from the start.

As with the subversion of unity-as-closure, the subversion of classical concepts of order that is found in the overall structure of avant-garde performance works is also widely manifest in avant-garde literature, music, dance, and visual art. Taking literature once again as our example, in avant-garde texts in general (as in Mallarmé's work) order is partially undermined by semantic and syntactic ambiguity. When words are used so that their meaning appears fundamentally undecidable, the assertion of their sense becomes contingent on the reader, who must then ultimately determine which direction the literary message will take. Our preconceptions of the nature of literary order are still more radically subverted by the avant-garde literary text's characteristic inclusion of words that seem totally extraneous to its logical progression—whose meaning is not, consequently, merely "undecidable" but absolutely indeterminant, that is, totally dependent on whether or how the reader will integrate them into the signifying process of the text.

Finally, avant-garde literature's subversion of the classical ideal of order also manifests itself in various profound disruptions of conventional notions of sequence—e.g., in a lack of clear beginnings, middles, and endings (of works, paragraphs, sentences, words, and so forth). These disruptions force readers to choose where the signifying process starts and where it will finally go and to make their own decisions at every step along the way. It would be wrong, in my view, to conclude from avant-garde artists' persistent disruptions of order that they are less concerned than other artists have been with the problem of order. On the contrary, the testing and expansion of various concepts of order often seem to be their primary concern. The Book, for example, conceived as a collection of unbound fragments to be variously recombined and read in opposite directions, seems to test whether the universal order it reflects ("l'ensemble des rapports entre tout") is itself limited, or fixed. And like *The Untitled Event* and the *18 Happenings,* the Book finally suggests that art reflects a universal order that is unrestricted, or absolute—that is, one embracing disorder within it and possessing such extreme flexibility as to remain operable in any state.

The Reproduction of Reality in Art

Another classical convention with which *The Untitled Event* and the Book break is the notion that art is not the same as reality but, rather, only its representation. That Cage equates art with reality in all the prevalent senses of the term—i.e., the physical world, the ensemble of facts pertaining to ordinary existence, and metaphysical truth—is evident in the following remarks, in which (for reasons that will become clear) he generally refers to this complex form of reality as "life":

> In Zen Buddhism nothing is either good or bad. Or ugly or beautiful. The actions of man in nature are an undifferentiated and unhierarchical complex of events, which hold equal indifference to the ultimate factor of oneness. No value judgements are possible because nothing is better than anything else. Art should not be different than life but an act within life. Like all of life, with its accidents and chances and variety and disorder and only momentary beauties. Only different from life in this sense: that in life appreciation is passive like listening to a sound complex of bird, waterfall and engine, whereas in art it must be a voluntary act on the part of the creator and of the listener. (Duberman 1972, 349)

As these remarks clearly indicate, what occurs in art for Cage is not, as classical aesthetics have long dictated, either the imitation of reality or its (positive or negative) transfiguration but, rather, the process by which reality, through the simple fact of its recognition, or "appreciation," is aesthetically reproduced. Cage's insistence that art is different from life because it is a voluntary or an intentional act seems difficult to reconcile with the general thrust of his thought, which rejects such binary oppositions as voluntary/involuntary, or intentional/unintentional. This seeming contradiction is, however, highly significant, for his writings consistently suggest that the intention to re-cognize and thereby to reproduce reality is at once the sole act of intentionality desirable in and the sole requirement for making works of art. He thus described his aim in producing *The Untitled Event* as one of "purposeful purposelessness" and on that basis distinguished it from the (more controlled) "happenings" later designed by Kaprow and others. The announcement for Kaprow's *18 Happenings* indicates, however, that their central purpose was also simply to take place, or to provide for the possibility of their own execution. "The actions will mean nothing clearly formulable so far as the artist is concerned. It is intended, however, that the whole work is to be intimate, austere, and of a somewhat brief duration" (Kirby 1965, 68.) That the primary aim of *18 Happenings* was, like that of Cage's *Untitled Event* and of Mallarmé's Book, to literally bring about a reality and to rivet our attention on the strangely elusive fact of its concrete spatiotemporal presence is also strongly suggested by the heading of the published script, which reads, "Something to take place: a happening." This heading seems an anachronistic response to "Rien n'aura eu lieu que le lieu," the secondary motif of Mallarmé's *Un coup de dés,* a text that the entire *18 Happenings* script resembles in its use of space and typography, as Kirby has pointed out (54).

In *Le Livre,* as we saw, Mallarmé constantly confronts the various aspects of his ideal Book in order to prove the fact of their respective existences through the process of their reciprocal reflections. And the laborious establishment of all these internal correspondences seems to demonstrate, as Scherer (1977) remarks, that the Book in its totality amounts to something intrinsically true to itself and therefore "real." As I suggested further, a primary purpose of the Book's performance is to allow for the presentation of this intrinsically constructed reality to others, whose witnessing would afford it the value also of an extrinsically proven reality, or truth. As Mallarmé (1977) writes at one point in the manuscript, "On ne prouve que quant aux autres" [189 (A)]. Thus, the Book in its totality—i.e., its double literary-theatrical state—does not present itself merely as a limited or intrinsically constructed reality or as the representation of a reality that remains extrinsic but, rather, as the reproduction, or reconstruction, of the process of reflection by which reality becomes reality and truth can be recognized as truth.

Undoubtedly, few artworks of any kind have been as obsessively guided as Mallarmé's Book by the ambition both to bring truth and reality into being and to demonstrate their relative and arbitrarily determined nature. Although we saw that art in the context of ritual generally aims to bring realities about through their symbolization, it is more characteristic of modern performance works to attempt this, as Mallarmé's Book does, even while exposing the various processes by which truth and reality are consecrated as such, or are made.

A striking example of avant-garde performance artists' ambition both to internally prove and to externally consecrate the real, or true, existence of their work is an event, or series of events, orchestrated by Yves Klein, a French painter turned performance artist who categorized himself as a "nouveau réaliste." Klein's art, by virtue of its spiritual-material aesthetic and its perpetual conjurations of the void, is, in fact, very similar in its effect to the poetry of Mallarmé. In the 1960s, more or less concurrently with his work on body art (the *Anthropométries*, in which nude models were not painted in the ordinary sense but, rather, dragged through the paint), Klein created a number of invisible art works, which he called "zones de sensibilité picturale immatérielle." To prove the existence of these "zones" and therefore their value on the plane of material reality, Klein determined that the "pure" spiritual worth of each one would materially correspond to, or be reflected in, 20 grams of pure gold leaf. In a number of ceremonial sales transactions he exchanged receipts for these "zones" for the calculated amount of gold leaf. But as the worth of the zones was fundamentally spiritual rather than material in nature, the material transaction once performed, its material evidence was also destroyed. Klein scattered half of the gold leaf into the Seine (saving the other half for eventual incorporation into his material *monogolds*) as the buyer burned the receipt (Millet 1983, 48). Thus, as in Mallarmé's Book, the reality, or authenticity, of Klein's work was established both intrinsically, through the reciprocal reflection and exchangeability of its constituent (material and immaterial) aspects, and extrinsically, by means of the ritual sales transactions.

Avant-garde performance works, by arresting our attention on the simple fact of their own spatiotemporal existence and by variously bringing into play what we generally accept as manifestations, or measures, of reality (e.g., material presence, economic value, truth arrived at by consensus through accepted processes of verification and proof), have consistently aimed, as exemplified above, to dislodge the conventional view that art is distinct from reality. In this process they have naturally afforded new angles of perception on the nature of reality itself.

The Interpenetration of Art and All Other Aspects of Human Life

Given Cage's remarks on the relationship between art and life, it is not surprising that his *Untitled Event* provided not only for the intermixture of all the arts but also for the incorporation within art of a wide range of mundane, traditionally nonaesthetic activities, such as casual conversation, the playing of popular music (apparently Edith Piaf records), the pouring of water from one bucket to another (Cage's "water music"), and the gallivanting about of an excited little dog. Moreover, the inclusion in Cage's own lecture of metaphysical issues (primarily allusions to Zen Buddhism and Meister Eckhart) as well as his discussions of Zen with Olson undoubtedly served to illustrate his own perception of art's identity-in-difference with the most (as well as the least) profound dimensions of human life (Cage 1967, 95–111). Thus, despite his having no clearly defined sociopolitical or religious agenda, Cage should no more than Mallarmé be considered a proponent of an "art for art's sake" philosophy that holds art in isolation from the rest of the world's affairs. Cage's view that music inherently encompasses all facets and planes of existence is obvious in such pronouncements as "the entire world must be made into music" (1981, 204), which echoes Mallarmé's "tout, au monde, existe pour aboutir à un livre" (1945, 378).

That Mallarmé's Book, like Cage's *Untitled Event,* sought to embrace *all aspects* of human reality was particularly striking in "le mythe de l'invitation" where major social institutions (hospital, market, school, factory, and prison) and various forms of ritual or public celebration (burial, marriage, and baptism; and hunting, balls, yachting, and fireworks) were presented as integral and interrelated aspects of the Work. It must of course be recognized that if the all-inclusive Book were to be achieved, it would somehow have to contain the entire universe— "l'hymne, harmonie, et joie . . . des relations entre tout" (Mallarmé 1945, 378).

Needless to say, no avant-garde artwork has ever achieved this ideal, but several have pointed to it as unequivocally as Mallarmé's Book. In 1961, for example, the Italian performance artist Piero Manzoni attempted to seize the world as his aesthetic property by simply erecting its sculptural pedestal, called *Base of the World* (Goldberg 1988, 14). Similarly, Klein, in his *Journal d'un seul jour,* announced a full (if temporary) appropriation of the universe:

> Dans le cadre des représentations théâtrales du Festival d'Art d'Avant-garde de novembre–décembre 1960, j'ai décidé de présenter une ultime forme de théâtre collectif qu'est un dimanche pour tout le monde . . . le théâtre des opérations de cette conception du théâtre que je propose n'est pas seulement la ville, Paris,

mais aussi la campagne, le désert, la montagne, le ciel même, et
tout l'univers même, pourquoi pas? (Millet 1983, 45).

Without necessarily going to such extremes, avant-garde performance
artists have consistently underscored that artists, artworks, and the pro-
cess of creating and interpreting art are not remote from other kinds of
people, things, and activities. Variously emphasizing, as Mallarmé did in
his plans for The Book, the intermingling of the roles of the artist and the
public, of highbrow and lowbrow art forms (ballets and parades, dramas
and circuses, poetry and journalism), and finally of art's functions as
entertainment and as religious and secular ritual, performance art in
general has refused to set itself apart from human reality in all of its
aspects and has striven to extend its boundaries to include everything
that is.

If we can continue, nevertheless, to consider avant-garde performance
as art, it is because, as in Le Livre, it generally falls short of realizing its
own aesthetic ideals, and necessarily so. As the aesthetic principles of
performance art in fact imply the negation of all those principles by
which art has been traditionally defined, their full implementation could
not lead elsewhere than to the death or dissolution of art. Though many
avant-garde performances have, like Le Livre, an apocalyptic quality,[1]
they have hardly brought about a death of art. Rather, their persistent
deconstruction of classical aesthetic conventions has resulted in a dra-
matic proliferation of new hybrid art forms and a radically expanded
concept of what a work of art is.

It is important to underscore, moreover, that performance works,
paradoxically, have done much to perpetuate the life of the very classical
conventions that they seem to have set out to destroy. Performance art
prolongs itself (and art in general) by partially adhering to the conven-
tion that the value of art lies in its particular products, performances,
and messages; by preserving a certain degree of closure and of restricted
order; and by provisionally maintaining shades of distinction between
itself and the complex reality of human life.

1. For an excellent discussion of Le Livre's apocalyptic quality, see Louis W. Marvick's
"Two Versions of the Symbolist Apocalypse: Mallarmé's Livre and Scriabin's Mysterium
(1986, 287–306). See also my presentation of Le Livre as a turn-of-the-century rite in
Rhétoriques fin de siècle (1992b).

The Birth and Development of
Twentieth-Century Performance

The beginnings of performance art are generally traced to the radical theatrical performances of such early twentieth-century movements as Futurism, Dada, and Surrealism. Many of the most important figures of these movements had matured under the influence of Wagner and the Symbolists. And while these figures often presented themselves as reacting directly against Wagnerian and Symbolist aesthetic principles, they often continued, in fact, to apply them but in an extreme, or absolute, manner, as Mallarmé himself had done in *Le Livre*. It is interesting, moreover, that whereas several of these revolutionary artists perceived themselves as having left behind the aestheticism and the cult of art that had become synonymous with the name Mallarmé, they actually retraced his thinking and experimentation in *Le Livre,* a work of which they were almost certainly unaware.

Although Futurism, Dada, and even Surrealism were essentially theatrical in their earliest manifestations, the founders of these movements were not performing artists but poets and painters who, like Mallarmé, turned to performance to put some of their most radical ideas about their own arts into practice.

A good example is the founder of Italian Futurism, the poet Filippo Tommaso Marinetti, who in 1914 became one of the first translators of Mallarmé's poetry into Italian. Deeply influenced by the French Symbolists and himself initially a French vers-librist (similar in style to Mallarmé's disciples: Gustave Kahn, Jules Laforgue, Emile Verhaeren, and Francis Vielé-Griffin), Marinetti pushed the Symbolists' dislocation of words from the constraints of versification and syntax to its radical extreme in his *Parole in Libertà*. In fact, he pushed the pulverization of literary language several steps further than his predecessors by incorporating into his poetic lexicon many vocables that were not words.

Marinetti (1980, 117) did not openly acknowledge his debt to Mallarmé; indeed, he unequivocally renounced him (along with Poe, Baudelaire, and Verlaine) for his nostalgic attachment to the Ideal. But there are many striking parallels between Marinetti's texts and theatrical works and those of Mallarmé that we have been examining. Marinetti's *Parole in Libertà* text *Zang Tumb Tuuum* (1912), for example, has important formal similarities with *Un coup de dés*, although it is clearly un- and even anti-Mallarmean in subject and tone.

Asserting from the incipit lines its own absolute originality, *Zang Tumb Tuuum* is an onomatopoeic war poem, screaming out in disjointed phrases the birth of (a new) poetry through the violent exploratory penetration of both the real and imaginary worlds.

> Nessuna poesia prima di noi
> colla nostra immaginazione senza fili parole
> in libertà vivaaaaAAA il FUTURISMO fi-
> nalmente finalmente finalmente finalmente
> finalmente
> FINALMENTE
> POESIA NASCERE
> (Marinetti 1983, 643)

Yet as the poem evolves, it is clear that it derives its meaning from an iconoclastic attack on Symbolist poetic ideals—the ubiquitous Symbolist "luna," and Mallarmé's "azzurro invisibile" (Marinetti 1983, 681)—an attack that is all the sharper and more efficacious for Marinetti's borrowing of Symbolist weapons, or poetic techniques. But however one may wish to measure the originality of Marinetti's style against that of the Symbolists, it must be recognized that the most innovative formal aspects of his words-in-freedom texts—the use of space and typography— are already present in *Un coup de dés*. *Zang Tumb Tuuum* is not the first but the second of modern concrete poems.

Moreover, like *Un coup de dés*, *Zang Tumb Tuuum* presents itself not merely as a visual text but also as a *score for oral performance*. Marinetti frequently performed his own and other Futurist poems, eventually proclaiming for himself "il indiscutibile primato mondiale di declamatore di versi liberi e di parole in libertà" (Marinetti 1983, 123). He described his style of declamation as dynamic and synoptic, asserting that it required wide variances in intonation and movement of the arms and legs. And *Zang Tumb Tuum*, like *Un coup de Dés*, offers natural images of disorder and wholeness-in-fragmentation on the level of its thematic content:

> NAVIGAZIONE DI
> MONTAGNE MALLEABILI
> deformazione
> incorporarsi
> strati strati strati di nuvole disfa-
> cimento   reincarnasi
> analisi di cumuli   contorsioni
> smembramento brandelli condensazione
> SINTESI sofferenza e rimorso del-
> l'UNITA
> (682–83)

Although as early as 1905 Marinetti had written a Symbolist play, *Le Roi Bombace* (inspired by and reminiscent of Alfred Jarry's *Ubu Roi*), when he returned to Italy to begin his Futurist movement in earnest, he searched for a new kind of performance unrestricted by conventional theatrical structures, one that would enable him to operate in conjunction with others who were revolutionizing their art forms along the same lines as he.

He found sympathetic collaborators in the Futurist painters: Umberto Boccioni, Carlo Carra, Luigi Russolo, Gino Severini, and Giacomo Balla, who affirmed their adherence to the ideas expressed in his first Futurist manifesto of 1909 in a manifesto of their own the following year. Among other things, their manifesto (Marinetti 1980) asserted the primacy in Futurist painting of:

1. Presenting art as open-ended process, as the reproduction of dynamic sensation: "Le geste que nous voulons reproduire sur la toile ne sera plus un *instant fixé* du dynamisme universel. Ce sera simplement la *sensation dynamique* elle même" (171–72).
2. Achieving structural wholeness-in-fragmentation: "il ne peut aujourd'hui exister de peinture sans Divisionisme. . . . Le Divisionisme, pour le peintre moderne, doit être un complémentarisme inné" (174).
3. Showing the relative and arbitrary character of reality both in and outside of art: "Tout est conventionnel en art. Rien n'est absolu en peinture. . . . Qui peut donc croire encore à l'opacité des corps?" (172)
4. Installing the spectator at the center of the painting: "Les peintres nous ont toujours montré les objets et les personnes placés devant nous. Nous placerons désormais le spectateur au centre du tableau" (173).
5. Revitalizing the connection between art and life: "Nous voulons à tout prix rentrer dans la vie" (173).

Balilla Pratella's "Futurist Music Manifesto" recommended a similarly innovative approach to music, affirming the necessity of "la polyphonie harmonique, fusion logique du contrepoint et de l'harmonie"; of "l'enharmonisme," which utilizes "toutes les plus petites subdivisions de tons"; of "la liberté polyrythmique"; and of introducing into music "toutes les nouvelles métamorphoses de la nature . . . la glorification de la Machine, le règne victorieux de l'électricité" (185). Out of Pratella's Futurist music evolved Russolo's "Art of Noises," anticipating much of Cage's experimentation by reproducing through specially invented instruments the sounds of motors, trains, and shouting crowds.

Marinetti's aesthetic principles were eventually applied to all of the arts (particularly cinema, dance, and pantomime) and led to the development of a new type of synthetic variety theater in which, paradoxically, distinctions between art forms could no longer be made. These mixed-media Futurist performances typically presented no storyline. Their central purpose was neither that of Wagnerian music-drama—to tell a story of profound significance in the most comprehensive and effective way—nor that of conventional variety theater—merely to entertain. Rather, they sought to coerce active participation from audiences that, constantly provoked by the Futurists' exploitation of new elements of surprise, generally responded to these shock treatments with missiles of food.

Futurist performance manifestos emphasize the importance of demonstrating the correspondence between the "simultaneity" and "copenetration" of all arts (and all things in the world) and the "syncretism" inherent to the spectator's soul. Through the establishment of this correspondence, the Futurists felt, they were able to create between themselves and their public "una corrente di confidenza senza rispetto," which allowed the general transfusion to the public of the "dynamic vivacity" of their theater (Marinetti 1983, 121).

The stated aim of Marinetti's performances was "to destroy the Solemn, the Sacred, the Serious, the Sublime of Art with a capital A" (1983, 86), an aim that appears to be contrary to that of Mallarmé's Book, which was to consecrate the truth of his texts and establish a cult, or religion, of art. And yet Marinetti and Mallarmé went about achieving their aims in much the same way and, in the process, produced strikingly similar works. Marinetti's use of the radio to explore the structure of silence and his creation in 1917 of a "livre en fer blanc" seem, for example, realizations of Mallarméan aesthetic ideals (Marinetti 1980, 61).

What is perhaps more important, however, than the many formal parallels between Marinetti's and Mallarmé's works is the fact that, in the final analysis, their ambitions for art were not as incompatible as they might appear. Just as the "solennités" sketched out in Mallarmé's Book implied important elements of farce, the antics of Marinetti, the trickster, ultimately fed a serious goal. Working ceaselessly, as Mallarmé had, toward the dissolution of all boundaries in art, Marinetti would eventually assert that "thanks to us [the Futurists] the time will come when life will no longer be a simple matter of bread and labour, nor a life of idleness either, but a *work of art*" (Goldberg 1988, 30), a claim (like that cited earlier by Cage) conveying much the same idea as several of Mallarmé's statements on the scope and purpose of the Book.

Although distinctly colored by their varying national origins and divergent political orientations, the performances of early Russian Futurism and Dada developed similarly to those inspired by Marinetti. Acknowledging their debt to him, Russian Futurist poets and painters (such as Vladimir Mayakovsky, Alexei Kruchenykh, Kasimir Malevich, and David Burlyuk) and Dadaists (such as Hugo Ball, Richard Huelsenbeck, Tristan Tzara, Kurt Schwitters, Jean Arp, Max Ernst, and Marcel Janko) devised new forms of multimedia performances in the streets, cafés, galleries, and theaters of St. Petersburg, Moscow, Munich, Zurich, Berlin, and other European cities.

Like the performances of the Italian Futurists, those of the Russian Futurists and the Dadaists strove to free the arts from all conventions. These artists used fragmentation, simultaneity, chance, and the radical modernizing of their works (usually through mechanization) to jolt audiences into recognizing that fundamental transformations were taking place within both modern art and the modern world. And they persistently sought to undermine distinctions between art and reality.

Goldberg presents the 1913 opera *Victory Over the Sun,* by Kruchenykh, Mikhail Matyushin, and Malevich, as exemplary of the flavor of early Russian Futurist performance. The cast for this opera, which depicts a band of "Futurecountrymen's" conquest of the sun, was drawn, like that of many contemporary performance works, primarily from nonprofessional performers. Having grown accustomed to the rioting that Futurist events inevitably provoked, police in St. Petersburg lined the exit of the theater in advance. That the creators of the opera perceived their work, as Mallarmé had perceived his Book, as a depersonalized transcription or transformation of themselves (a "majoration devant tous du spectacle de soi") (Mallarmé 1945, 370) is evident in Malevich's description of the opening scene:

> The curtain flew up, and the spectator found himself in front of a white calico on which the author himself, the composer and the designer were represented in three different sets of hieroglyphics. The first chord of music sounded, and the second curtain parted in two, and an announcer and troubadour appeared and an I-don't-know-what with bloody hands and a big cigarette. (Goldberg 1988, 36)

Although the various elements of the opera were disconnected and logically incoherent in terms of traditional literature, music, and visual art, they were closely correlated. Corresponding to Kruchenykh's fragmentary, nonsensical libretto, Malevich's geometric stage designs and puppetlike figurines implied a "complete displacement of visual relationships" and introduced new concepts of relief, weight, form, and color. The composer Matyushin described the opera as "the first performance on a stage of the disintegration of concepts and words, of old staging and musical harmony" (Goldberg 1988, 36–37).

In later years, with Mayakovsky's orchestrated political demonstrations, Nikolai Foregger's renaissance of the circus and mechanical dances, and Vsevolod Meyerhold's unification of "bio-mechanical" movement and constructivist sets, Russian Futurism, far from being destructive and chaotic in its overall thrust, expanded to include several different varieties of rigorously formal yet socially oriented theater.

Dada performances, although by definition nihilistic and anarchical, were very similar to the more politically directed ones of Italian and Russian Futurism. The famous disputes that occurred within the inner circles of Dada (in Zurich between Ball, Huelsenbeck, and Tzara, in Paris between Francis Picabia, Tzara, and André Breton) consistently brought to the fore a problem central to the very existence of Dada: the impossibility of maintaining its "purposeful purposelessness," that is, its status as a gratuitous vehicle for absurdity and for attacks on old and new philosophical principles, social values, and artistic conventions. Constantly on the verge of signifying something, of moving toward one or another coherent and constructive form of affirmation or negation, all Dadaists were eventually forced to recognize the necessary ephemerality of Dada and abandon it, channeling their energies in other directions.

Ball, the founder of the celebrated Cabaret Voltaire in Zurich, was, like Marinetti, a poet become producer. What interested him primarily was not the re-creation of his own or others' "original" artworks but, rather, the activity of production in the more profound Artaudian sense of bringing things into existence. Thus, it is not surprising that the "tendencies" of Ball that would cause him to eventually break with Dada were not those of political activism (as with others such as Huelsenbeck and Raoul Haussman) but, rather, his strong penchant for metaphysics and mysticism.

Going further still, perhaps, than Marinetti in his pulverization of literary language, Ball was certainly among the first of modern poets to create and perform "verse without words." The extremism of his assault on language was, to use Arp's terms, more "positive" than "negative" in its ultimate aim. His understanding of so basic a convention as the foundation of poetry on the unit of the word was (like Mallarmé's undermining of the alexandrine) not undertaken with a view toward the ultimate destruction of this convention. Rather Ball's ultimate objective was simply to arrive at "the secret alchemy of the word," to revitalize its "original magic" by renouncing from the outset "the language devastated and made impossible by journalism" (Ball 1974, 71).

Breaking markedly with the chaotic bawdiness that characterized most Dada events, the somber, ceremonial performance in 1916 of "Karawane," Ball's most famous "sound poem," already suggested his increasingly ritual orientation. Resembling, by his own account, an obelisk—dressed in a tubular cardboard costume draped by a great collar, which he flapped up and down like wings, and decked by a high witch doctor's hat—Ball, with the pomp and solemnity of Mallarmé's *opérateur*, read his text from music stands placed on three sides of the stage. In his *Diary*, he explains that in the course of the performance and in response to the conditions of reading that he had set up for himself, he was mystically guided toward the appropriate manner of delivery: "my voice had no choice but to take on the ancient cadence of priestly lamentation, that style of liturgical singing that wails in all the Catholic churches of East and West" (Ball 1974, 71).

Ball's partner, the Romanian-born poet Tzara, was paradoxically the staunchest advocate of the nonprincipled, or "going nowhere," character of Dada and the strongest force in establishing it as an artistic movement. That Tzara perceived Dada as the ultimate attainment of a kind of gratuitous, self-propagating aesthetic ideal—that is, a phenomenon that could continue to exist eternally "for its own sake"—was evident in his constant efforts to create anthologies and journals for Dada's preservation and expansion and to codify its lack of precepts in his numerous manifestos, the majority of which are masterpieces of self-generating contradiction. Naturally, Tzara's first official Dada manifesto of 1918 explicitly capitalizes on the contradiction inherent in his engagement in such activities:

> I write a manifesto and I want nothing, yet I say certain things, and in principle I am against manifestoes, as I am also against principles. . . . I write this manifesto to show that people can perform contrary actions together while taking one fresh gulp of air; I am against action; for continuous contradiction, for affirmation too, I am neither for nor against and I do not explain because I hate common sense. (Lippard 1971, 14)

Like the success of Futurist performances, that of Dada performance was measured primarily by its capacity to provoke aggressive audience participation. Successful Dada performances consistently implied their solicitation of violent reactions from audiences, who far from being random and innocent victims, willingly subjected themselves to performances from which they knew very well what to expect.

This adversarial yet strangely complicitous artist-public relationship seems to be one of the most original features of early twentieth-century avant-garde performance. Certainly, it is not consistent with the passive yet mutually respectful relationship to which we are accustomed in most Western art. The provocation of spectators by performers (and vice versa) is, however, not unique to avant-garde performance. As Schechner has pointed out, it is an important part of many rites, and it also figures prominently in Mallarmé's plan for the Book. Representations of the poet's difficulty in communicating with a slumbering, uncomprehending public (which nevertheless beseeches him to perform) arise consistently in *Le Livre*. And in "le mythe de l'invitation" this problem is finally resolved through the symbolization of an act of aggression preposterous even by Dada standards, the poet's devouring of the lady ("la foule") who has provoked him to such extremes by withholding from him her "food" (symbolic, as we saw, of those elements of "la cité" under the crowd's jurisdiction).

The difference between Futurist and Dada performances and *Le Livre* is that in the latter the problem of strained artist-public relations does not remain peripheral to theatrical events but rather is symbolically incorporated within them. Not only "le mythe de l'invitation" but also all of the myths sketched out in *Le Livre* revolve around the description of theatrical events in which communication is severely impeded owing, in part, to a symbolic confusion of the artist-performer's and public's respective roles and domains and, in part, to a blurring of the spatio-temporal boundaries that normally separate theatrical events from aspects related to their preparation and reception. It is interesting to note that the problems of strained artist-public relations and obstructed communication that were inevitably provoked by early Futurist and Dadaist performances would also become frequently theatricalized, or symbolically integrated into the theatrical events themselves, as Futurism and Dada dissolved as rebellious, marginal movements.

The dissolution of Dada as a "movement" began with its transportation (by Tzara) to Paris, where the way had been well prepared by such important individual artists as Guillaume Apollinaire, Pablo Picasso, and Erik Satie, who had already been applying Futurist and Dadaist aesthetic principles in their respective disciplines for some time. Although these artists did not form a movement as cohesive as Futurism or Dada, they were in constant communication with one another through participation in various groups and collaboration in journals, exhibitions, and multimedia performances. (The best known of the latter were produced by Sergey Diaghilev.)

Apollinaire, for example, still far more widely read today than either Marinetti or Ball, has been credited with making as significant a contribution as they did to restoring concreteness and vitality to modern poetry. In 1917, he called for the invention of a new language, one that would express thought "synthetico-ideographically" rather than "analytico-discursively" (Apollinaire 1952, 144). His own efforts to move poetic language in these directions are clearly reflected both in his *Calligrammes* and his Surrealist drama, *Les mamelles de Tirésias*. Literary champion of the Cubist painters and their theories and an ardent and powerful proponent of modernism in all the arts and of new kinds of alliances between them, Apollinaire announced the realization of his aesthetic ideal and the emergence of a "new spirit" (for which he first coined the term "surrealism") in his program note for the 1917 Ballets Russes's production of *Parade*.

Apollinaire affirmed that *Parade* with Satie's transposition of Jean Cocteau's scenic poem into music and "its alliance between dance and painting, between the plastic and mimetic arts," heralded the birth of "a comprehensive art" that would "bring about profound changes in our arts and manners through universal joyousness" (Apollinaire 1972, 452). Indeed *Parade*, because of its wholeness-in-fragmentation, its ordered anarchy, and its radically new approach to realism, has long been regarded as one of the first important twentieth-century performances to break away from the influence of Wagner. Proposing a new nonsynthetic model for the convergence of the arts, *Parade* is far more similar in its overall structure and thematics to today's avant-garde theatrical performances than to the Wagnerian *Gesamtkunstwerk*. It is also strangely similar to *Le Livre* in several respects.

Cocteau described *Parade* as "realistic" and felt that this realism was confirmed by the multiple correspondences between his scenario, Picasso's cubist costumes and scenery, Léonide Massine's choreography, and Satie's music. His libretto, which was originally designed to be read during the ballet through holes in the scenery (that is, as an *autonomous yet integral part* of the ballet) revolves around the problem of a crowd's mistaking the performers' parade ("a comic act, put on at the entrance of a traveling theater to attract a crowd") for the circus act, the spectacle itself (Shattuck 1958, 121). The crowd's symbolic confusion of the parade with the main theatrical event (and thus, the substitution of the former for the latter occurring in the ballet itself) brings to mind numerous instances of parallel confusion for readers of *Le Livre*—that which results, for example, from the circular theatrical structure of "le mythe des deux femmes." There, what seems to constitute the main action, the initial *mise en scène* of two women reaching toward each other on a beach, is both mirrored and brusquely interrupted by a balletic interlude, or "entracte" (whose spatiotemporal theatrical context receives more attention than the divertissement itself). And when after this parenthesis the main action is finally resumed, it is once again simply repeated but in the radically different symbolic register of animals jumping through hoops in a circus act. Moreover, as is the case in all of the myths in *Le Livre,* the problem of impeded communication between artists and public is central to the thematics of *Parade.* In both works the accomplishment of the performers' act is represented as dependent on their ability to draw the spectators into the center of their work, spectators whose communion with the artists is blocked by their inability not only to interpret but also to identify the artists' performances or to know precisely what their performances consist of.

Reminiscent of one of the scenes from "Le mythe des deux femmes" (Mallarmé 1977, 22A–25A), Picasso's opening backdrop for the ballet is a cityscape with a miniature theater in its center. And the ballet itself consists, as does *Le Livre,* of a kind of collage of modern myths. The characters of the ballet include three Managers (one American, dressed as a skyscraper); the Chinese Prestidigitator (played by Massine); a Little American Girl who cranks up her car, catches a train, and foils a bank robber; two tumbling acrobats and a horse "formed by two dancers, one of whom does the steps of the forelegs and the other those of the hind legs" (Apollinaire 1972, 453). The internal dehiscence of the structure of *Parade* results, in part, from the fact that it includes within its confines (like the Book and *The Untitled Event*) an extraordinarily wide range of objects and activities from everyday modern life. This is strikingly apparent in the intrusion of jazz, noise music, typewriters, bells, and the like in Satie's revolutionary score. Finally, like the myths sketched out in *Le Livre* (and the totality of the Book there conceived) the ballet evolves cyclically rather than linearly, the Finale recalling various themes from earlier sequences and ending with the little American girl in tears as the crowd still refuses to enter the circus tent and take part in the show.

The aesthetic principles applied in *Parade* were greatly exaggerated in one of the last Dadaist performances, *Relâche,* a 1924 collaborative effort of Satie, Picabia, Jean Borlin, Man Ray, Marcel Duchamp, Rolf de Maré, and René Clair. Once again central to the thematics of this performance was the confusion of its own spatiotemporal confines. As in *Parade,* the importance of this confusion is underscored by the title. *Relâche* indicates "no performance," or a break in performances, rather than the presence of a show, and the irony of this title was fully exploited by the cancellation of *Relâche*'s first highly publicized scheduled performance. A blurring of the spatiotemporal boundaries of theatrical performance was also achieved in the internal structure of *Relâche* by its presentation of Clair's and Picabia's famous cinematic "Entracte" as the highpoint and centerpiece of the show. Keeping the audience captive inside the theater, the film shows the performers leaving it in a farcical presentation of the most solemn of rituals, the funeral procession. Following a camel-drawn hearse, the procession ends with the birth of a dandy—the breaking open of the coffin by a grinning corpse—an uncanny inversion recalling the *ouvrier's* emergence from the tomb in Mallarmé's "truc de la mort de faim." As was generally the case with the various stages of Mallarmé's myths, the two live acts of *Relâche* also developed around a number of role reversals and logical inversions— presenting, for example, a chain-smoking fireman pouring water into buckets; the dancers revolving in darkness while Man Ray measured the stage floor; and Duchamp in the role of Adam (à la Cranach) in a *tableau vivant*. Audience participation in the forms of both a complicitous chorus and intrusive heckling and laughter was ensured from the outset by Satie's prelude, which was based on "The Turnip Vendor," a well-known student song. The event came to a close, as "driving a midget five-horsepower Citröen, Satie popped out on stage, took a turn around the track, and ironically greeted the worthy audience whom he had just ridiculed magnificently" (René Dumesnil, cited in Shattuck 1958, 137).

Relâche, although it clearly amounted, in Picabia's words, to "beaucoup de coups de pieds dans beaucoup de derrières consacrés ou non" (Beaumont 1938, 684), was nonetheless received by serious artists as the realization of a thoroughly modern total artwork. The reasons are clear: its innovative mixture of such a wide range of art media and genres (it was apparently the first time film had been incorporated into a ballet), the simultaneity of its events, and its abrupt and arbitrary transitions amounted to an all-pervasive onslaught on conventional concepts of structure and order.

As mentioned earlier, *Le Livre* was undoubtedly unknown to the collaborators of *Relâche*, but several of them were familiar with texts such as *Igitur* and *Un coup de dés*, wherein a radically new, nonsynthetic model of combining the arts is suggested, and multiple layers of irony function to undermine the difference between seriousness and farce. Roger Shattuck (1958, 115) has described Satie's 1914 *Sports et divertissements* as "the sole example of a modern work that combines, precariously but successfully, calligraphy, painting, poetry, and music."

Yet, the manner in which Satie combined poetry, music, and visual art in meticulously prepared scores (resistant to performance), his persistently ironic use of extramusical content, and his insistence on the simultaneous autonomy and interdependence of the musical and nonmusical aspects of his work ("I prohibit any person to read the texts aloud during the period of musical performance") convey an aesthetic whose only precedent may lie in Mallarmé's theatrical texts.

One of Man Ray's last films, *Les mystères du château du Dé* (1929), was in part a playful homage to Mallarmé. Duchamp frequently avowed that Mallarmé was his preferred poet and that his penchant for Mallarmé was more than an idiosyncratic inclination toward the beauty of verses that he did not (as he put it) "completely understand." This point is evident in his avowal that the origin of his own work was poetic and that "modern art must return to the direction traced by Mallarmé" (Paz 1970). Although Mallarmé's impact on Duchamp has yet to be thoroughly explored, in *Marcel Duchamp or the Castle of Purity* (1970) and "Mallarmé and Duchamp: Mirror, Stair, and Gaming Table" (1980) Octavio Paz and Mary Ann Caws have prepared the way for such a study, pointing to various analogies between the two artists' work.

One highly significant point of juncture between Mallarmé and Duchamp lies in the analogous nature of their respective masterworks. Duchamp's *La mariée mise à nu par ses célibataires, même* and *Le Livre* are similar not solely in their meticulously calculated, yet unfinished, character but also in that their lack of completion and inherent decomposition are, to a large extent, determined by the fact that they were designed as performance works.

As is well known, when Duchamp abandoned his magnum opus in 1923, having brought it "to a state of incompletion," it consisted not only of the *Large Glass* but also of the accompanying notes of the *Green Box* and of plans for a sonic counterpart. The ultimate composition of Duchamp's masterpiece—like that of *Le Livre,* unfinished and inherently decomposed—is left to the reader-spectator who, Duchamp often asserted, makes the work of art. That Duchamp perceived a correspondence between the wholeness-in-fragmentation of *La mariée mise à nu par ses célibataires, même* and the unity-in-duality of mind and body inherent in the spectator's being (which the *Large Glass* quite literally reflects) is apparent in his notes explaining how the work should be received:

> Le verre en fin de compte n'est pas fait pour être regardé (avec les yeux "esthétiques"), il devait être accompagné d'un texte littéraire aussi amorphe que possible qui ne prit jamais forme; et les deux

éléments, verre pour les yeux, texte pour l'oreille et l'entendement devaient se compléter et s'empêcher l'un et l'autre de prendre une forme esthético-plastique ou littéraire. (Duchamp 1975, 34)

As in my discussion of the relationship between Mallarmé and Marinetti, in drawing parallels between *Le Livre* and the works of such important anti-artists, or art iconoclasts, as the Dadaists, Satie, and Duchamp, I do not wish to pass lightly over an important difference between them: the fact that *Le Livre* seems to point unequivocally toward the sanctification of art, and the other artists' work, to its desanctification. I do wish to underscore, however, that as Victor Turner and others have pointed out, iconoclasm (in the sense of the destruction of all that is sacred) constitutes an important stage in many rites and that the deritualization of early twentieth-century art can be regarded as a similarly important stage in the historical process of its reritualization. Futurism, Dada, and Surrealism led to the development of new kinds of multimedia performance in which the sociometaphysical efficacy of art—its ritual-like capacity to shape reality and to have a lasting impact on the thoughts and behavior of spectators and participants—was highly stressed. Evolving out of these movements we find, for example, both Bertolt Brecht's political theater and the metaphysical theater of Antonin Artaud, extremely influential models for contemporary avant-garde performance, whose points of juncture with Mallarmé's aesthetics have already been discussed.

Generalizations are usually dangerous. Yet I think it safe to say that the second generation of avant-garde performances—which began after World War II with events such as *The Untitled Event* and has extended to the slick multimedia performance works of the Next Wave—is highly derivative of the first, and often self-consciously so. According to Cage, *The Untitled Event* itself was inspired by his readings of Artaud and Schwitters' descriptions of Dada theater. Thus, even were we to assume that contemporary performance artists have known little of Mallarmé's texts (which is unlikely),[2] in applying the aesthetic principles discussed in this chapter, these artists have not been avant-garde in the literal sense. Rather, they have been rediscovering, developing, and expanding on what avant-garde artists of the early twentieth century had done before.

In the present context this point is significant, for it goes directly to the

2. Many of the artists here discussed have referred to Mallarmé's texts—e.g., Cage (1981, 180) to *Le Livre* as a precedent for his own according of primacy to chance and Olson to the preface of *Un coup de dés* as a clear exposition of his own theory of projective verse (Boer 1975, 63).

question of whether contemporary performance art is fundamentally iconoclastic, as were Futurist and Dada performance works, or functions, rather, in the manner of ritual and Mallarmé's Book to consecrate and celebrate our society's most profound and revered beliefs. To answer this question we must ask ourselves, among other things, whether the performance aesthetic (by which I mean the aesthetic based on the five principles here discussed) is now, in fact, as "unconventional" as it is generally held to be. As I suggested earlier, my own feeling is that it is far too widespread both in the high-culture art world and in popular forms of entertainment to be considered marginal today. The adoption of a significant measure of the "unconventionality" characteristic of performance works has become one of the most prevalent aesthetic conventions of our time. Thus, while it is somewhat frustrating, it is not altogether inappropriate that Goldberg's discussion of performance art in the 1970s treats phenomena ranging from the punk rock of the Sex Pistols to Yvonne Rainer's minimalist dance and presents the 1976 Robert Wilson/Philip Glass landmark opera, *Einstein on the Beach,* as belonging to the "performance fringe." In a documentary film made on the occasion of this work's revival in 1984, Glass himself remarked on the dramatic increase in the general public's ability to perceive and understand *Einstein* since its initial production, concluding from its newfound acceptance that audiences were finally recognizing in its music-theater the art form appropriate to our time (Obenhaus 1987). That performance art has, indeed, acquired a broad-based appeal is, moreover, clearly enough reflected by the penetration of its distinct sensibility into such consumer-oriented products as advertising and music videos. Thus, it is not surprising that, while young people (my own students, for example, in a course on avant-garde multimedia art) may find theories of performance art arcane, they tend to find performance works themselves extremely effective and not necessarily strange.

If the mixing of media and genres, wholeness-in-fragmentation, and the ordered disorder of performance art are now more widely appreciated than rejected, it is undoubtedly, in part, because these aesthetic practices are fully consistent with, are indeed the formal expression of, the "postmodern" precepts prevailing in contemporary philosophy, psychology, and the social sciences. Thus, as might be expected, the term *postmodern* has been frequently used to describe contemporary performance works, and this label is, in my opinion, especially well suited to them in view of the fact that they so often present themselves as derivative, not only with respect to the performances of Europe's early twentieth-century avant-garde but also in relation to the art practices either known or imagined of far more distant places and times. As

Wilson states in program notes for his own postmodern theatrical rendi-
tion of the Babylonian *Epic of Gilgamesh* (1200 B.C.), "the avant-garde
is rediscovering the past, the classic, and in some ways that's [its] respon-
sibility" (Wilson 1988).

The postmodern, backward-glancing character of much contempo-
rary avant-garde performance brings it curiously still further in line with
ritual (as earlier defined in this book), for as soon as this quality is
recognized, the similarity between the two no longer appears merely in
such formal aspects as their supplementary alliances of verbal and non-
verbal languages and their paradoxical equation of the symbolic with the
real. Performance art also appears similar to ritual in being partially
determined by participants' need to *authenticate* and *make present* the
metaphysical principles in which they believe. The symbolic realization,
or consecration, of our society's metaphysical principles is, after all,
what occurs in most contemporary avant-garde performance works,
however negative the casting of these principles may be (e.g., the post-
modern preoccupation with the absence of the origin, the impossibility
of knowing, and the unapprehensible, decentered subject, or self).

Here one might object that while avant-garde performance works may
reflect our most profound collectively held beliefs, they are sharply distin-
guishable from most ritual performances in that they lack that authentic
mythology which, in most rites, acts as the symbolic cultural carrier of
such abstract metaphysical principles or beliefs. Indeed, contemporary
performance works often remain exceedingly abstract either because
their mythical aspects are not linked to well-defined cultural traditions
(as in Mallarmé's Book) or, conversely, because they are attached to
plural systems of belief. What the superimposition of strains of disparate
mythologies (such as occurs in Lee Breuer's mixture of Japanese Bun-
raku puppet theater with West African griot, Caribbean reggae, and
European epic poetry in *The Warrior Ant*) generally achieves is not, as
critics have rarely failed to point out, the authentic mythology of any
given community but, rather, that highly personal mythology of the
synthesizing artist himself or herself. Yet what form of communal cele-
bration could be more appropriate to those of us belonging to the "me"
generation than the sharing of personal mythologies that call into ques-
tion the very possibility of community, focusing, rather, on the presence
of communities within each self?

It may be that in representing this isolated yet pulverized modality of
being in a collective, interactive, and relatively controlled environment,
contemporary performance art constitutes a form of what Victor Turner
(1974, 37–41) refers to as "redressive" action, that is, action aiming to
repair the threatening breach in norm-governed social relations that this

self-centered yet decentered modality of being implies. If this were the case, it might also be argued that avant-garde performance, paradoxically, has like many ancient rites the function of preserving an element of balance and continuity both in our social behavior and our perceptions of the world and ourselves—i.e., of maintaining a necessary status quo. I perceive avant-garde performance works not only as being determined by the social and psychological trouble caused by the transgressive ideas they represent but also as attempting to amelioratively respond to it. There is nothing extraordinary about this perception. As Schechner (1976) as well as others has pointed out, the evasion or resolution of crises through their reenactment on a symbolic plane has always been at the heart of all human performance:

> Performances are liminal events existing to mediate, explain, or explore for pleasure those interactions that are potentially most disruptive. Where transitions/transformations are dangerous what van Gennep calls the "rites of passage" are invented. Where trouble is liable to break out, where communication, clarity, and fun can help to get through a difficult confrontation, there develops ritual, ceremony, and theater. (194)

For many contemporary artists, as for Mallarmé, it seems that survival in a world without God, or the metaphysical Idea, represents a terribly dangerous transition, for just as his texts are haunted, today's art world is fraught with performance works bringing one or another form of it back into existence.

Discussion of the extent to which representations of the world by contemporary performance artists are linked, as in much ritual and in Mallarmé's texts, to the artists' perception of the mind/body duality is beyond the scope of this book. Performance artists' constant explorations of conceptual and material aesthetic extremes, of verbal and corporeal languages, and of the relationship between them within symbolic frameworks that mediate dichotomies suggest, however, that this link could be fruitfully studied.

Bibliography

Alain. 1926. *Système des beaux-arts.* Paris: Gallimard.

Alland, Alexander, Jr. 1977. *The Artistic Animal.* New York: Anchor Books.

Amiot, Anne-Marie. 1974. "*Hommage* ou contre-hommage à Richard Wagner? Une poétique Mallarméenne de l'ambiguité." In *Etudes et recherches de la littérature générale et comparée,* 219–32. Paris: Les Belles Lettres.

Apollinaire, Guillaume. 1952. *Le guetteur mélancolique.* Paris: André Salmon.

———. 1972. *Apollinaire on Art: Essays and Reviews, 1902–1918.* Ed. Leroy C. Breunig. New York: Viking Press.

Artaud, Antonin. 1964. *Le théâtre et son double.* Paris: Gallimard.

Austin, J. L. 1975. *How to Do Things with Words.* Cambridge, Mass.: Harvard University Press.

Austin, L. J. 1951. " 'Le principal pilier': Mallarmé, Victor Hugo, et Richard Wagner." *Revue Littéraire de la France* 51:154–80.

Bachelard, Gaston, 1944. "La dialectique dynamique de la rêverie mallarméenne." *Le Point,* special issue (February–April 1944): 40–44.

Ball, Hugo. 1974. *Flight out of Time: A Dada Diary.* Ed. John Elderfield. New York: Viking Press.

Barko, Carol. 1977. "The Dancer and the Becoming of Language." *Yale French Studies* 54:173–87.

Barthes, Roland. 1953. *Le degré zéro de l'écriture.* Paris: Seuil.

Barzun, Jacques. 1958. *Darwin, Marx, Wagner: Critique of a Heritage.* New York: Anchor Books.

Baudelaire, Charles. 1925. *L'art romantique.* Paris: Louis Conard.

———. 1955. *Oeuvres complètes de Baudelaire.* Vol. 1. Paris: Le Nombre d'Or.

———. 1982. *Les fleurs du mal.* Ed. and trans. Richard Howard. Boston: David R. Godine.

Beaumont, Cyril W. 1938. *The Complete Book of Ballets.* New York: G. P. Putnam's Sons.

Benjamin, Walter. 1969. *Illuminations.* New York: Schocken Books.

Benveniste, Emile. 1966. *Problèmes de linguistique générale.* Paris: Gallimard.

Bernard, Suzanne. 1959. *Mallarmé et la musique.* Paris: Nizet.

Bersani, Leo. 1982. *The Death of Stéphane Mallarmé.* New York: Cambridge University Press.

Blanchot, Maurice. 1955. "L'expérience d'Igitur." In *L'espace littéraire.* Paris: Gallimard.

———. 1959. *Le Livre à venir.* Paris: Gallimard.

Block, Haskell M. 1963. *Mallarmé and the Symbolist Drama*. Detroit, Mich.: Wayne State University Press.

Boas, Franz. 1955. *Primitive Art*. New York: Dover Publishing.

Boas, Franzisca. 1944. *The Function of Dance in Human Society*. New York: The Boas School.

Boer, Charles. 1975. *Charles Olson in Connecticut*. Chicago: Swallow Press.

Bonnefoy, Yves. 1977. "The Poetics of Mallarmé." Trans. Elaine Ancekewicz. *Yale French Studies* 54:9–21.

Borie, Monique. 1981. *Mythe et théâtre aujourd'hui: Une quête impossible?* . . . Paris: Nizet.

Boulez, Pierre. 1966. *Relevés d'apprenti*. Paris: Seuil.

Bowie, Malcolm. 1978. *Mallarmé and the Art of Being Difficult*. Cambridge: Cambridge University Press.

Brecht, Bertolt. 1977. *Brecht on Theater*. Trans. John Willet. New York: Hill & Wang.

Brown, Calvin S. 1971. "The Musical Analogies in Mallarmé's 'Un coup de dés.' " *Comparative Literature Studies* 10: 67–79.

Cage, John. 1967. *A Year from Monday*. Middletown, Conn.: Wesleyan University Press.

———. 1981. *For the Birds: John Cage in Conversation with Daniel Charles*. Salem, N.H.: Marion Boyars.

Caws, Mary Ann. 1980. "Mallarmé and Duchamp: Mirror, Stage, and Gaming Table." *L'esprit créateur* 20:51–64.

Cazeneuve, Jean. 1971. *Sociologie du rite*. Paris: Presses Universitaires de France.

Chastel, André. 1948. "Le Théâtre est d'essence supérieure." *Les lettres* 3, special issue (June): 93–105.

Claudel, Paul. 1965. "La catastrophe d'Igitur" in *Oeuvres en prose*. Paris: Gallimard.

Cohn, Robert Greer. 1951. *L'Oeuvre de Mallarmé: Un coup de dés*. Paris: Librairie de Lettres.

———. 1981. *Mallarmé: Igitur*. Berkeley and Los Angeles: University of California Press.

Compagnon, Antoine. 1979. *La seconde main ou le travail de la citation*. Paris: Seuil.

Cooperman, Hasye. 1933. *The Aesthetics of Stéphane Mallarmé*. New York: Koffern Press.

Copeland, Roger, and Marshall Cohen, eds. 1983. *What Is Dance? Readings in Theory and Criticism*. New York: Oxford University Press.

Crowley, Roseline. 1977. "Toward the Poetics of Juxtaposition: L'Après-midi d'un Faune." *Yale French Studies* 54:33–43.

Davies, Gardner. 1953. *Vers une explication rationnelle du "Coup de dés": Essai d'exégèse mallarméenne*. Paris: José Corti.

———, ed. 1959. *Les Noces d'Hérodiade, Mystère*. By Stéphane Mallarmé. Paris: Gallimard.

———. 1978. *Mallarmé et le Rêve d'Hérodiade*. Paris: José Corti.

Delfel, Guy. 1951. *L'esthétique de Stéphane Mallarmé*. Paris: Flammarion.

Derrida, Jacques. 1967. *De la grammatologie*. Paris: Minuit.

———. 1972. *La dissémination*. Paris: Seuil.

Descartes, René. 1979. *Méditations métaphysiques*. Paris: Garnier-Flammarion.

Diderot, Denis. 1967. *Paradoxe sur le comédien*. Paris: Garnier-Flammarion.

Duberman, Martin. 1972. *Black Mountain: An Exploration in Community.* New York: Dutton.

Duchamp, Marcel. 1961. *Duchamp du signe: Ecrits Marcel Duchamp.* Paris: Seuil.

Duncan, Isadora. 1969. *The Art of the Dance.* New York: Theatre Arts Books.

Durkheim, Emile. 1965. *The Elementary Forms of Religious Life.* New York: Free Press.

Eco, Umberto. 1984. *The Role of the Reader.* Bloomington: Indiana University Press.

Eliade, Mircea. 1959. *The Sacred and the Profane.* New York: Harcourt, Brace and World.

Evans, Calvin. 1963. "Mallarméan Antecedents of the Avant-Garde Theater." *Modern Drama* 6:12–19.

Florence, Penny. 1986. *Mallarmé, Manet, and Redon: Visual and Aural Signs and the Generation of Meaning.* Cambridge: Cambridge University Press.

Fowlie, Wallace. 1953. *Mallarmé.* Chicago: University of Chicago Press.

Fraenkel, Ernst. 1960. *Les dessins trans-conscients de Stéphane Mallarmé.* Paris: Nizet.

Franko, Mark. 1981. "An Intertextual Model for the Interaction of Dancer and Spectator in the Renaissance." Ph.D. diss., Columbia University.

Gautier, Théophile. 1948. *Oeuvres de Théophile Gautier.* Paris: Alphonse Lemerre.

Geertz, Clifford. 1973. *The Interpretation of Cultures.* New York: Basic Books.

Genette, Gérard. 1962. "Bonheur de Mallarmé?" *Tel Quel* 10:61–65.

Ghil, René. 1886. *Traité du Verbe.* Paris: Giraud.

Goldberg, RoseLee. 1988. *Performance Art: From Futurism to the Present.* London: Thames and Hudson.

Goodkin, Richard E. 1984. *The Symbolist Home and the Tragic Home: Mallarmé and Oedipus.* Amsterdam: Benjamins.

Gould, Evlyn. 1989. *Virtual Theater from Diderot to Mallarmé.* Baltimore: Johns Hopkins University Press.

Guillaume, clerc de Normandie. 1970. *Le bestiaire divin.* Ed. C. Hippeau. Réimpressions des éditions de Caen et Paris, 1852–1877. Geneva: Slatkine Reprints.

Hanna, Judith Lynne. 1979. *To Dance Is Human: A Theory of Non-verbal Communication.* Austin: University of Texas Press.

Hanson, Thomas. 1977. "Mallarmé's Hat." *Yale French Studies* 54:215–27.

Hardin, Richard. 1983. " 'Ritual' in Recent Criticism: The Elusive Sense of Community." *PMLA* 98(5): 846–58.

Harris, Margaret Haile. 1979. *Loïe Fuller: Magician of Light.* Richmond: The Virginia Museum.

Harrison, Jane Ellen. 1913. *Ancient Art and Ritual.* London: Norgate.

Hegel, G.W.F. 1975. *The Philosophy of Fine Art.* Trans. F.P.B. Osmaton. New York: Hacker Art Books.

Hertz, David Michael. 1987. *The Tuning of the Word.* Carbondale: Southern Illinois University Press.

Hugo, Victor. 1967. *Oeuvres poétiques.* Vol. 2. Paris: Gallimard.

———. 1969. *Les contemplations.* Paris: Garnier Frères.

———. 1972. *Poésie.* Vol. 2. Paris: Seuil.

Huot, Sylviane. 1977. *Le "Mythe d'Hérodiade" chez Mallarmé.* Paris: Nizet.

Ionesco, Eugène. 1954. *La cantatrice chauve / La leçon.* Paris: Gallimard.

Johnson, Barbara. 1981. *The Critical Difference.* Baltimore: Johns Hopkins University Press.

Kaufmann, Vincent. 1986. *Le Livre et ses adresses.* Paris: Méridiens Klincksieck.

Kealiinohomoku, Joann W. 1981. "Dance as a Rite of Transformation." In *Discourse in Ethnomusicology II: A Tribute to Alan P. Merriam,* edited by Caroline Card et al., 131–52. Bloomington, Ind.: Ethnomusicology Publication Group, Indiana University.

Kermode, Frank. 1962. "Poet and the Dancer Before Diaghilev." In *Puzzles and Epiphanies,* 1–28. London: Literistic.

Kirby, Michael. 1965. *Happenings.* New York: E. P. Dutton.

Kostelanetz, Richard. 1968. *The Theater of Mixed Means.* New York: Dial Press.

Knapp, Bettina. 1977. " 'Igitur or Elbehnon's Folly': The Depersonalization Process and the Creative Encounter." *Yale French Studies* 54:188–213.

Kravis, Judy. 1976. *The Prose of Mallarmé: The Evolution of a Literary Language.* Cambridge: Cambridge University Press.

Kristeva, Julia. 1974. *La révolution du langage poétique.* Paris: Seuil.

Laban, Rudolf von. 1974. *The Language of Movement: A Guidebook to Choreutics.* Boston: Plays.

La Charité, Virginia. 1987. *The Dynamics of Space: Mallarmé's Un coup de dés jamais n'abolira le hasard.* Lexington, Ky.: French Forum.

Langer, Suzanne K. 1953. *Feeling and Form.* New York: Charles Scribner's Sons.

Last, Rex W. 1973. *German Dadaist Literature: Kurt Schwitters, Hugo Ball, Hans Arp.* New York: Twayne Publishers.

Leach, Edmund R. 1968. "Ritual." *The International Encyclopedia of the Social Sciences* 13:520–26.

Leconte de Lisle, trans. 1864. *Idylles de Théocrite et Odes Anacréontiques.* Paris: Poulet-Malassis et de Broise.

Levinson, André. 1923. "Mallarmé, métaphysicien du ballet." *La Revue musicale* 5:21–33.

Lévi-Strauss, Claude. 1962. *La pensée sauvage.* Paris: Plon.

———. 1964. *Le cru et le cuit.* Paris: Plon.

———. 1971. *L'homme nu.* Paris: Plon.

Lewis, Gilbert. 1980. *Day of Shining Red: An Essay in Understanding Ritual.* Cambridge: Cambridge University Press.

Lewis, Paula Gilbert. 1976. *The Aesthetics of Mallarmé in Relation to his Public.* Cranbury, N.J.: Fairleigh Dickinson Press.

Lhombreaud, R.-A. 1951. "Deux lettres de Mallarmé's à Edmund Gosse." *Revue de littérature comparée* (July–September): 355–62.

Lippard, Lucy. 1971. *Dada on Art.* Englewood Cliffs, N.J.: Prentice-Hall.

Mallarmé, Stéphane. 1945. *Œuvres complètes.* Ed. Henri Mondor and G. Jean-Aubry. Paris: Gallimard.

———. 1953. *Propos sur la poésie.* Ed. Henri Mondor. Monaco: Editions du Rocher.

———. 1959. *Les Noces d'Hérodiade, Mystère.* Ed. Gardner Davies. Paris: Gallimard.

———. 1959. *Correspondance: 1862–1871.* Ed. Henri Mondor and Jean-Pierre Richard. Vol. 1. Paris: Gallimard.

———. 1961. *Pour un "Tombeau d'Anatole."* Ed. Jean-Pierre Richard. Paris: Seuil.

———. 1965. *Correspondance: 1871–1885.* Ed. Henri Mondor and Lloyd James Austin. Vol. 2. Paris: Gallimard.

———. 1977. *Le "Livre" de Mallarmé.* Ed. Jacques Scherer. Paris: Gallimard.

———. 1983. *Œuvres complètes de Stéphane Mallarmé: Poésies.* Ed. Carl Paul Barbier and Charles Gordon Millan. Paris: Flammarion.

Marchal, Bertrand. 1988. *La Religion de Mallarmé*. Paris: Corti.
Marinetti, F. T. 1980. *Le futurisme*. Ed. Giovanni Lista. Lausanne: L'Age d'Homme.
———. 1983. *Teoria e invenzione futurista*. Ed. A. Mondadori. Milan: I Meridiani.
Martin, John Joseph. 1980. *The Dance*. New York: Tudor Publishing Company.
Marvick, Louis W. 1986. "Two Versions of the Symbolist Apocalypse: Mallarmé's *Livre* and Scriabin's *Mysterium*." *Criticism: A Quarterly for Literature and the Arts* 28:287–306.
Mauron, Charles. 1951. *Introduction à la psychanalyse de Mallarmé*. Neuchâtel: A la Baconnière.
———. 1964. *Mallarmé par lui-même*. Paris: Seuil.
Mauss, Marcel. 1968. *Œuvres*. Vol 1. Ed. Victor Karady. Paris: Minuit.
McDonald, Christie. 1986. "Unsettling the Score: Poetry and Music." *Romantic Review* 77:254–63.
Millet, Catherine. 1983. *Yves Klein*. Paris: Art Press Flammarion.
Mondor, Henri. 1941. *Vie de Mallarmé*. Paris: Gallimard.
———. 1948. *Histoire d'un faune*. Paris: Gallimard.
Moutote, Daniel. 1988. *Maîtres livres de notre temps: Postérité du "Livre" de Mallarmé*. Paris: Corti.
Nelli, René. 1948. "Igitur ou l'argument ontologique retourné." *Les Lettres*, special issue, 3:147–54.
Nettl, Bruno. 1956. *Music in Primitive Culture*. Cambridge, Mass.: Harvard University Press.
Nietzsche, Friedrich. 1967. *The Birth of Tragedy and the Case of Wagner*. Trans. Walter Kaufmann. New York: Random House.
Noulet, Emilie. 1940. *L'Oeuvre poétique de Stéphane Mallarmé*. Paris: Droz.
Obenhaus, Mark. 1987. *Einstein on the Beach: The Changing Face of Opera* [Film]. Direct Cinema Limited.
Paz, Octavio. 1970. *Marcel Duchamp or the Castle of Purity*. Trans. Donald Gardner. London: Cape Goliard Press.
Peirce, Charles S. 1966. *Selected Writings*. Ed. Philip P. Wiener. New York: Dover Publications.
Polieri, Jacques. 1971. *Scénographie, sémiographie*. Paris: Denoël-Gonthier.
Poulet, Georges. 1952. "Mallarmé." In *La distance intérieure*, 298–355. Paris: Plon.
Pridden, Deirdre. 1952. *The Art of Dancing in French Literature from Théophile Gautier to Paul Valéry*. London: Adam & Black.
Richard, Jean-Pierre. 1961a. *L'univers imaginaire de Mallarmé*. Paris: Seuil.
———, ed. 1961b. *Pour un tombeau d'Anatole*. By Stéphane Mallarmé. Paris: Seuil.
———. 1964. "Mallarmé et le rien: D'après un fragment inédit." *Revue d'histoire littéraire de la France* 64:633–44.
Riffaterre, Michael. 1978. *Semiotics of Poetry*. Bloomington: Indiana University Press.
———. 1983. *Text Production*. Trans. Terese Lyons. New York: Columbia University Press.
Rimbaud, Arthur. 1960. *Œuvres*. Paris: Garnier Frères.
Rivière, Jacques. 1983. "Le sacre du printemps." In *What Is Dance?* edited by Roger Copeland and Marshall Cohen, 115–23. New York: Oxford University Press.
Rolland de Renéville, André. 1938. *L'expérience poétique*. Paris: A la Baconnière.
Rottenberg, Pierre. 1967. "Une lecture d'Igitur." *Tel Quel* 37:74–94.

Roulet, Claude. 1943. *Elucidation du poème de Stéphane Mallarmé: Un coup de dés jamais n'abolira le hasard.* Neuchâtel: Aux Ides et Calendes.
Rousseau, Jean-Jacques. 1963. *Essai sur l'origine des langues.* Bordeaux: Ducros.
Ruwet, Nicolas. 1972. *Langage, musique, poésie.* Paris: Seuil.
Ryan, Marie-Laure. 1977. *Rituel et poésie: Une lecture de Saint-John Perse.* Berne: Peter Lang.
Sachs, Curt. 1943. *The Rise of Music in the Ancient World.* New York: W. W. Norton.
———. 1963. *World History of the Dances.* New York: W. W. Norton.
Sartre, Jean-Paul. 1988. *Mallarmé, or the Poet of Nothingness.* Trans. Ernest Sturm. University Park, Pa.: The Pennsylvania State University Press.
Saussure, Ferdinand de. 1972. *Cours de linguistique générale.* Ed. Tullio de Mauro. Paris: Payot.
Schechner, Richard, 1977. *Essays on Performance Theory 1970–1976.* New York: Drama Book Specialists.
Scherer, Jacques. 1947. *L'expression littéraire dans l'œuvre de Mallarmé.* Paris: Droz.
———, ed. 1977. *Le "Livre" de Mallarmé.* Paris: Gallimard.
Schwartz, Paul J. 1972. "Les Noces d'Hérodiade." *Nineteenth Century French Studies* 1:33–42.
Searle, John R. 1971. "What Is a Speech Act?" In *The Philosophy of Language,* edited by John R. Searle, 39–53. Oxford: Oxford University Press.
Shakespeare, William. 1967. *Macbeth.* Ed. G. K. Hunter. Middlesex, Harmondsworth, England: Penguin Books.
Shattuck, Roger. 1958. *The Banquet Years.* New York: Harcourt, Brace & Co.
Shaw, Mary. 1992a. "Mallarmé, Pre-postmodern, Proto-dada." In *Mallarmé, Theorist of Our Times,* special edition of *Dalhousie French Studies.*
———. 1992b. Introduction to *Rhétoriques fin de siècle.* Ed. Mary Shaw and François Cornilliat. Paris: Christian Bourgois.
Sollers, Philippe. 1966. "Littérature et totalité." *Tel Quel* 26:81–95.
Sonnenfeld, Albert. 1977. "Mallarmé: The Poet as Actor as Reader." *Yale French Studies* 54:159–72.
Sorell, Walter. 1951. *The Dance Has Many Faces.* Cleveland: World Publishing.
Sperber, Dan. 1974. *Le symbolisme en général.* Paris: Hermann.
Stoïanova, Ivanka. 1978. *Geste-texte-musique.* Paris: Union générale d'éditions.
Stravinsky, Igor. 1947. *Poetics of Music.* Trans. Arthur Knodel and Ingolf Dahl. Cambridge: Cambridge University Press.
Thibaudet, Albert. 1926. *La Poésie de Stéphane Mallarmé.* Paris: Gallimard.
Todorov, Tzvetan. 1978. *Les genres du discours.* Paris: Seuil.
Turner, Victor. 1967. *The Forest of Symbols.* Ithaca: Cornell University Press.
———. 1969. *The Ritual Process: Structure and Anti-structure.* Chicago: Aldine.
———. 1974. *Dramas, Fields, and Metaphors.* Ithaca: Cornell University Press.
———. 1982. *From Ritual to Theatre.* New York: Performing Arts Journal Publications.
Ubersfeld, Anne. 1981. *L'Ecole du spectateur: Lire le théâtre II.* Paris: Les Editions Sociales.
Valéry, Paul. 1924. *Variété.* Paris: Gallimard.
———. 1950. *Ecrits divers sur Stéphane Mallarmé.* Paris: NRF.
———. 1957. "L'âme et la danse." In *Oeuvres.* Vol. 2. Ed. Jean Hytier. Paris: Gallimard.

Van Gennep, Arnold. 1960. *The Rites of Passage*. Trans. Monika B. Vizedom and Gabrielle L. Caffee. Chicago: University of Chicago Press.

Verdin, Simonne. 1975. *Stéphane Mallarmé le presque contradictoire*. Paris: Nizet.

Verlaine, Paul. 1891. "Art poétique." In *Jadis et Naguère*, 19–21. Paris: Léon Vanier.

Wigman, Mary. 1966. *The Language of Dance*. Trans. Walter Sorell. Middletown, Conn.: Wesleyan University Press.

Wilson, Robert. 1988. Program notes for *The Forest*. Performed at the Brooklyn Academy of Music, December 1988.

Wolf, Mary Ellen. 1987. *Eros under Glass: Psychoanalysis and Mallarmé's Hérodiade*. Columbus: Ohio State University Press.

Index

270 Index

Ernst, Max, 247
Essays on Performance Theory (Schechner), 230

fashion, 49, 201
Faune, intermède héroïque, Le (Mallarmé), 125, 143
"Fausse entrée des sorcières dans Macbeth, La" (Mallarmé), 98–101
Feeling and Form (Langer), 52, 58 n. 10
Fin d'Antonia (Dujardin), 33
Flaubert, Gustave, 106 n. 5
"Fleurs, Les" (Mallarmé), 109 n. 9, 112
Florence, Penny, 178 n. 6
Foregger, Nikolai, 248
Forest of Symbols, The (Turner), 11
Fort, Paul, 71, 126
For the Birds (Cage), 229
Fraenkel, Ernst, 178 n. 6
France, Anatole, 71 n. 4, 126 n. 4
free verse, 33
frivolous/superficial versus sacred/profound, 49, 201
Fuller, Loïe, 3, 52, 57 n. 9, 59–64, 65, 66, 67, 174 n. 3, 185, 226 n. 20
Function of Dance in Human Society, The (Boas), 64 n. 16
Futurism, Italian, 5, 243–47, 250, 255, 256
Futurism, Russian, 247–48
"Futurist Music Manifesto" (Pratella), 245

Gautier, Théophile, 31, 32, 55
Geertz, Clifford, 20 n. 8
generic ambiguity, 73
"Genre ou des modernes, Le" (Mallarmé), 72
genres, purity of, 71–73
Gesamtkunstwerk, as synthetic work of art, 1, 3, 88–91, 96, 251
Ghil, René, 29
Glass, Philip, 256
Goldberg, RoseLee, 230, 231, 247, 256
Gomringer, Eugen, 2
Goncourt, Edmond de, 71
Goncourt, Jules de, 71
Goodkin, Richard E., 74
Gosse, Edmund, 42
Graham, Martha, 4, 52, 67–68
Green Box (Duchamp), 254
Grotowski, Jerzy, 95

"Guignon, Le" (Mallarmé), 127
Guillemot, Maurice, 117

Hamlet (Shakespeare), 74, 175
Hanna, Judith Lynne, 60 n. 13
happenings, 5, 230
Happenings (Kirby), 231, 236
Harrison, Jane, 52
hat, symbolism of, 200–201, 202
Haussman, Raoul, 248
Hegel, Georg Wilhelm Friedrich, 30, 43
Heine, Heinrich, 106 n. 5
"Hérésies artistiques: L'art pour tous" (Mallarmé), 30
Hérodiade (dance), 68
Hérodiade (Mallarmé). See also *Noces d'Hérodiade, Mystère, Les* (Mallarmé)
  ambiguity between writing and performance in, 105, 127, 171
  conventions of poetry in, 112–16
  language in, 103
  literature and performing arts in, 97, 101, 105, 171
  mind/body dichotomy in, 109–12, 123–24
  narrative sequence of, 105–12
  performance notes to, 116, 118–22, 158, 161
  performance of, 104–5, 116–24
  publication of, 104
  subversion of mimesis in, 115–16
  synchronic approach to time in, 113–14
  titles of sections in, 116–17, 158
  unity-in-duality in, 112, 122–23
  virtual theater in, 18 n. 7
  writing of, 103, 104
Hertz, David Michael, 34
hieroglyphs, 54
"Hommage [to Wagner]" (Mallarmé), 87 n. 1
Homme nu, L' (Lévi-Strauss), 24
How to Do Things with Words (Austin), 12
Huelsenbeck, Richard, 247, 248
Hugo, Victor, 44, 87 n. 1, 90, 128, 156
hymen, 140, 143, 197

"Ibo" (Hugo), 156 n. 8
iconoclasm, 255, 256
Idea (*l'Idée*)
  in dance, 4, 55–56, 58, 62, 67